the wines of
AUSTRALIA

the wines of
AUSTRALIA

D A V I D   P E A R C E

SALAMANDER

A SALAMANDER BOOK

Published by Salamander Books Ltd
8 Blenheim Court Brewery Road
London N7 9NY
United Kingdom

© Salamander Books Ltd, 2003

A member of **Chrysalis** Books plc

ISBN: 1 84065 444 9

Printed in China

Picture Credits

Australian Wine Export Council
2, 8, 9, 10, 11, 12, 14, 15, 16, 17, 18, 26, 27, 28, 29, 30,
34, 35, 38, 39, 42, 43, 44, 45, 47, 48, 49, 52, 53, 54, 55,
56, 62, 63, 64, 65, 66, 67, 68, 69, 70, 72, 73, 74, 75, 76,
78, 80, 81 top, 82, 85, 86, 87, 90, 91, 92, 93, 95 top, 97,
98 bottom, 99, 102, 103, 104, 105, 107, 108, 109, 110,
114, 116, 117, 120, 121, 123, 127, 130, 131, 132, 133,
134 top, 135, 138, 139, 140, 141 bottom, 142,
143 top, 144 top, 145, 150, 151 bottom,
155 top, 156

Corbis
84, 125, 134 bottom, 141 top, 143 bottom, 144 bottom,
147, 151 top, 154, 155 bottom

Contents

MAP   6

INTRODUCTION   8

GRAPES & VINES   11

HOW WINE IS MADE   14

HOW TO BUY WINE   18

VINTAGE CHART   20

HOW TO SERVE WINE   22

WESTERN AUSTRALIA   24

MARGARET RIVER   26

GREAT SOUTHERN   35

OTHER AREAS   38

SOUTH AUSTRALIA   40

BAROSSA   42

MCLAREN VALE   53

CLARE VALLEY   63

COONAWARRA   72

ADELAIDE HILLS   80

OTHER AREAS   85

VICTORIA   88

YARRA VALLEY   90

HEATHCOTE   100

GOULBURN VALLEY/MACEDON   104

BENDIGO   106

RUTHERGLEN   108

MORNINTON PENNINSULA   112

BEECHWORTH   116

OTHER AREAS   118

NEW SOUTH WALES   128

HUNTER VALLEY   130

CANBERRA   139

MUDGEE   144

OTHER AREAS   146

TASMANIA   148

QUEENSLAND   156

INDEX   158

ACKNOWLEDGEMENTS   160

TIMOR SEA

DARWIN

INDIAN
OCEAN

Broom

TANAMI DESE

GREAT SANDY DESERT

NO
T

PILBARA

GIBSON DESERT

MAC

Murchison R.

**WESTERN
AUSTRALIA**

GREAT VICTORIA DESERT

SO
AUST

INDIAN
OCEAN

Swan District

Perth Hills

PERTH

GREAT AUSTRALIAN

Bunbury
Geographe
Blackwood Valley
Great Southern
Margaret River
Pemberton
Albany

SOUTHERN OCEAN

0   500 km

Ocean, Sea:	TIMOR SEA
Deserts, Mountains:	*GIBSON DESERT*
Rivers:	*Thomson R.*
States, Territories:	QUEENSLAND
Capital Cities:	● SYDNEY
Smaller Cities, Towns:	● Geelong
Wine-producing Regions:	● Clare Valley

Introduction

Being asked to write a book about the subject you love has to be one of life's greatest pleasures, albeit a frantic one with deadlines to meet! I will start with a disclosure - my day job is the Managing Director of a wine merchants that specializes in Australian wines. Some people (mainly wine critics) will disapprove of this, and say it is impossible to be impartial in this position. They are quite right, but will have missed the point. This book is not a critique and does not set out to criticize, but a work about the wine regions of Australia and the people who run them.

If some of the greatest winemakers in Australia invite me to stay with their families whilst I am in a particular region, then I would be foolish to turn them down. It is a unique opportunity to see the inner workings of the business and how major changes are made, over a fine bottle of wine. It is, of course, far better as well to be sitting down with fine food when tasting old and precious bottles that have been dusted off from the cellar, than standing around in a cold cellar. This book is based on my knowledge of 15 years in the wine business and visits to virtually all the wine regions in Australia. My research trip for this book lasted for five weeks (I would have liked it to have been longer, but with a wife and young family to look after, it did not prove possible) and I drove 7000 kms covering 23 regions, 112 wineries and over 1000 wines.

ABOVE Australia produces a range of wines that have proved very acceptable both to new wine drinkers and old alike.

It was quite some undertaking, but I loved every minute of it. My thanks must go to Qantas for providing me with a greatly reduced fare, without which this trip would not have been financially feasible.

Australia is going through a golden age, with year-on-year sales increasing and export markets developing well. The UK has always dominated the export side, through such brands as Jacobs Creek, Penfolds, Hardys, Rosemount and Lindemans, which are also now taking hold in the United States and the

ABOVE *A Kookaburra in a vineyard - something that can only been seen in Australia. Since the vineyards are basically open agricultural areas, most of the indigenous wildlife of Australia has adapted well to their presence.*

ABOVE Vineyards in Hunter Valley, New South Wales. Grape vines only produce a crop once per year and it takes four years for the vine to develop enough to give a good quantity of fruit. Many Australian vineyards will produce better wines in the next few years.

rest of Europe. This does have its problems though. Wine is an agricultural product derived through the growing of grapes (amazingly not everyone knows this), which come from vines that produce a crop once per year and take four years to develop enough to give a good crop of fruit. To satisfy market needs (read shareholders' needs), acres of vineyards have been planted in recent years to satisfy demand. So much so in fact, that at one point it was suggested that 80% of Australian vineyards were less than five years old. This is an

ABOVE Sauvignon grapes. To satisfy market needs, acres of vineyards have been planted in Australia in recent years.

incredible fact, but one which means that in time, the quality of fruit taken from these vines will improve. This of course means even better wines in the next few years.

The 2002 figures from the Winemakers Federation of Australia show another record year. The estimated vintage crush was estimated at 1.65 million tonnes, or in layman's terms, approximately 123 million cases of wine, depending on the levels of pressing. Shiraz alone showed an increase of ten million cases. This demonstrates the dominance that this variety is achieving over Cabernet Sauvignon, which only saw a modest increase. Interestingly, the largest up-trend in wine grape intake from the previous year was Petit Verdot, at 147%, followed by Barbera, at 47%. Both are rarely bottled alone, but used as blending material to enhance other varieties.

On a world scale, Australia is a very small producer but by 2002 had nearly overtaken France as the country with the highest market share in the United Kingdom at around 22%. This is a formidable feat considering Australia only has around 1500 (a new one starts every 72 hours currently) wineries. By way of comparison, Bordeaux in France alone has 7000 Chateaux. So what makes Australia so popular in world markets? It is certainly not just one element, but a multitude of ideologies and marketing ideas that, when bought together, resulted in a product that was acceptable to new wine drinkers and old alike. What was the total sum of all the parts? Well they say simplicity is often genius and this is what Australia

ABOVE *A kangaroo in a vineyard. The wildlife roaming free in the vineyards can be an extra attraction at those wineries that are open to the public, as tourists enjoy seeing all the indigenous animals and birds.*

has achieved. You actually know what you are drinking. In an age of increased consumer awareness, we all like to know what we are consuming. Australia tells us this, and has developed a paper known as 2025, which sets out a blueprint of where the Australian wine industry as a whole should be by that year. It outlined ways to accomplish this and what targets to meet. The wine industry is well on its way to meet these already. The basic principle behind Australia's success has been in the style of the wines and the labelling of them. Instead of being named after the region that the wine originated in, and then the producer in small print below, they promoted the grape variety in large type. Why would this be so successful? The answer is simple in my opinion. If you were going to buy a tin of beans you would probably like to know which variety they where - butter, flageolet, kidney, black eye, cannelloni, etc. The same principle applies to wine. How many of the average people who casually buy a bottle of wine know which grape variety goes into the bottle of Beaujolais (it is Gamay) that they have just purchased? Not many, so when they go back to the wine store, they cannot make a lateral purchase of another bottle of Gamay - and so it goes on. The next stage, once the wine has been purchased is in enjoying the flavour of it. The majority of Australian wines are fruit-driven, which focuses on the primary flavours of a wine (secondary flavours come from the wine making itself), and those wines from the warmer climatic regions of the country are

quite alcoholic as well. Many professional wine journalists frown upon this, saying that the wines have no elegance or finesse. They are missing the point though. Although elegance can be found, especially in the Yarra Valley and other cool regions in Victoria, in my opinion that is not what the full style of Australian wine is about - they are meant to be big, fruity and immediately enjoyable. You may see a French vigneron drive around in a small car; his Aussie counterpart will no doubt have a massive 6-litre truck or 4WD instead. The same philosophy seems to apply to wine as well. In these circumstances, I see no reason to compare the two side by side - it would be akin to a motoring journalist road-testing a Ferrari against a Rolls Royce. Both are cars, but they are built for very different purposes.

Bearing in mind some of the points above, I hope you will find the information contained within these pages helpful. For those whose knowledge of Australian wine is limited to what is available on the supermarket shelf, I hope you will find some interesting new wines to try. And for those who already know something about the subject, I hope you will enjoy finding out a little more.

Due to the size restrictions of this book, I have had to focus on the major areas of wine production in Australia, where there are a number of producers making an excellent product. This has meant that I have had to leave out a number of the smaller regions to whom I apologise.

Grapes and Vines

Australian vignerons are very fortunate when compared to their European counterparts, because they can effectively plant what they like in the location of their own choice. The Europeans, on the other hand, are restricted due to laws that dictate what can be grown and where, which are based on centuries of trial and error. Although decreeing laws of this kind that are fundamentally based on tradition are admirable, with today's modern viticultural methods and vast improvements in winery machinery, they do not necessarily dictate the best policy. This is demonstrated in Tuscany, where to make a wine labelled DOCG (the highest legal ranking a wine may achieve in Italy) it must come mainly from the Sangiovese grape. Yet some of the most revered wines from the region are made from Cabernet Sauvignon, and therefore have to be labelled Vino da Tavola (table wine). Australia has no such labelling restrictions, relying on the Label Integrity Programme, which ensures that information on the label is correct.

Although Australian winemakers have the freedom to plant what they like, most will do so with a deep understanding of which vines are most suited to the soils, and a commercial reality of what will sell. For instance, with land prices being so high, it would be rather naive

ABOVE *Cabernet Sauvignon grapes.*

to plant Graciano in the Barossa, which is famed for its fine Shiraz - who would buy it and at what price? Saying this though, most wineries have experimental plots of various varieties that they will either discard or sell at the cellar door. Some of these are really quite interesting and make a refreshing change, but it is unlikely that we will ever see any commercial bottlings of most of them.

When planting a vineyard from scratch, the first step a vineyard manager will undertake is to decide what they wish to grow and if it would be consistent with the winery's long

ABOVE *Low-growing grafted Merlot vines.*

ABOVE *Old Grenache bush vines in the Barossa Valley, South Australia.*

ed to his land. The results will be analysed and the required number of vines needed will be calculated and then ordered from a vine nursery. Before the vines arrive the land will be fully prepared by deciding the spacing between the vines, called the density, and how the canopy is going to be managed. Factors such as the method of harvesting have to be taken into consideration (mechanical or hand) and the aspect (in which direction the rows will be planted along the ground), so the grapes receive the maximum amount of sun and light that is possible.

Irrigation systems, if required, will need to be put in place so that they will be able to start work as soon as the vines are planted. These enable the winemaker to drip water onto the vines as and when needed. This is a system usually employed by wineries wishing to make a more commercial wine (or in very arid areas), as it can be utilised to increase yields and therefore production per acre. Although the system

term goals and anticipated future market trends. When the variety of grape has been chosen, a soil analysis will be conducted to see which strain of rootstock and vine is most suit-

Grapes

Commercially it only makes sense in Australia to grow certain grape varieties for general sale and export. The rest are mainly experimental and may never be sold outside the cellar door. The main varieties grown are:-

White Wines

GRAPE VARIETY	MAINLY GROWN
Chardonnay	Everywhere but excels in cooler and maritime climates like Margaret River
Riesling	Most regions but best in the Clare and Eden Valleys of South Australia
Semillon	Most regions but particularly good when aged from the Hunter Valley and the Barossa when young.
Sauvignon Blanc	Excels in the cool climate Adelaide Hills
Verdelho	Very tasty and fresh in the Hunter Valley and good examples from Langhorne Creek
Viognier	South Australia
Muscat	Rutherglen

Red Wines

GRAPE VARIETY	MAINLY GROWN
Shiraz	Everywhere
Cabernet	Everywhere
Merlot	Best in South Australia
Pinot Noir	Best in the Yarra Valley
Malbec	Used to blend with Cabernet Sauvignon to give extra body and earthiness
Cabernet Franc	Fills out Cabernet Sauvignon
Grenache	Tremendous from the McLaren Vale and Barossa bush vines
Mouvedre	Used mainly for blending.

ABOVE *Chardonnay grapes*

Factors to consider when planting Merlot

James Irvine from the Irvine Estate has compiled a 41 point list of factors that need to be considered when planting Merlot:-

1 Why Merlot, Which Clones?
2 Why in this site?
3 Which row direction?
4 What trellis to achieve desired style?
5 How far apart within the row?
6 How many vines per panel?
7 How high?
8 How irrigated if at all?
9 How much irrigation?
10 What crop level?
11 Which pruning technique?
12 What Baume level to pick at?
13 Pick by Hand or machine?
14 Do we green pick?
15 What time of day to pick?
16 Into which bins, trailers or boxes?
17 Do we add back stalks and if so how much and why?
18 Do we acid adjust?
19 What fermentation temperatures?
20. Is the winemaking different for each clone?
21 How long on skins?
22 Do we add tannin during fermentation?
23. Do we cap sink?
24 Do we barrel ferment?
25 Which yeast?
26 Do we add malolactic culture or use a natural source?
27 Do we clarify pre-wood?
28 What acid adjustment pre malolactic?
29 What sulphur dioxide adjustments?
30 Which oak, how old and where from?
31 Which toasting level for the oak?
32 Will we barrel rack or stillage?
33 How long will the wine stay in wood?
34 How often will we top up the barrels?
35 How often will we rack and return?
36 Do we humidify the storage?
37 Will we add sulphur dioxide after each rack?
38 What adjustments are needed for the final blend?
39 Will we filter the wine pre bottling?
40 How long will be store it for?
41 What should the price be?

As you can see the process is a long and drawn out one that cannot be taken lightly. It takes a great deal of thought and planning if one intends to establish a premium vineyard - something that is essential if the end product is to be one of quality.

---

may be in place in wineries making a more serious wine, it will only be used when absolutely necessary in the driest of years and to a minimal extent. The effect of doing without irrigation systems is that the vines suffer some stress, and this encourages the roots to dig deep to find a source of underground water, which will hopefully contain numerous minerals to enhance the quality of the grapes. It is generally considered that vines grown in this manner (called dry growing) produce wines of a superior quality. There are three main types of irrigation practiced today. The most advanced is drip irrigation, in which the pipes running alongside the vines drip water constantly or at pre-selected intervals. This has recently been taken to the next level, by utilising satellite technology to predict weather patterns, and the placing of underground sensors to measure the soil's moisture and control the water added to the exact specifications of the vineyard manager. Other methods include flood irrigation, in which the vineyard is flooded regularly and the dry ground soaks up the water, and the use of sprinkler systems spaced at regular intervals around the vineyard.

Posts are spaced at intervals between the vines, with wires between them on which to train the vines as they grow. One of the most widely used systems is called VSP or Vertical Shoot Positioning which gives the grapes maximum exposure to the sun during the long hot summer. This also makes life considerably easier for the hand harvesters, as they do not have to bend down for the majority of the harvest. In the Barossa and McLaren Vale there are still some 100-year-old Grenache bush vines, which grow like bushes, low to the ground, making the process of harvesting a very physical one. Other systems include Scott Henry, in which the canopy is split vertically and the shoots are parted and trained to the left and right, along the wires, with one facing up and the other down on each side. This is commonly used in the New World, because it allows for good yields and is ideal for mechanical harvesting. The most widely used system of training in Bordeaux is one invented in the 1860s by a Frenchman named Dr Guyot, who gave his name to it. The Guyot system comprises of a single or double cane which has 6-10 canes growing from it in an upright fashion.

How Wine is made

Many beverages, in today's somewhat silly array of drinks, service the young drinker's demands of high-profile, well-marketed, and generally sweet-flavoured Alcopops. Wine is different, in that it is still made from fruit, grown in a vineyard that has been nurtured and looked after for years. White wine is generally far easier to make than red, due to the fewer components required to make it. Naturally it all starts in the vineyard, where the viticulturalist is faced with many decisions all year round. Should they hand or machine prune during the winter? How much to prune? Do they add fertiliser? Is a green harvest implemented - and of course when to harvest the grapes? To pick at optimum ripeness, the sugars must be high enough and the phenols (although this is more important in red wines) fully developed. Think of them as a being mature, as opposed to in their adolescence. It is important for the grapes to reach the winery as soon as possible after picking, to stop deterioration.

The first piece of equipment that the fruit will be put through is the crusher/de-stemmer. The grapes initially go through a series of rollers, which crush the berries and then separate them from the stalks by revolving them in a slotted cage - the grapes fall through whilst the stalks are collected and ejected at one end. In some instances the grapes are not crushed

ABOVE *Boxes full of freshly-picked ripe grapes arrive to be crushed and destemmed.*

but fermented in whole bunches, using a process known as Carbonic Maceration (Beaujolais is the most common wine that is made in this manner). The matter that is collected from the crushed grapes is called the must, and this may be passed through a long spiral pipe, which is the inner core of another containing very cold brine. The purpose of this is to cool the must of white grapes down.

The major difference in how red and white wines are made now comes into play. For white wine, crushed grapes are placed in a press, and the juice and pulp extracted from the must. It is very important when making white wine to have a very gentle press, to avoid crushing the pips and remaining stems, which would release bitter tannins into the wine. Most wineries these days have a pneumatic press, which is essentially a cylindrical stainless steel tank with an air bag inside. The bag is inflated slowly, which in turn gently presses the pulp against the sides and releases the juice to be drained into a new tank. The juice is left to settle, and when all the solid components have reached the bottom of the tank it is racked (the juice is taken from the tank, whilst leaving the solids behind) into the fermentation tanks. The wine at this stage may be filtered, but this can result in the loss of flavour compounds and adversely affect the overall quality of the wine.

The fermentation vats are either wooden barrels or stainless steel tanks. It is common for more illustrious wineries to ferment their wines in barrel, when the grape variety will benefit from it. The most obvious example of

ABOVE *Waiting for the next load to arrive and be tipped into the crusher.*

LEFT *As the grapes are crushed, the stalks are ejected at one end.*

BELOW *Many items of historic equipment are still in use, like this old crusher/destemmer.*

this would be Chardonnay and the least Riesling, in which you would wish to preserve the delicate pure flavours as much as possible. The major advantage of stainless steel is that you can easily regulate the temperature. Ideally, an extended fermentation at a cool temperature (around 10ºC) would be ideal for less naturally-flavoursome grapes, whilst a slightly higher one for grapes like Chardonnay can add extra complexity and longevity to the finished wine. Fermentation is the conversion of the natural sugars to alcohol, which is activated by yeasts. These may be natural, or as in most cases in the New World, cultured. The benefit of cultured yeasts is that different strains can provide the wines with different flavour compounds. It is common to purchase yeast that will combine well with the grape variety in question, and also provide the desired flavours.

The make up of grapes contains hundreds of different chemicals, one of the major groups

ABOVE *When making red wine, the cap must be plunged into the juice regularly.*

being various types of acids. In warm regions where natural sugar ripeness is high, it is essential to have a good acidity to balance a wine. However, in some cool climate regions where the sugar is less ripe, the acid level may be too high, and this needs to be addressed by the wine maker. The harshest of these acids is known as Malic Acid, which can be converted to a softer Lactic Acid. As the name suggests, this can make the wines taste a little milky just after the conversion. The process is initiated by Lactic bacteria, which are found readily in old wineries but need to be introduced in newer ones. It usually happens naturally in spring, when the temperature rises a few degrees (if not then the barrels/tank are placed in a separate storage facility and heaters are turned on to encourage the conversion). The Lactic bacteria can be added to the must shortly after fermentation, or it can happen naturally when wine is placed in old wooden barrels where malolactic fermentation has taken place before because the bacteria will still be present. In cooler climates, the juice and equipment may be sterilised before use to ensure that this process does not occur, either in the winery - or more importantly in the bottle, as the result would be a cloudy wine!

The next stage is the clarification of the wine after fermentation. This can be done by

ABOVE *Crushing grapes at Pepper Tree Wines, New South Wales. The resulting matter is called the must, and for white wine it needs to be cooled down.*

using modern machinery utilising a number of filters, or by bentonite clay. The wine is pumped through the latter, which collects remaining particles and yeast cells. The wine may also be cooled to below zero to enable the tartrate crystals to "drop out" of the wine. Wines which may benefit from maturation in oak barrels are often placed in them for up to 18 months. The oak can add many different flavours to a wine, most notably wood and vanilla. How the winemaker wishes his final wine to taste will affect the type of barrel used (this is covered in more detail in the section on how red wine is made).

Finally, when the wine is ready to be consumed, which may be after a couple of months in the cases of Sauvignon Blanc or Riesling, the wine is bottled. This is performed either at the

ABOVE *Wooden caskets give the wine its final flavour and structure.*

winery, or in some cases in the New World at a specific bottling plant at a different location.

The difference in making red wine is that the grapes miss the pressing stage, and go straight into a vat or barrel to ferment, complete with their skins (which have been split in the crushing process) and pips. This is when the wine achieves its colour (all grape juice is clear) and extraction. The fermentation process is usually carried out in open fermenters, so that the cap can be broken and plunged down through the juice at regular intervals. This is accomplished either by hand with a paddle, or if in an enclosed vat, electronically with paddles that go up and down the tank, turning the juice at preset intervals. Fermentation will usually start naturally 2-3 days later, and the temperature may rise to 30°C. Ideally it should last for 6 days or so, after which the must is left to macerate from 1-3 weeks, depending on the wine makers objectives. Once the fermentation is completed the clear juice at the bottom (known as the free run juice) will be pumped out. The remaining mass of pulp may be discarded or pressed. The pressed wine is harsher than the free run juice, and may or may not be added to the final wine. Depending on the wine, it will be aged in oak barrels or stainless steel tanks. If oak is chosen, as it is for the majority of serious wines, then the choice is paramount to the

ABOVE *Wine racks at Coonawarra, South Australia. At most wineries you can try different varieties free of charge.*

final flavour and structure of the wine.

When considering wooden barrels, firstly, you must choose not only which country to purchase your oak from, but also the forest within it. American oak generally has larger pores, giving a more robust flavour and imparting more vanilla and sweetness to a wine. French oak is more refined, and imparts a more elegant flavour to the wine, as it has small, tight-grained pores. Once the type of wood is decided upon (which may be many from different sources, to add to the complexity of the wine) the degree of toast needs to be considered. Barrels are formed over a small fire and the cooper must constantly turn and shape them during final construction. The fires singe the wood, and the degree to which they do so is known as the toast. The higher the toast, the more apparent it will be in the flavour of the wine.

The wine will be racked and fined before being placed in barrel. Once in the barrel, Malolactic fermentation will almost certainly be carried out to soften the wine and add complexity. It will be left in barrel for up to two years, during which time it will be racked every few months to remove it from its sediment and allow some aeration.

Once the wine is ready to be bottled, it will go through assemblage, a process where the wine making team will taste through each individual barrel in a laboratory, to determine the final blend or which wine will go into each cuvee. Once this has been completed, the wine is then ready for bottling.

Depending on the winery (or sometimes the cashflow) situation, the wine will either be stored until it is deemed mature enough to enjoy and then shipped, or sent out to their distributors immediately.

How to Buy Wine

A rather simple matter you may think - but is it? As someone who is reading this book, it is probably safe to assume that you have more than a passing interest in Australian wines or wine in general. As with all hobbies and pastimes, it is nice to get the maximum benefit from it that you can. To enable you to do this, you may want to divide your wine collection up into departments: wines for drinking now; for the medium term; and for lying down for a long period. Which wines should you buy and what quantity? This all depends of course, on your personal preferences and your budget, but I will outline here a few guidelines that you may find useful.

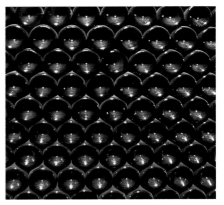

ABOVE *Wine bottles at Chateau Tahbilk, Goulburn Valley,*

To start, it is worth remembering that the majority of wines purchased, and especially whites, are made to be drunk upon release. They simply will not evolve and transform to a glorious wine worthy of a higher price point. As a general guide you should expect that the more expensive a wine is, the better it chances of longevity are.

If based in Australia, you are blessed with cellar doors where you can try most wines free of charge before making a purchase. This is ideal, as often the winemaker will be around and able to discuss cellaring potential with you. One of the most important factors to consider is the balance of the wine. If the fruit, tannin and acids are all in harmony in an expensive bottle, then the chances are you will be able to lay it down for a while. What if you are unsure about how more mature wines

taste? Ask the person at the cellar door to open one and give it a try - they may refuse, due to limited stocks, but it is worth a go. If you are a long way from a wine region then your local bottle shop will have a good selection, or you can purchase via mail order from a company like Baily and Baily (www.bailys.com.au) in Adelaide, who have one of the most comprehensive ranges in the country.

The US is not the easiest of places to buy Australian wines if you are based outside of California or New York states, due to the antiquated liquor laws imposed throughout the country. I would suggest contacting Joshua Tree Imports in Pasedena for a list.

As the largest importer of Australian wines in the world, it would seem logical that the UK would also have the largest choice. Although

ABOVE *The cellar door at Peter Lehmann Wines, Barossa Valley, South Australia. Sometimes it may be possible to try more mature wines at cellar doors if you are choosing a wine to lay down.*

Which wines to choose

WINES FOR IMMEDIATE DRINKING - Generally applies to cheaper bottles.

Hunter Verdelho
Barossa Semillon
Almost all Rieslings
Adelaide Hills Sauvignon Blanc
Most Chardonnay
Chambourcin
Pinot Noirs
Shiraz
Cabernet

WINES FOR MEDIUM TERM STORAGE (5-10 YEARS)
- Generally applies to medium priced bottles.
Margaret River Chardonnay
Clare and Eden Valley Rieslings
Hunter Semillon
South Australian Shiraz
Margaret River Cabernet
Great Western wines from Bests
Central Victorian wines from Tahbilk and Heathcote wineries.
Barossa Shiraz
McLaren Vale Shiraz

WINES FOR LONG TERM STORAGE (10+ YEARS)
- Generally applies to the best examples of each.
Hunter Semillon
Leeuwin Estate Chardonnay
Clare and Eden Rieslings
Tahbilk Marsanne
Rutherglen special and rare sweeties which will last forever in bottle
Yarra Pinot Noir
Yarra Cabernet blends
Bests Great Western range of reds
Coonawarra Cabernets (especially Wynns)
Barossa Shiraz

this may be the case, it is worrying that the big three have the monopoly in most supermarkets and chains of wine merchants where the majority of wine is purchased. This is due to economies of scale and the healthy marketing budgets of these multi-national companies. It is far easier for the supermarket to deal with a few suppliers, than tens for each product category. Between them, the big three own most of the world-known brands. Southcorp own Penfolds, Lindemans, Rosemount and Wynns. Orlando owns Jacobs Creek, Gramps and Wyndham. BRL Hardy owns Hardys, Banrock Station, Houghton and many more like them. I suggest that you seek out independent wine merchants with a good range, who cannot only provide advice but work directly with you to build your collection. It would be foolish of me not to recommend myself, at www.winevault.co.uk, as I have one of the largest collections in the country and I am able to export worldwide.

Auctions are a good way to buy mature stocks of upmarket wines, but be careful not to buy over-the-hill wines. Sometimes prices can be inflated, due to positive reviews by Robert Parker, the influential American wine critic. This leads to a sudden worldwide demand for these wines, which are usually made in minute quantities. Once the initial furore has calmed down and merchants realise that they can no longer sell the wines at previous levels, you may be able to pick them up at a good price. There is no substitute, though, for buying on release on your own or an expert wine merchant's advice.

Vintage Charts

VINTAGE	1998 White	1998 Red	1999 White	1999 Red
WESTERN AUSTRALIA				
Margaret River	★★★★	★★★★	★★★★	★★★★★
Swan District	★★★★★	★★★★★	★★★★	★★★★
Great Southern	★★★★	★★★	★★★★	★★★★
SOUTH AUSTRALIA				
Clare Valley	★★★★	★★★★★	★★★★	★★★★★
Barossa Valley	★★★★	★★★★★	★★★	★★★
McLaren Vale	★★★★	★★★★★	★★★★	★★★★
Coonawarra	★★★★★	★★★★★	★★★★	★★★★★
Adelaide Hills	★★★★	★★★★	★★★★	★★★★
VICTORIA				
Yarra Valley	★★★★	★★★★★	★★★	★★★
Mornington Peninsula	★★★★★	★★★★★	★★★★	★★★★
Geelong	★★★★	★★★★	★★★	★★★★
Bendigo	★★★★★	★★★★★	★★★	★★★★★
Nagambie Lakes	★★★★★	★★★★★	★★★★	★★★★
Grampians	★★★★	★★★★★	★★★★	★★★★★
NEW SOUTH WALES				
Lower Hunter Valley	★★★★	★★★★	★★★★	★★★★
Upper Hunter Valley	★★★★★	★★★★	★★★★.	★★★★
Orange				
TASMANIA				
North	★★★★	★★★★★	★★★★★	★★★★★
South	★★★★	★★★★★	★★★★	★★★★
QUEENSLAND				
Granite Belt	★★★	★★★★	★★★	★★★★

These vintage charts offer a representation only of each area. It is impossible to give totally accurate accounts as it can differ between each producer. The 2002 ratings are based upon anticipated quality in relation to the vintage in the area.

2000 White	2000 Red	2001 White	2001 Red	2002 White	2002 Red
★★★★	★★★★★	★★★★	★★★★	★★★★	★★★★
★★★	★★★★	★★★★	★★★★	★★★★★	★★★★★
★★★★	★★★★	★★★★★	★★★★	★★★★	★★★★
★★★★	★★★★	★★★★	★★★★	★★★★★	★★★★★
★★★	★★	★★★	★★★★	★★★★	★★★★★
★★★	★★★	★★★	★★★★	★★★★	★★★★★
★★★★	★★★★	★★★★	★★★★	★★★★	★★★★★
★★★	★★★	★★★★	★★★★	★★★★★	★★★★
★★★★	★★★★★	★★★	★★★★	★★★★	★★★★
★★★★	★★★★	★★★★	★★★★	★★★★	★★★★
★★★★	★★★★	★★★	★★★	★★★★	★★★★
★★★	★★★★	★★★★	★★★★★	★★★	★★★
★★★★	★★★★	★★★★	★★★★	N/A	N/A
★★★★★	★★★★	★★★★	★★★★	★★★	★★★
★★★★★	★★★★★	★★★★	★★★	★★★★	★★★★
★★★★★	★★★★	★★★★	★★★	N/A	N/A
★★★★★	★★★★★	★★★★	★★★★	★★★★	★★★★
★★★★★	★★★★★	★★★★	★★★★	★★★★	★★★★
★★★★★	★★★★★	★★★★	★★★★	★★★★★	★★★★★

How to Serve Wine

The packaging of wine is currently under-going a major change. Depending on who you listen to, around 5% of wine sold today is tainted by trichloranisole - we refer to such wine as being corked. It is not the fault of the wine maker but of the cork itself, and it can only be detected in its raw state if an analy-sis is carried out on each and every batch sold, which is nearly impossible to do. Although it is perhaps more prevalent in the mass-market bulk wines, which use an inferior grade of cork, it can even happen to the most expensive bottles as well. Many different closures have been invented to prevent it from happening, but none is used to such a great extent as Stelvin, which is a form of screw-cap. Some people argue that unscrewing a bottle of wine does not have the same romanticism as listen-ing to the sound of a cork popping out of a bottle, and that it downgrades the perception of the wine to a non-alcoholic beverage. Although I can understand this, I am sure that many people would sacrifice those 30 seconds of romantic idealism, in order to have a bottle of wine that is in the exact condition the wine-maker had intended. These screw-caps are still permeable down to a maximum of 0.05% penetration, which is consistent with that of a top-graded cork. Considering that 90% of all wine made is drunk within 48 hours of pur-chase, I am totally in favour of them.

It is unfortunate that in today's society it is generally expected that white wines will be served very cold. Although this is fine for some wines like Sauvignon Blanc and Champagne,

it has the effect on other wines of putting flavours and nuances into hibernation. A gen-eral rule is that the more expensive a bottle of white wine is, the warmer it should be served. Red wines suffer from the reverse problem - they are served too warm. It used to be accept-ed that red wines should be served at room temperature, but this was when rooms were around 17-18ºC. With today's modern heat-ing systems, the temperature of a dining room is more likely to be around 20ºC, which has the effect of accentuating the alcohol levels in the wine and making it appear unbalanced.

The best way to chill white wine is too leave it in the fridge for a few hours before you intend to drink it. If you need to chill it down in a hurry, then place it in a bucket of ice cov-ered with water - this is far quicker than put-ting it in just ice. Red wine can be brought straight from the cellar (if you are fortunate to have one), otherwise place it in a cool room the morning before you will need it. In an emer-gency, it is quite acceptable to take the capsule off the bottle and place the wine in a microwave for 30 seconds. This will have no adverse effect on the wine - although I would not recommend it on a 1952 bottle of Penfolds Grange Hermitage!

If serving an old bottle of red, be careful when handling it as sediment may have devel-oped in the bottom of the bottle. This is quite natural and is caused by the changes in the wines chemical make-up during maturation. Anthocyanins and phenols aggregate together, and when they become too heavy to be sus-pended in the wine they drop out. To ensure the wine is served without the sediment, decant the wine carefully into a clean decanter alongside a candle, so you can see when the sediment reaches the neck.

To get the most enjoyment from a bottle of wine, always use a large glass. The flavours of a wine are more pronounced when it comes into contact with oxygen, so the larger the surface area the better. Ideally, glasses should be thin and clear (not made from cut glass or crystal) and be bowl shaped at the bottom, narrowing to the rim. Swirling the wine around the glass allows oxygen to penetrate into the wine and release flavours for you to nose. If you do not feel embarrassed, then roll the wine around in your mouth and draw in air - this will bring out all the flavour compounds and increase your enjoyment.

There has been a lot of talk about wine and

ABOVE *To get the most enjoyment from a bottle of wine, always use a large glass.*

food matching in the press in recent years, and although this does have a place I would not devote too much time worrying about it unless you are an expert wine taster and accomplished cook. Why do I say this? Simply because most people already know and follow the time-tested guide lines that have been established throughout years of culinary and vinous experiment. It does not matter if you do not subscribe to them, as you will ultimately get far more enjoyment by following your own preferences. If a Riesling with roast beef is what you like, then there is nothing wrong with it - and you should not feel pressurised into having a bottle of Cabernet Sauvignon just because it is correct. If you would like to take it further and develop a

ABOVE *The vast majority of wine you buy is ready for drinking immediately.*

knowledge, it is always worth remembering that wines that come from a region will usually be best suited to a food that originates from that region. For example, a Pinot Noir with Beef Bourguignon. This, of course, becomes more difficult when you are eating foods from Asia or South America. What does go with them? To help you choose, I have compiled a table below that should act as a base point for your experiments.

Wine is the only consumable commodity that can, and often does, improve with age. There is not enough room in this book to go into the subject in detail, so I shall only out line it here. The vast majority of wine you buy is ready for drinking immediately, but a small percentage can benefit from being laid down in a dark and cool space. As a very general rule of thumb, the more expensive a bottle the longer it is likely to cellar for. This, of course, depends on how the wine is made and the vin-

tage in question. For suggestions on a few suitable wines to lay down, see the chart on page 19. The danger of laying down wine, of course, is that you can see it in your storage facility and you may be tempted to pull the cork. I would suggest placing your selection (buy the best you can afford) in long flat wine boxes, and taping them up. On the box write the year that it can be opened. After a few years you will have a rolling stock of mature wine that will contain many bottles you had forgotten about years before.

Wine can also be used to create an ideal party game. Make up a blindfold, and hold a wine-tasting competition. The idea is that you have a selection of red and white wines, and the blindfolded person has to identify which colour each wine is. It may sound easy but, if the wines are all served at the same temperature (try it at around 13ºC), even the professionals can be fooled.

A Brief Guide To Food and Wine Matching Guide

ANTIPASTO - Try a Pinot Gris, perhaps from Mount Langi Ghiran

ASIAN/CHINESE - A Traminer or Gewürtztraminer

BEEF STEAK - The more expensive the cut, the finer the wine. Try a Coonawarra or Margaret River Cabernet.

CAESAR SALAD - Not easy on wine, perhaps a full bodied Chardonnay.

CURRY - A gutsy but cheap Shiraz.

FISH - Depending on the sauce, a good Chardonnay from a cool climate region like the Yarra.

GUACAMOLE - Something with nice acidity, like a Clare Riesling.

MELON - A big ripe Chardonnay.

LAMB - Top quality Pinot Noir

OYSTERS - Cool climate Chardonnay or Sauvignon Blanc which is not too perfumed.

PASTA - Depends on the sauce - if cream, then something refreshing like a Semillon; if in a meat sauce, try a Sangiovese or other Italian grape variety.

PIZZA - A nice full Shiraz, but not too expensive as tomato is one of wine's enemies.

Prawns - Expensive food needs expensive wine. Try a Margaret River Chardonnay.

Western Australia

It is almost impossible for me to say which out of the three main wine-producing states in Australia is my favourite, or to rank them, but if I really had to, Western Australia would have to come in at third. Why? Not because of the quality of the wines, but because the area as a whole does not have the quantity of great wine-making regions that the others do. Once you move beyond Margaret River and the Great Southern, you certainly have respectable regions - but not ones that could really be called world-class.

Western Australia is so far removed from South Australia and Victoria, that it might as well be in a different country. However, it is here that some of the most revered wines are made. Critics the world over applaud the Cabernets produced in Margaret River, which can be so much more elegant and refined than those to the east, with the exception of Victoria. The Chardonnay grape also prospers here, with some of the country's finest being produced at Leeuwin Estate.

Although by itself the Sauvignon grape is not exquisite, when blended with Semillon it comes into its own, making it Margaret River's premium white blend. Shiraz, the country's most popular variety, tends to flourish in the Great Southern area, especially around Mount Barker. Cabernet Franc is also performing well here, at wineries like Garlands.

In Australian terms, Western Australia is the new kid on the block, as it has only been cultivating grapes for wine production since the 1960s. It was only after Dr John Gladstone did a thorough study of the Margaret River region in 1965 that the first vineyards were planted. The wine-producing area has grown considerably since then, mainly in the south west of the state around Geographe Bay, and moving in an easterly direction. Serious plantings have also happened north of Perth in the Swan Valley, which is almost an outer suburb of the city now.

Tourism plays a major part in the economy of the south west, and this has led to serious investment being made here in cellar doors and restaurant facilities. The new money being invested has naturally bought employment to the area, and therefore makes it more desirable for employees, so we will see growth continuing for some years to come before saturation points are met. I believe it was Len Evans who stated that Australia may not have found its best vineyard sites yet, and if this is true then I would strongly suspect that Western Australia could be the state to find them in. Unlike Victoria, Western Australia in mostly desert, so any new discovery is likely to happen in the south west where maritime climates dominate and the climate is a little wetter.

Overall, Western Australia produces some very fine wines that are all relatively well priced compared to the superstar wines of the Barossa. All it will take is for the next wave of wine writers to get behind it and emphasise just how good it is. The only stumbling block they may face is the price, because most of the wineries here fall into the boutique bracket and there are, as yet, no major players marketing a generic wine from this region.

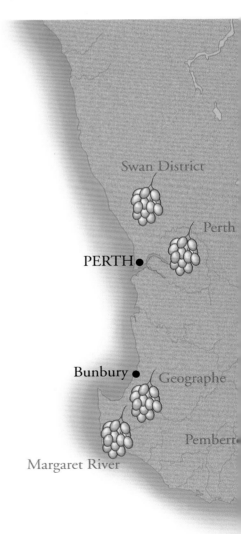

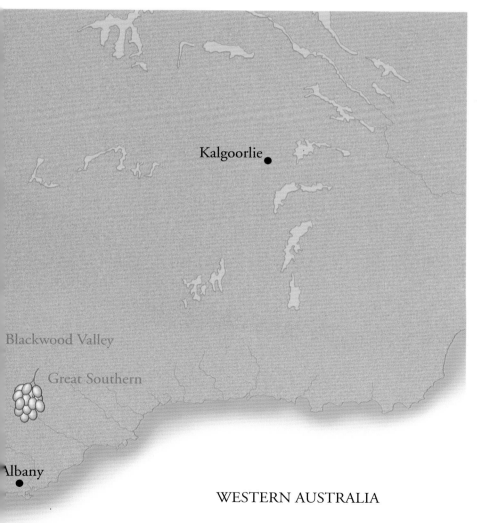

Kalgoorlie

Blackwood Valley

Great Southern

Albany

WESTERN AUSTRALIA

Margaret River

Margaret River is one of my favourite wine regions in Australia, perhaps because it was the first one I visited in the country and I ended up working a vintage there (well for one week, anyway, as it was back breaking!). The region has grown up since then, much like the rest of Australia, possibly due to its appearance on the world stage for the year 2000 Olympic Games in Sydney. Although closer to Singapore than it is to the cities on the east coast, the transformation from a lively, although slightly behind the times, region to its modern self has been rapid. It is truly a cosmopolitan area with, a strong Asian influence and a temperate climate that makes it an ideal place to live. That is if you do not mind being a three hour plane journey from the next large city.

Margaret River is situated around 200kms south of Perth, near Geographe Bay and Cape Naturaliste. It is a beautiful part of the world covered in large eucalypt trees (you can climb one - the Gloucester Tree which reaches up 60 metres) and surrounded by idyllic beaches that if you are lucky, you can still have all to yourself. The town offers a number of restaurants, but in no way can be called large. It attracts a lot of travellers en-route to Adelaide via the Nullabor plain, and surfers who come from around the world to catch the fearsome waves. It runs along the rolling hills of the Leeuwin-Naturaliste Ridge, which extend for around 54 miles. To the west is the Indian Ocean - go out to sea and the first city you will reach is Cape Town in South Africa. Most vineyards are located along the major water routes that flow

west into the ocean and can be found within one and three miles from the coast.

The climate here is often compared to that of Bordeaux in France, as the Heat Summation days are similar. The maritime location and good weather ensure that frosts are not a problem (an amazing amount of people from this part of Australia have never seen real snow). Soil types are very important here and can make or break a wine. One vineyard that I visited had dug up their Chardonnay and replanted with Shiraz, as the former was not performing well. The neighbouring block a couple of metres away was producing their best Chardonnay grapes!

The foundations for the finest vineyards, lateritic gravel loams, can be traced back to around 2000 million years ago when this part of the country was detached from the mainland by an island of granite stretching 60 miles north to south. This is now linked by the Whicher Range of low lying hills. It was first discovered by the French, but in they paid little attention to it apart from collecting a few samples of plants here and there. On one of the expeditions though, a sailor by the name of Vasse got left behind. No one knows what happened to him but one can only imagine that he either perished or was taken in by the Aboriginals who had been here for 50,000 or so years. It was not until 1830 that the first white settlement began, with dairy farmers and loggers. Its viticultural roots only began in 1965, when Dr John Gladstone concluded that the soils and climate of the south west in

ABOVE *In 1965 Dr John Gladstone concluded that the soils and climate of parts of the south-west were ideal for viticulture and singled out Margaret River, as it was less prone to extremes.*

ABOVE *Sandalford Wines, Margaret River. Sandalford is the oldest family-owned winery in WA, having been founded in 1840.*

places were ideal for viticulture. He singled out Margaret River, as it was less prone to extremes. The first vineyard was planted by a Perth surgeon named Tom Cullity, who called it Vasse Felix. Shortly afterwards Dr Bill Pannell founded Moss Wood in 1969, and Dr Kevin Cullen his eponymously-named vineyard in 1970 (they had originally planted a trial acre in 1966). At this time the region was becoming known as a hippy commune, as two or three groups had set up camp, possibly due to the excellent surf. One imagines that they provided a lot of the labour force in the early days, so it was a feat in itself to harvest the grapes. Ironically it is these very same people who became professionals and invested heavily in the region during the 1980s and 90s and are now opposed to development. This has not stopped the gradual expansion of the wine industry, as there are about 50 wineries now and the area attracts 1.5 million visitors per year. Almost half of Western Australia's grape crush is done here, which equates to around 25,000 tonnes. Virtually all of this is premium fruit, making it WA's answer to Coonawarra in quality terms, and also the country's specialist Cabernet Sauvignon region. The most interesting facet of the region, and one which will help propel it to even greater heights, is that the average age of the vines here is only nine years, enabling the district to have a potential golden period over the next 20 years and beyond. Although some of the larger companies may venture here from SA, I do not foresee it ever becoming another Barossa. This is the home of the boutique wineries and the large companies will only ever use wines made here in premium labels. The area will expand

dramatically, though, over the next years, as it has done in the past ten. In the early nineties, the cellar doors were relatively basic and usually contained within the winery itself. Today this has all changed, with multi-million dollar facilities replacing the old tin shack that was once quite sufficient. Although this has come about due to the increased awareness of the wines, it is also due to a vast improvement in the marketability of the region as a tourist destination. It is almost unrecognisable now from ten years ago, especially the outlying town of Dunsborough, which acts as the western gateway to the Caves Road where the majority of wineries are located. This is a positive improvement, although I am concerned that investors will focus on the dollars created through tourism and open up spectacular wineries,

ABOVE *Cabernet Sauvignon, 'Cape Mentelle', Margaret River, Western Australia.*

restaurants and homesteads, whilst not paying close enough attention to the wines. This has happened to a certain extent in the Hunter Valley, although it does not seem to have a detrimental effect as long as you plan beforehand which cellar doors to visit.

The fame of David Hohnen of Cape Mentelle was originally derived from his New Zealand winery, Cloudy Bay, for its superb Sauvignon Blanc that put the country onto the wine-making map in world terms. It is here, though, that his finest and most complex wines are made. David previously worked for the Portet Brothers at Clos du Val in California and Taltarni in Australia (Dominique currently has his own winery in the Yarra Valley), gaining a wealth of experience and a passion for Zinfandel, which he now grows successfully at Cape Mentelle. For someone who studied Oenology at Fresno

ABOVE *Cullen Wines is one of the top six wineries in the Margaret River region. Vanya Cullen was one of the first female show judges.*

University in California, but did not complete the course, he has done remarkably well carving his name out as one of the finest winemakers in the country. The vineyard was first planted in 1970, making it one of the first in the region. Today the area under vine is over 225 acres, and they crush over 1000 tonnes per year in their winery, which was constructed in 1977. Along with the Zinfandel, it is the Cabernet Sauvignon and Semillon/Sauvignon blends that lead the way and have the most appeal from the range. A second label, Ironstone, was introduced to allow people to try his wines at a lower price point, and this has proved very successful. Helping David out is senior winemaker John Durham, who graduated from Charles Sturt in 1984, having worked a Lindemans, amongst others. Interestingly, John has a passion for Pinot Noir, which he makes from his own vineyard and markets under the Vertumnus label.

Diana Cullen of Cullens was one of the first of a new breed of female winemakers. She retired from physiotherapy to focus on the family winery in 1981, and became the first woman to win a prize at the Royal Perth Wine Show with a Sauvignon Blanc. She had used oak in the making of it - the first time this had been done successfully in Western Australia. Diana carried on in this mould until 1986, when she made the decision to stop putting her wines into shows - they were good enough to stand up by themselves. Cullens had gained a reputation for the quality of the wines at the time, so this move made sense. In 1989 Diana's daughter, Vanya , who has a BSc in Zoology as well as well as a diploma in wine, took over the helm as senior winemaker, and instead of exhibiting in shows, became a show judge of which she was one of only two women. If you visit the winery and restaurant you might still be able to catch Diana for a quick chat, as she keeps her eye on things as the chairperson of the business.

Vanya and the rest of the family believe that great wine comes from the vineyard and as such, minimal intervention is applied in the winery. When planting new vineyards great care is taken to find the most suitable site for the variety. The soils at Cullen are old, granite and gravely, sandy loam, overlaying lateritic subsoils. The vines are dry-farmed and low-yielding to enhance quality, and are both pruned and harvested by hand. The vineyard is in the process of going organic, like a number of other prominent wineries in the region.

Good vineyard management is essential in the farming of quality grapes, and as such the Sauvignon Blanc and Semillon, with their high vigour, are on a Lyre trellis. This gives a bigger area for the leaves and fruit to grow on, thereby enabling the fruit to reach proper physiological ripeness. The Chardonnay has been put on a vertical-shoot-positioned trellis, as this variety seems to favour it. The red grape varieties, Cabernet Sauvignon, Merlot and Cabernet Franc, have been converted to a Scott Henry Trellis to increase ripe flavours and develop higher quality tannins.

The Fermoy Estate takes its name from the town of the same name in County Cork Ireland. It was first planed in 1985 by John and Beryl Anderson, with cuttings from Moss Wood, Evans & Tate and Pierro. They also had the luxury of being able to build a winery to the specifications of Michael Kelly, the wine maker. He naturally chose to combine the latest wine-making equipment with the use of traditional methods. Fermoy is situated in the Willyabrup sub-region of Margaret River, where the soils are deep and fertile gravely loams. One reason why this site was chosen is that they believe the Cabernet Sauvignon finds its most pure expression here, with the climate and soils, and it produces a wine of good structure whilst maintaining its finesse. They do possess rich, ripe fruit, but these are elegant wines with ripe tannins, giving silky smooth textures, rather than jammy.

Palandri is the new name on the block in Margaret River, and it made a big splash in the international marketplace on its launch in 1998. The intention was to create a range of varietal wines from Margaret River, at a more assessable price than was generally on offer. The striking images on the labels, which depict reptiles, have made the brand stand out. The Palandri family have had a long association with Western Australia after Rob Palandri's father, Giovanni, migrated there in 1949 from Modena in Italy, to join his brother who owned a timber mill. It took just one year of working for his brother for Giovanni to earn enough money to purchase a small farm near Margaret River, which he duly planted with vines he had bought with him from Italy. By the 1960s the region was being discovered by other winemakers. Vasse Felix was the first to arrive in 1967, and Giovanni started working for them from the outset, and then for Cape Mentelle, Moss Wood and Sandalford until his death in 1986. His help in the formative years of these vineyards was substantial; he possessed experience and knowledge of vine pruning as

ABOVE *Leeuwin Estate, Margaret River, Western Australia.*

ABOVE *Vasse Felix, the first vineyards in Margaret River. The name comes from a sailor called Vasse, who was left behind when French expeditions first discovered the area.*

RIGHT *Hand picking Chardonnay at Margaret River, Western Australia.*

well as wine-making, which was rather lacking in this far south-western corner of Australia at the time. It is easy to see how Rob became more interested in the wine business, rather than following a traditional route having completed his degree in commerce from the University of Western Australia. After graduation, Rob joined Penfolds as a salesman and became friends with John Duval in 1980, which was the start of his career proper.

Although it takes their name, Palandri is not a family business - its major shareholder and chairman is Darrel Jarvis and it was formally a public unlisted company. Unlike most wine start-ups, Palandri purchased the vineyard that Giovanni had owned. This gave them a small 12 acre plot with 24-year-old vines, which has been used to make reserve wines. This will prove very valuable to them in the long term, as they will be able to throw more money at them without having to worry too much about meeting certain price points. Do not be fooled into thinking they are a small operation with one vineyard though - they make around 250,000 cases per year, which must make them one of the largest in the area.

Leeuwin Estate was founded in 1974. The 1485 acre ranch was purchased by Denis Horgan in 1974, with the help of Californian supremo Robert Mondavi. Today there are some 61 acres planted to Chardonnay (in eight blocks), along with plantings of Riesling, Cabernet Sauvignon, Pinot Noir and Sauvignon Blanc. Mondavi's ties ended in the late 1970s, when viticulturist John Brocksopp and winemaker Bob Cartwright joined the team. This wine-making team is still together at Leeuwin Estate after 22 years; undoubtedly this is a vital factor in the consistency of the wines, as it gives them a deep understanding of how to achieve what they want given the conditions of each vintage.

Leeuwin Estate wines come in three different ranges, starting with the Siblings Sauvignon Blanc/Semillon, made for drinking upon release. Then comes the Prelude range, consisting of a Chardonnay and a Cabernet/Merlot, wines designed to be expressive of their fruit and drunk soon after release. At the very top comes the Art Series comprising a Riesling, a Sauvignon Blanc, a Chardonnay, a Pinot Noir, a Shiraz and a Cabernet Sauvignon whose labels depict a different work of contemporary Australian art each vintage. These wines are made from a selection of the best fruit, and in the case of the Chardonnay and Cabernet Sauvignon, have a reputation for being extremely long-lived.

Leeuwin's Art Series Chardonnay is acclaimed as perhaps the finest Australia has to offer. I would have to agree, although the likes of Pierro, Petaluma (with their Tiers), Giaconda and Penfolds (with their sought-after Yattarna) may disagree. Leeuwin has a long history of world-class Chardonnay, which demonstrates their sheer quality over a sustained period of time. The Art Series is always a very complex wine, with the ability to age for 20 years or more in good vintages. Though this sounds like extraordinary longevity for an Australian Chardonnay, it is the unique terroir that makes this wine and offers some explanation. 50% of the grapes come from the Block 20 vineyard, which is established on old, leached soils offering excellent drainage and deep root penetration. The vines are now 25 years old and are cooled in the summer by the sea breeze from the Indian Ocean, which surrounds them on three sides. I am convinced this is a vital component (whilst working the '94 harvest in Margaret River, we had to finish at midday as the sun was simply too hot to continue). The yields are low - virtually always under 40 hectolitres per hectare - and the grapes achieve high sugar ripeness whilst delivering some 8-9 grammes per litre of natural acidity. Not only does this provide the backbone to the wine, but it ensures a long life.

The skills demonstrated in vineyard management are extensive too. Leeuwin believes that the quality of a wine comes first and foremost from the vineyard. Careful thought and planning has resulted in some very clever prac-

ABOVE *Winemaker Bob Cartwright of Leeuwin Estate, who has worked with viticulturalist John Brocksopp for more than 22 years.*

tices. For example, to prevent damage to the buds as they develop, cereal rye has been planted between every third row to act as a wind break. To further demonstrate a desire to produce wines of a world class level, sunflowers have been planted around the perimeter of the vineyard for parrots to feed on instead of their precious grapes! This level of viticultural detail undoubtedly aids the such success of the finished wine.

Once the grapes are picked, each block is kept separate. Most are whole-bunch pressed with additional skin contact. Fermentation takes place in French barrels (from Troncais and Allier oak), and malolactic fermentation is carried out selectively as appropriate; normally on around 20% of the wine. The wine stays in barrel for up to 17 months, depending on the block. Regular stirring of the wine on its original lees takes place, and the wine is only pumped at the bottling stage so there is minimal disturbance.

Although I have tasted the wines of Leeuwin Estate many times, in several vintages, I had never before had the opportunity for a vertical tasting across nine years as I did in 2002. The sheer quality and consistency was testament to the skills of Bob Cartwright and John Brocksopp. Writing tasting notes became very difficult, as the wines all possessed the same characteristics - albeit it in a complex manner. This is Australian wine-making far removed from the big label brands, whose main aim is often to achieve year-on-year uniformity. The thing that struck me most was the freshness of the wines even after 15 years in bottle,

ABOVE *Leeuwin Estate Shiraz. Each vintage depicts a different work of contemporary Australian art on the label.*

and some obvious signs of development.

Saracen is based in the Willyabrup area on the Caves Road, between Cullens and Vasse Felix - not a bad place to be. The Cazzolli and Saraceni families who own the business have enlisted Bill Crappsley, as the winemaker who possess over 25 years of experience in wine-making in McLaren Vale and Margaret River. Starting in the industry in 1964 as a cellar hand with the Houghton Wine Company, he worked under the legendary Jack Mann. His progression was quick - after 18 months he was appointed Cellar Foreman and he continued in this position until 1968, when he left for South Australia, to further his experience. He joined a winery consulting firm and spent two years working vintages at Seaview, d'Arenberg, Redmans and Tullochs in the Hunter - a total of seven harvests in two years, which is what you might call being on the fast track. After this, Bill moved to the Barossa to work at Basedow for six years. In this time Bill won an amazing collection of medals, which totalled over 3250 show awards and trophies for a number of different wine styles. Whilst working at Basedows, Bill was a consultant to John Tate, co-founder of Evans & Tate, and was instrumental in the development of the now legendary Gnangara Shiraz. He returned to Western Australia to live at the end of 1977 and took up the position of Wine Maker/ Winery Manager at Evans & Tate. In 1993 Bill moved on once again to seek new challenges - this time Sandalford was his choice, one of the largest family-owned vineyards in the region. He rejuvenated the vineyard, and kept win-

Recommended Producers

Abbey Vale   A strong range throughout.

Arelewood Estate   The wines here are made by Cliff Royale from Voyager Estate, although they plan to double production in the next five years to 5000 cases, when they will consider the possibility of building their own winery.

Brookwood Estate   A new winery that has seen acclaim for its Shiraz, but also makes a good selection of white wines.

Cape Mentelle   One of the most respected wineries in the region. Very good wines across the range and an interesting Zinfandel, which suggests that the region may be well suited to the variety.

Clairault   Back in the days when the cellar door here was literally a tin shack, it was one of my favourite wineries. Today it is a multi-million building, which houses a restaurant and spectacular cellar door facility. Unfortunately the lady in charge of the tasting facilities was only willing to let me taste their most basic range. This is a shame as I disclosed who I was and the wines had always impressed.

Cullen Wines - One of the top six wineries in the region, along with Leeuwin, Cape Mentelle, Moss Wood, Vasse Felix and Pierro. Vanya Cullen is now at the helm and her judicious wine-making skills are apparent throughout the range on offer.

Deep Woods Estate   Award-winning wines, with the Shiraz and Semillon/Sauvignon picking up most of them.

Devil's Lair   Now part of the Southcorp empire, so hopefully the impressive track record they have enjoyed will be preserved.

Evans & Tate   A large operation that enjoys a worldwide reputation.

Fire Gully   Ownership by Michael Peterkin of Pierro gives these wine pedigree.

Garlands   A winery on the move. The best Cabernet Franc in Australia?

Gralyn Estate   This estate is rapidly gaining a reputation for its red wines, which are made in a style that could attract the attention of Robert Parker.

Green Valley Vineyard   Keith Mugford from Moss Wood makes these wines.

Hamelin Bay   As well as spectacular wines, the views from the estate are some of the finest in the region.

Happs   The story of Happs winery is a very interesting one - the winery was built by Erl Happs himself. Erl is a consummate professional and is at his happiest leafing through various technical manuals to overcome problems; he has always had a very hands-on approach.

Howard Park   A very impressive new winery and tasting facility has been built here, with a most impressive driveway. The wines follow in the grandeur of it all and show well.

ABOVE *Cape Mentelle Vineyard, Margaret River.*

Juniper Estate   Going through a period of revitalisation under new ownership. A lot of work has been carried out in the vineyard and major investment has been made in the winery. Next door to Vasse Felix.

Killerby   The Killerby family were some of the first settlers in the region and their experience shows in their stunning Shiraz wines.

Leeuwin Estate   Quite simply the finest producer of Chardonnay in Australia, with its Art Series bottling. The other wines on offer are equally impressive.

Lenton Brae   A family-run vineyard, where I once worked the 1994 harvest. The Sauvignon/Semillon and Chardonnay are the stars of the show.

Moss Brothers   Great pedigree, with the owners hailing from Moss Wood

Moss Wood   Exemplary wines and very sought after Cabernet Sauvignon.

Pierro   Along with Giaconda and Leeuwin Estate, a producer of one of the top Chardonnays. Although it doesn't have the longevity of the Leeuwin Chardonnay it is still excellent.

Redgate   One of the most southern vineyards in WA, being less than two miles from the Indian Ocean. Bill Ullinger has undergone some difficult times since setting up the winery in the late 1970s, not least because of the bank manager. A war veteran, Bill had the inner mettle to see the project through, however, and the winery has won over 100 medals in the past seven years.

Sandalford   Sandalford is the oldest family-owned winery in Western Australia, having been founded in 1840. In fact it was on Land Title No 2 in the State - although this is near the Swan River region, just north of Perth. The family also own a thirty-year-old vineyard in the Willyabrup region of Margaret River, from which the fruit is transported to the winery in Swan River.

Saracen Estate   Founded in 1998, this winery goes from strength to strength.

Suckfizzle   Although the name is funny, along with one of their labels Stella Bella, the wines are actually rather good.

Vasse Felix   Another top winery. The Heytesbury range in particular should be singled out for the sheer quality on offer. Cabernet at its best.

Willespie   Willespie has historically done very well in the Margaret River show, having won the award for the top wine in 1983. Unfortunately the shows stopped after this, and did not recommence until 2002. The owners who made this wine, Kevin and Marian Squance, are still here, although they are now helped by various staff. They initially planted the vineyard in 1976, and in 1982 were one of the first to plant Verdelho, which is made as a dry table wine and marketed as a flagship wine.

Xanadu   A winery that has grown enormously over the past 10 years. An impressive cellar door facility is now in operation, where you can taste most of the range on offer.

ABOVE *Fermentation vats at Evans & Tate Limited, Margaret River. From here the majority of red wines and some white wines will be transferred to 225-litre oak barriques for maturation.*

ning medals until his departure in 2000 to develop a consultancy that includes being the winemaker at Saracen.

Green Valley Vineyard is in one of the most picturesque locations in the Margaret River region, in the bush of the Boranup forest. It is owned by ex-weatherman Ed Green and his wife Eleonore. Ed was mostly involved in the Civil and Military Weather services, and was awarded a Australian Public Service Medal. He is now the general manager of the vineyard whilst Eleanor, a former Oral Surgeon, is the viticulturalist. The vineyard was originally designated a Gelignite Block by the premier of WA, Sir James Mitchell, and it covers approximately 30 acres of which 20 is under vine. It was first planted in 1980, with the most recent vines being planted in 1995 on north-facing slopes, ensuring insulation and gentle ripening. The vineyard is also ideally situated, having favourable topography that steers the West Coast trough showers and thunderstorms away from it. This has the added benefit that at Green Valley they can continue harvesting when others within three miles cannot due to heavy rainfall (not that this happens too often!) As well as the lateritic gravel, karri loam can be found here, with sands on top of loam and gravel. The vines are hand-pruned, thinned and picked, which helps Keith Mugford of Moss Wood, their contract winemaker, to make the best possible wines.

Moss Wood was founded in 1969 by Bill and Sandra Pannell, at the same time that Cape Mentelle was being formed. The first vintage was in 1973, when just 250 cases of Cabernet Sauvignon were made. Pinot Noir and Semillon were next to be planted, as until 1976 no suitable cuttings of Chardonnay were available in Western Australia.

It did not take long for Moss Wood to establish itself as one of the leading wineries in the region, and in 1978 it was selected as the winery from which the Australian Governor of the time, Sir Wallace Kyle, would select wines to serve to the Queen during her tour. Keith Mugford was employed in 1969, after he graduated from Roseworthy College. He obviously did not miss South Australia too much, as he purchased the property in 1985 with his wife Clare. The business has been evolving ever since, and many strategic problems have had to be resolved. One of the largest concerns for the Mugfords was providing a future for their four children within the framework of the business. This could have been to the detriment of current staff, who would not have been able to advance their career with the company, because the senior roles would eventually be taken by family members. The solution was found by purchasing an established vineyard, located 1.5 miles from Moss Wood, and creating a new label. This also fitted in with their long term plan of establishing a new Cabernet Sauvignon to fit into their portfolio, as the worldwide demand for Moss Wood Cabernet had escalated the prices beyond the reach of some of their domestic customers, who had supported the wines since their inception. The new Cabernet is also from a different clone, ensuring that each label has its own nuances.

Great Southern

Alkoomi is a family-owned and operated vineyard; the name when translated means "the place we chose" and was given to it by the original owners in 1900. The property has been in the Langes family since 1946, when Merv Langes' father purchased it for farming, including grain, sheep and cattle. Wool prices declined in 1960s so Merv decided to explore different ways of utilising the land to best effect. The Western Australian Department of Agriculture had been testing trial plantings of Cabernet Sauvignon and Riesling in nearby Mt Barker. This prompted Merv to plant Riesling, Cabernet Sauvignon and Shiraz on the property in 1971. Over the years there have been many subsequent plantings here, including Chardonnay, Sauvignon Blanc, Semillon, Merlot, Malbec, Viognier, Petit Verdot and Sangiovese. In all, the estate now comprises some 200 acres of vines. Today Merv and his wife Judy are in charge of the management of the business, with their son Wayne in charge of the vineyard. Their son-in-law, Rod Hallett, runs the winery, whilst Michael Staniford has been in charge of the wine-making since 1995. Michael came with very good experience, having worked for Max Lake from Lakes Folly in the Hunter Valley and this shows in the wines. One of the nicest aspects of this business is that the Langes have borrowed no money at all from the bank, which I think is wonderful.

Chatsfield is owned by Ken Lynch, a medical practitioner of some 50 years who read a book by a French GP on the merits of good French wine. The author had been the sole GP in a village and had found out, via his practice and autopsies, that his patients never died of either heart disease or liver failure if they drank no more than one litre of good wine per day. Ken has been intrigued ever since, especially since modern medicine seems to support his hypothesis - although our anglo-saxon christianity decrees that anything that gives pleasure must be bad, and so we are reluctant to go as far as one litre spread over 24 hours! However, due to this Ken took an interest in a vineyard in 1995, and in 1988 bought it outright.

Ken strongly believes that this area is the sleeping giant of wine regions in Australia. It has always produced more fruit than Margaret River, and exported more fruit to that region than the region produced itself, until five years ago. It is also said that the climate is better, especially inland from the sea, and the fruit is much more delicate and elegant than in the southwest.

A lot of the soils in the region are gravely loam - including that of Chatsfield, situated as they are on the western side of the Porongurup

ABOVE *A view of the vineyard at Goundrey Wines, in Mount Barker, Western Australia. Goundrey produce an impressive line-up of wines, across a wide range. It was at Mount Barker that the WA Department of Agriculture did trial plantings of Cabernet Sauvignon and Riesling.*

range, which is over one million years old - in fact next to the Australian alps, it is the oldest mountain range in Australia. Ken is determined to make wines of moderate alcoholic strength, and is starting to see others follow as they have seen how elegant his wines can be.

Frankland Estate is a family-owned and operated winery, located in the Frankland River region. It is one of only four Australian producers listed in Jancis Robinson's global list of up-and-coming producers, which is published in her Concise Wine Companion. The renowned US wine writer Robert Parker, on his first visit to Australia in 2001, urged Australian winemakers not to try and copy European styles, but to make distinctively Australian wines. Asked by wine writer Huon Hooke to nominate such a wine, he singled out Frankland Estate's Olmo's Reward, and described it as a distinctive wine with its own personality, which he loved.

In 1988, Frankland Estate was the second winery to be established in the region, with red

wine varieties deliberately chosen for the vineyard, to enable the production of a red wine blend of predominantly Cabernet Franc and Merlot. It is not just the reds that dominate here though - Riesling is also high on the agenda. To promote it The Frankland Estate Riesling Scholarship is awarded annually to a member of the Australian wine or hospitality industries who, through their commitment to the variety, have contributed to greater appreciation and enjoyment of Riesling wines. Every two years they hold a Riesling tasting, with examples from around the world, to give a general overview and point of discussion on the variety. The estate itself produces three Rieslings, all from separate vineyards, to emphasise the effect of different terroirs.

Galafrey is another family-run vineyard, making around 12,000 cases per year. Ian, Linda and their daughter, Kim Hardy, all help out in the running of this 35-acre property, with particular success with their Art Label Semillon/Sauvignon blend. Ian is an industry veteran, who sits on numerous boards and committees to help promote the region. Some of the most distinctive labels are to be found here, having been painted by Kim, an accomplished artist.

Trevelen Farm is the most northerly wine producer in the Great Southern region. It is owned by the Sprigg family, whose forefathers emigrated to Australia in 1839. John and Katie have spent some 32 years in agriculture, together diversifying into wine-making around 1994. The vineyard was established in 1993 around 100km north of Albany, which means that they are not affected to such a great extend by coastal weather and spray (there are big waves in this part of the world making it very popular with surfers). The Riesling and

Recommended Producers

Alkoomi   Look out for the Jarrah and Black Butt wines

Castle Rock Estate   Robert Diletti, the winemaker here, can remember planting his first vines as a six-year-old in 1983. He went on to successfully complete a winemaking degree at Charles Sturt. A couple of years spent working elsewhere has given him the experience needed to come and run the family vineyard.

Chatsfield   A good range, including Shiraz and Cabernet Franc.

Ferngrove   A new winery in 2000 will help Murray Burton achieve his goal of making wines of indisputable quality.

Frankland Estate   Located in the Frankland River region, the Olmo's Reward is well worth seeking out.

Galafrey   Quite large wines for the area.

Garlands   The best Cabernet Franc in Australia?

Gilberts   Magnificent wines that are made at Plantagenet under contract.

Goundrey   An impressive line up across the range.

Merrebee Estate   If you are lucky you can sometimes purchase mature wines from this estate, which continues to develop.

Plantagenet   This winery consistently makes wines to a very high standard. The Pinot Noir in good years can be outstanding, as is the Shiraz in most vintages.

Trevelen Farm   A multi agricultural business that makes fine wines of exceptional value.

West Cape Howe Wines   Brenden Smith runs this winery located in the Denmark area, which is considered to be the jewel in the crown of the region. The wines have good structure and balance, coming from vines grown on lateritic gravel loams over clay, which are common for much of the region.

Zarephath Wines   The name means refinement; these wines are made by a monastic community of the Christ Circle Inc and the labels convey a spiritual message. The vineyard is the most easterly in the region.

Sauvignons are the winners here, both gaining many medals on the show circuit.

Garlands was formed just outside of Mt Barker in 1996 by Michael and Julie Garland, with the splendid Pornguups as a backdrop to the vineyard. Although Michael has only recently graduated from the Charles Sturt University in Oenology, he has worked in the past for Plantagenet, gaining the experience and expertise needed to run his own winery. The results so far have been impressive, particularly so with his Cabernet Franc, which is quickly establishing itself as one of the best in the country. The style they are aiming for here is based upon elegance, and to accomplish this they hand-craft their wines and make them in a traditional manner. The vineyard was originally planted in 1988, enabling them - along with their neighbours Craig and Carolyn Drummond - to get off to a running start. As with all businesses cash is vital, and the two families were fortunate to have a chance visit from Patrick and Christine Gresswell in 2002, who put forward an investment plan that they accepted. This has enabled the business to grow greatly and find European markets - a far cry from their beginnings, when they operated on a shoestring. The first vintage was made in a shed that measured only 6x6 metres, but this did not stop the wine, a Cabernet Franc, from getting a gold medal. This further fuelled the family's ambition and proved their conviction about the site. After this success, they set about custom-building a winery, which today processes around 150 tonnes of fruit. Craig and Carolyn are retiring from their careers, as a GP and physiotherapist respectively, to focus on the wine business. Craig is also undertaking the Master of Wine examinations, which are discussed in more detail in the McLaren Vale section.

Ferngrove Vineyard was started by Murray Burton, who mortgaged his family farm at Walpole in 1996 to purchase an area of land to the north of the Frankland River. It took a year to establish the vineyard - but the vines thrived, leading to the acquisition of more land in 1998. One of the attractions of this region is the nightly breezes that come in from the Southern Ocean, making it one of the coolest regions. This means that the grapes are harvested much later in the year, which gives the wines more intensity.

Western Australia Other Areas

It may come as a surprise to learn that the oldest winery still in operation today is located not in the eastern states but in the Swan Valley, north of Perth. It was here in 1829 that vines were planted, and a cellar built at Olive Farm, which is still in operation today. For some 150 years the Swan Valley enjoyed the reputation of being the largest wine region in the west. It is quite a unique area, having the highest mean January temperature, the lowest summer rainfall, the lowest relative humidity and the most sunshine hours per day of all the major regions in the country. The most famous winery located here is Houghton, due to their "HWB" logo that actually stands for Houghtons White Burgundy - although this has had to be dropped to meet EU labelling laws. It could be argued that it was this wine that really put Western Australia on the viticultural map to other Australians, due to the sheer volume of it that was sold. Although sold in large quantity it is a quality wine, and leads you up to the ultra premium Jack Mann Cabernet blend, which, when purchased in magnums, comes in its own wooden presentation case. One winery that has entered a new era in its 160-year history is Sandalford, founded by John Septimus Roe, Western Australia's first Surveyor General. A new winery has been built, which has seen Sandalford maintain its position as the largest winery in WA, producing around two million bottles annually. Still some way off from this impressive total is Aquila wines, who have grown from crushing 37 tonnes in 1992 (their first vintage) to over 350 now, although most of the grapes are purchased from Margaret River and the Blackwood Valley.

As its name would suggest, the Perth Hills are in close proximity to the Western Australian capital city of Perth. In fact if you are on the road to the Pinnacles tourist area some hours to the north, you could quite easily pass through the region without noticing it. Although classified as having a Mediterranean climate, this is not necessarily true of an evening. The region is subject to regular easterly winds blowing after dusk which can drop the temperature down to 12°C or less, even in summer. It is a diverse region, which is still in its infancy. It is similar to the Yarra Valley, in that there are a variety of soils (mainly gravely loam/sand at a depth of 1-3 metres over a clay base) and micro-climates throughout the region. It is quite common for vineyards in the valleys to receive less sunshine during the day making them substantially cooler. Due to the relatively young age of the area it is still experimenting with various grape varieties to determine which are the most suited. So far, it would appear that Semillon, Shiraz and Merlot are doing well, although it is too early to say if these grapes will reach the same heights as they do in other states. One flavour descriptor that does occur quite frequently with wine from here is "earthy" - perhaps this could be terroir showing through.

Although as yet there are no real superstar

ABOVE *Vineyards in Swan Valley, Western Australia. The first vines were planted here in 1829, and the first cellar at Olive Farm is still in operation today. For 150 years it was the largest wine region in the west.*

ABOVE *A view of the vineyard at Houghton Wines, Swan Valley,*

RIGHT *Shiraz is doing well in some areas of Western Australia.*

wineries here, it may only be a matter of time. The region is lucky enough to have James Elson, who owns Carosa and has a wealth of experience as a winemaker in Rutherglen, the Barossa and Great Western. Although James only makes a small amount of wine under his own label, he does make it for five other Perth Hills wineries also. This should give, if conditions allow, the potential to make some serious wines in the future. However, it is unlikely these will ever make a big splash on the market, as the wineries are all reasonably small and they are prevented from expanding by the city encroaching upon them.

Heading south along the coast towards Margaret River, there are a few wineries of note. The first one you pass, located between Perth and Freemantle, is Paul Conti Wines. Established in its current form in 1948 (vines were first planted in 1927) on the South West Coastal Plain, this winery is know for its Mariginiup Shiraz, made from vines planted in 1958. The region itself is a thin strip, which at its maximum is 2.5 mile wide and extends from Yanchep to the Ludlow Tuart Forest near the old port of Busselton, some 110 miles to the South. The soils of the region are dominated by fertile sandy topsoils over a limestone base, and the massive Eucalypt Tuart trees. Being close to the Indian Ocean, it benefits from a mild maritime climate with no frosts during the growing season. Like a number of WA wine regions the wines are refined, a factor that Paul Conti puts down to the limestone content of the soil. Another producer of fine Shiraz from the region is Peel Estate, located some way south of Paul Conti. The wines here are made to age gracefully and the winemaker, Will Nairn, holds a tasting every year of six-year-old Shiraz from various wineries. This is a confident move to make, and is testament to the quality of these wines.

The last well-known name that you reach is Capel Vale, located just south of Bunbury and officially in the Geographe region. This winery has grown from operating out of a tin shed to a production of in excess of 150,000 cases, under the direction of Dr Peter Pratten, the winery's founder in 1974. There is a large portfolio of wines made here, at least 20, which must keep head winemaker Nicole Esdaile quite busy. The company's vineyards in Geographe (they are also in three other WA regions) are located on five-metre-deep red alluvial soils over limestone, and benefit from a very long growing season which can last up to seven months. The wines are well rounded and offer a nice spiciness, with the Chardonnay and Merlot being particularly successful.

South Australia

South Australia is the darling of the Australian wine scene at the moment. No other state has been glorified by the American wine critic Robert Parker as much, with dozens of scores in the nineties and a splattering of 100s. It would seem that South Australia has it all. For every grape variety commonly grown in Australia, it has a region that can grow it supremely well. In Barossa there are Shiraz and Semillon, Riesling in Clare; Pinot Noir and Sauvignon Blanc in the Adelaide Hills; Chardonnay and Grenache in McLaren Vale; and Cabernet Sauvignon in Coonawarra. What's more, many regions can grow several varieties equally as well. It is this ability to work with the environment that has enabled it to become the premier state for wine and wine tourism in the country.

There is a big move currently to promote regionality in Australian wines. Whilst this is fine in theory, it is perhaps not the ideal route to follow to achieve more sales - which is what it is ultimately about. For a start, it takes a real professional to tell the difference between a McLaren Vale Shiraz and a Barossa one. What I believe they should focus on, and promote, is which grape variety is most at home in each region and the style it makes there - for example, if it has cold or warm climate characteristics. This not only focuses the mind of the grower, it also enables the consumer to be more certain of the style of wine they are going

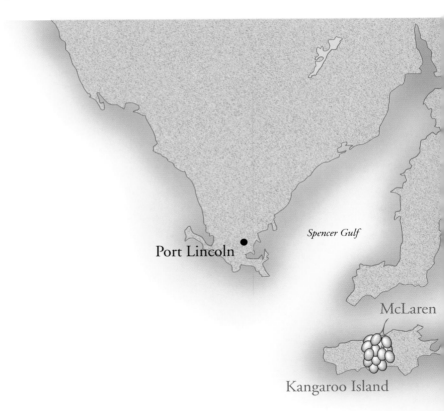

Spencer Gulf

Port Lincoln

McLaren

Kangaroo Island

SOUTH AUSTRALIA

to purchase. The other alternative would be to market the vineyards around Adelaide - McLaren Vale, Adelaide Hills, Barossa and Eden Valleys, and Clare Valley - as communes in the district of Adelaide. I am not in marketing so I do not know if this could work, but this same system has worked for centuries in Bordeaux.

One of the most appealing aspects of the state is the ability to tour the wine regions surrounding Adelaide with ease. All are located less than an hour from the city centre, and if you start in McLaren Vale you can work your way in a northerly direction into the Adelaide Hills and onto the Barossa and Eden Valleys. Just a short drive from here and you will find yourself in the Clare Valley. An altogether very pleasant way to spend a couple of weeks.

South Australia is also very fortunate in

that the planning people, all those years ago, decided that Coonawarra should fall here and not in Victoria, as it almost straddles the border. The benefits this has bought have been enormous, and have enabled the state to be considered one of the finest in the world.

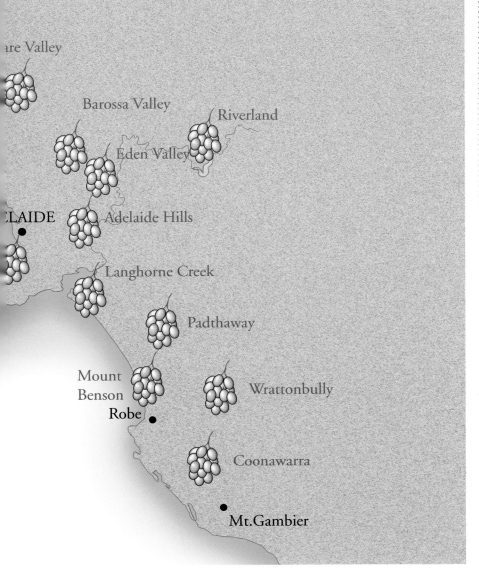

Barossa and Eden Valleys

The Barossa is without question the engine room of the Australian wine industry. No other region has so many great and historic names located within it. Virtually all the giants of the industry such as Southcorp, who own Penfolds, Rosemount and Lindemans, are based here, along with Orlando, makers of Jacobs Creek, and BRL Hardy, the owners of the Hardy's Stamp series of wines. It is also the land of the smaller independent winery, without whom the region would be nowhere near as interesting. It is all these idiosyncratic wines, which are crafted from vines that have been tended by four or five generations of grape-growing families, that provide the real interest. They offer so much more than the sometimes one-dimensional wines that the bigger companies have to make for commercial reasons. It is perhaps in the last 15 years that the region has come to be regarded as special on the world stage. Helped along by Penfolds Grange - arguably the finest red wines in Australia - and the influential American wine writer Robert Parker, names such as Torbreck, Greenock Creek, Three Rivers, Langmeil, Charles Melton and Veritas have all received international acclaim.

The Barossa Valley's name can be traced back to 1811, when Lieutenant General Thomas Graham (a Brit) defeated a French Marshal at Barossa Ridge in Andalusia, Spain during the Napoleonic War. It is located one hour north of South Australia's capital city, Adelaide, and comprises three main towns -

ABOVE *The Barossa Valley is named after the Barossa Ridge in Spain, where the British defeated the French in 1811.*

Tanunda, Nuriootpa and Lyndoch. It is hard to imagine that some of the world's finest winemakers live in these sleepy, but charming villages, where life seems to have continued on in the same fashion for the past 50 years or so. Walking through Tanunda in the afternoon, you will still find shopkeepers sitting behind a desk and chatting to customers as they sell whatever it is they sell. There is one sign of modernisation though - the tourist information centre has a touch-screen terminal and speaker system, to allow you to the find the location of your favourite winery or perhaps look at sample menus from the local restau-

ABOVE *The Barossa Valley not only holds the giants of the wine industry, but also several smaller, independent wineries.*

rants. All three towns lie along the Barossa Highway, which must count as one of the great wine roads of the world as it runs through some of the most prized vineyards in Australia, or indeed anywhere.

The Barossa was officially zoned in 1997 with a Geographic Indicator, to comply with European requirements to have a recognised system of identification of wines. This effectively split the Valley in two. To the east is Eden Valley, lying between 400 and 600 metres above sea level. The soils are quite acidic and rocky, with high winter rainfall that can be as much as 255mm more than the Barossa. Due to the high altitude, temperatures are the lowest in South Australia for grape growing, which leads to a longer growing season to enable the grapes to ripen fully. The soils here are ancient, consisting of yellow -brown and grey-brown podzolics, over mica schist and quartz reef - the least fertile soils in the State. It may not sound ideal to the layman, but one of the world's great wines is made here - Henschke's Hill of Grace. This vineyard is in the middle of nowhere in an idyllic valley overlooking a marvellous Lutheran Church, which is the location for many a photograph. This most famous of vineyards is not open to the public - you may only enter if accompanied by a member of staff. This will usually be Stephen Henschke, who quite rightly insists that you dip your boots in a solution to ensure that no pest can be carried onto the hallowed turf.

The Henschke family has long associations with the region. Johann Christian Henschke

ABOVE *Eden Valley in South Australia is a place of unspoiled beauty.*

arrived in 1841, after enduring a 98-day voyage from Germany. Although settling at Krondorf, he also purchased land in Bethany and by 1868 had made his first wines - all from white varieties. Henschke, a true grafter, built an underground cellar to house the fermenting grape juice, and soon expanded to red, to make a Bordeaux-style wine. As the demand slipped for dry table wines and increased for sweeter dessert wines, the family followed suit and started selling fortifying spirit to the Angas Park Distillery. However, when Cyril Henschke, a fourth-generation family member, joined the firm after leaving secondary school, he pursued his interest in making dry table wines. To gain vital experience he completed a vintage working for Hardys and came back full of enthusiasm to make a high-quality dry red wine. This was the beginning of the modern era for the Henschke family business, which is flourishing today. Cyril's determination to make some of the greatest wines in the land paid off. Today Stephen and Prue Henschke, the current owners, commemorate him by naming their top Cabernet Cyril Henschke. They also make a plethora of other wines, including a top class Riesling that is sometimes released under their Museum Programme (wines that are only put into the market when they have reached maturity). All have one continuous attribute - elegance. They are refined and supremely balanced, and act as benchmarks not only for the Eden Valley but for the whole of Australia.

ABOVE *Sunrise at Yalumba Wines, Barossa Valley*

Although clearly an area which has proved itself to be ideal for grape growing, it is very doubtful that the Eden Valley will be able to expand in the near future unless government policy changes. It has been decreed a "Proclaimed Water Restricted Area", which basically means that no further water can be taken to increase vineyard holdings from the amount held at 1999. Without this water, which is vital for irrigation, it would prove very difficult to establish a vineyard even with a higher rainfall than in the Barossa. One other important factor, which would have been of interest to grape growers wanting to follow an organic farming model, is that the area has very little problem from disease or pests. The light brown Apple Moth and Powdery Mildew can appear, but they are easily treated with natural sprays such as diluted milk or canola oils.

Although this region is mainly known for its superb Shiraz and Riesling-based wines, it has now been established that Merlot also grows very well here - as demonstrated by the Irvine Estate. Partly due to their enormous success with the variety others have followed suit, which has resulted in an increase from just one acre of Merlot in the entire Eden Valley in 1983, to around 100 in 2002. Irvine's 1992 Grand Merlot was judged World's Best Merlot at the Swiss World Merlot tasting hosted by Academie du Vin and Wein Wisser in 1997. It beat off competitors such as Petrus

ABOVE *A 140-year-old Shiraz vine at Yalumba Wines in the Barossa Valley.*

and Mondavi, in a field littered with superstar names. Not a bad achievement from a label only started in 1991.

The Barossa itself has an average altitude of less than 400 metres, with red-brown soils that are indicative of the region's climate, which is around 2°C higher than surrounding areas. This region, along with the rest of South Australia, is blessed by not having been affected by the pest Phylloxera, which attacks the

Grape Varieties

SHIRAZ - This is the grape of the region. Almost always full and intense, these wines display layers of dark fruits, sometimes with chocolate and hints of earthiness. The abundance of fruit can mask the sometimes savoury aspect.

CABERNET - Again, rich and full wines with lots of black fruits and chocolate. Cassis can be found from wines in the warmer valley floor of the Barossa, as opposed to the cooler Eden Valley.

GRENACHE - An intense earthy variety, which is best from the old bush vines. It can be spicy, with hints of tobacco and black fruits.

SEMILLON - Along with the Hunter Valley, this is possibly the best region in Australia for this variety. Unlike the Hunter, the wines are usually oak-matured, which adds

ABOVE *Shiraz grapes*

a new dimension to the citrus flavours found here. They have a good potential to age and take on more toasty and honeyed flavours as they develop.

RIESLING - Most of the Barossa Riesling hails from the cooler Eden Valley. Citrus and flora notes dominate here, although the wines are a little lighter than those found in the Clare Valley.

vines' roots, and which destroyed European vineyards in the late 1880s. Although disease is not a problem on the whole, in 1974 the region was affected by Downy Mildew, because the vineyards were too boggy to spray as a result of heavy rains.

The Barossa was first colonised in the 1840s by English settlers, who took advantage of the "Special Surveys" promotion from the South Australian Company. This enabled any prospective buyer to purchase up to 4000 acres, surveyed in 80-acre blocks. The blocks cost the princely sum of £1 per acre, so buyers bought large areas and leased out any land in excess of their requirements. The region was not wholly for wine at this stage, because around this time George Fife Angus was successfully farming crops and livestock. This attracted further settlers, especially migrants from Germany, who by 1847 numbered 2,500. Angus himself was a Scot who had succeeded in business, and was particularly adept at promoting South Australia in London. However, it was not the English that he was most successful in persuading to migrate to Australia - it was Lutherans who had fled Prussia. Showing great financial acumen, he lent them the money to purchase land in the Barossa at £10 per acre!

The arrival of vines to the area was instigated by Joseph Gilbert, a noted landholder in England who owned a manor house in the Vale of Pewsey, Wiltshire. Having spent time in France, he soon recognised the Eden Valley as having potential for viticulture. Being at a high altitude and considerable cooler than the rest of the Barossa, he found it ideal for the growing of mainly white varieties (how could

ABOVE *Vineyards in the Barossa Valley.*

he keep the fermentation temperatures down in the hotter valley next door?). By 1857 Gilbert had 15 acres planted to Cabernet, Shiraz, Red Frotignac, Riesling, Verdelho, Tokay and Gouais, an obscure grape from the Jura region of France. As the business grew, so did the stock holdings, as wine was only released four to five years after vintage. Gilbert utilised his strong connections with England, especially London, and almost 50% of his produce was exported there. He won numerous prizes at competitions, but the family suffered crippling taxes in 1929 when Joseph Gilbert died, and only six years later, with the advent of the great depression, the vineyard was grubbed up. It was not until the 1960s that winemaking returned to the area, when the Angas and Hill Smith (of Yalumba) families purchased 9000 acres of land, including the original Pewsey Vale vineyards. Eventually the

ABOVE *Frost fans at Barossa Valley. Although cooler temperatures suit many varieties of grape, such as Riesling, frost can damage the fruit as it forms.*

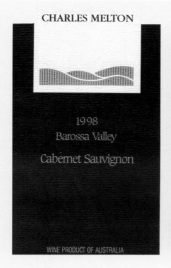

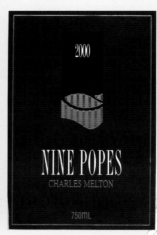

Hill Smiths bought out the Angas Parsons, and expanded the vineyards.

The next major name to come to the area was David Wynn. He was looking for an idyllic location that would have the right conditions to make wine. He found it in what is now known as High Eden, on the other side of the Boundary Road from the Eden Valley itself. The area as a whole was unspoilt (and still is) with no major dwellings. One of the main wineries in the area today is Eden Springs, a small operation that began life in 1972. However, it was only in recent times, since the acquisition of the property by Richard Wiencke and Meredith Hodgson, that it has been performing to its true potential. They produce only three wines, which are all 100% varieties of Cabernet, Shiraz and a Riesling. The vineyards are unique as they are planted on contours, including the shallow sandy yellow podzol soils on which their Riesling is grown. They believe that this makes a richer, more fruit-driven and less austere and acidic wine than other High Eden and Eden Valley Rieslings. Richard also pointed out in an interview that the area can be susceptible to Botrytis, if preventative measures are not taken in the vineyard. This is due to the Autumn rains arriving before the end of vintage, causing the disease to spread quickly throughout the vineyard (which can, of course, be great if you want it on the Riesling grapes).

The Barossa experienced strong growth between 1861 and 1891, when the land used for viticulture grew from 447 acres to 4,477 acres. This growth was fuelled by the "Work Act" which allowed more licensing of distilleries. This due to spirit being an essential preservative before electricity - and therefore refrigeration - were common place. The British Government also relaxed duty on wine entering the country, so that Australia could compete on price with France and other European countries.

At the Southern end of the valley is Rowland Flat, perhaps most famous for being the headquarters for Orlando, the makers and owners of Jacobs Creek. This area was first planted at Jacobs Creek in 1847 by Johann Gramp, an immigrant from Bavaria. Today the Orlando wine business is one of the largest in Australia, and it has a magnificent cellar door facility and restaurant that opened in 2002. Soils in the area vary between red-brown earth and black Biscay, with the former being the preferred choice for many, due to its ability to retain moisture and produce finer flavours. Amongst the first people to settle here and grow grapes was Benno Liebich, who started in 1919 with a business called Rovalley Wines. His family still live here today, with his granddaughter, Janet. at the helm of their eponymous-named winery.

Around Tanunda in the centre of the valley lie some of the most famous names in the Barossa - Charles Melton, Grant Burge, Rockford, Langmeil, Peter Lehmann and Veritas. Of these renowned names, only Veritas and Peter Lehmann have been established for more than 20 years. Peter Lehmann, who had worked for Yalumba as an apprentice and then as chief winemaker for Saltram, is a legend in the valley, and it is partly down to him that a lot of the wineries are still in existence today. In the late 1970s the major wineries reduced the amount of grapes they purchased from independent growers. This obviously left them in a precarious position, and one which could have resulted in financial ruin. Peter Lehmann stepped in with an offer to buy the excess grapes, make it into wine and then pay the growers once the wine had been sold. This worked so well during this hard period, that Lehmann formed a consortium which built the present day winery. In 1992 the financial backers had to pull out and he, along with his staff, friends and growers, bought the assets. Today his wines are exported worldwide, and they all receive consistent acclaim, from the approachable Barossa Vines range to the award-winning Stonewell Shiraz.

Charles Melton is a relative newcomer, having only been established since 1984 on the Krondorf Road. Frustrated by the vine pull scheme, he decided - along with other small Barossa winemakers - that the Shiraz and Grenache varieties that were being destroyed should, in fact, be savoured and looked after because of the tremendous wines they can produce. Following the classic blends of the Rhone, Charlie made a wine known as Nine Popes, a blend of the two grapes mentioned above, along with Mouvedre. This blend is now known simply as GSM throughout Australia. Charlie is not afraid to be adventurous in the winery, and often uses whole bunch presses and indigenous yeast in the fermentation process. The very low yields of around one tonne per acre, given by the plethora of vineyards that he uses throughout the valley, really add to the complexities of the wine.

Veritas, now owned and run by Rolf Binder and his sister, Christa Deans, was

ABOVE *Sunrise over the Barossa Valley.*

established in 1955. Rolf is an tremendously gifted winemaker and all round nice guy. When I visited him to taste and talk about his wines, I asked him to recommend the best restaurant in Tanunda for me to have dinner that evening (by myself). Straight away he invited me to join him and his family at his house. This is an opportunity that could not be passed up - how often do you get invited to one of the world's greatest winemakers for a bite to eat? Naturally the majority of the conversation was about wine, which prompted some interesting discussion. We enjoyed bottles of Rolf's Heysen along with a bottle of Torbreck's Factor; both showed very well and were drunk with pleasure. The Heysen is perhaps the greatest value wine in Australia. It is

ABOVE *Bethany Wines in the Barossa Valley. The Bethany family first planted a vineyard here in 1852, and today it is run by their descendants.*

ABOVE *As the casks are made, the cooper constantly turns them over a small fire. The resulting singeing of the wood, known as the toast, will affect the final flavour of the wine.*

of exceptional quality, and can be comfortably cellared for the medium to long term. The rest of the large Veritas range also regularly impresses me, with its earthy and deep Grenache and Mouvedre-based wines, through to the fortifieds. I cannot help but feel that Veritas is to the Barossa what d'Arenberg is to McLaren Vale.

It was Robert O'Callaghan who made the first quality sparkling Shiraz in the region. Robert, the son of a vineyard manger in Riverland, soon found himself in Rutherglen working for Seppelt for the 1965 vintage onwards. Whilst here, he made the whole spectrum of wines, from the famous dessert wines of the area to dry table wines and spirits. This continued for five years until 1970, when he was transferred to the Barossa in a move that would benefit the region greatly. He made sure that he knew the ways of the valley and the growers within it; what they grew and where. He used this considerable knowledge when he started the Rockford Winery in 1984. Then, as now, he did not own a vineyard but bought in quality fruit from the growers he had been working with for the past 14 years. His ambition was to maintain the distinctive Australian wine style that dated back to the 1880s. His problem was sourcing the correct grapes to make a base wine with which to build a solera system. A solera is the method used in Jerez, Spain, in the making of Sherry. Barrels are stacked 2-4 high, and wine for bottling is taken from the bottom layer. To stop oxidation and keep the barrels full, more wine must then be added from the layer above. Therefore, young wine is added to the top level of barrels and passed down to the ones below after each

bottling. This theoretically means that there will always be a portion of every year's wine still in every barrel, which helps nurture the younger wines along and matures them at a more rapid pace. Robert O'Callaghan was fortunate to be offered 500 barrels of old Shiraz, which he utilised as the base wine for the solera. Robert's approach differs slightly, in that he blends the base wine with an equal amount of Shiraz (chosen from the finest fruit of the vintage) that has been aged in oak barrels for three years. He then places half of this back in the solera, to ensure its continuation. Fermentation is induced with yeast and sugar in the remaining wine, which is disgorged a few months later. Rocky then adds a propor-

ABOVE *Stems are ejected to one side from the destemmer/crusher.*

tion of super ripe Shiraz "port" to the wines, to finish it. The resulting wine is quite extraordinary and unique. The company also produce, amongst others, a great basket-pressed Shiraz, which is considered a fine example of traditional dry-land wine making.

Moving north a few miles you pass by the Southcorp/Penfolds winery and arrive in Nuriootpa. It is in this area that some of the most prized of all Barossa vines are planted. Drive along Roennfeldt Road (actually a dirt track) and you pass some of the most prized vines in Australia. At 100 years and older, these produce the minuscule amounts of fruit that go into wines such as Penfolds Grange, Greenock Creek Roennfeldt Road and Torbreck's Run Rig, all of which cost in excess of A$250 per bottle. These wines are special though - especially Grange, which is the most revered wine in Australia. It was originally made in 1951 by Penfolds' winemaker, Max Schubert, whose bosses refuted it and told him to stop wasting his time. Fortunately he chose to ignore his superiors' orders and continued to make the wine in secret. Some years later the board of directors re-tried the wine and were highly impressed. A legend was born, and to this day it remains at the helm of Australian wines. Penfolds has accomplished so much for Australian wine worldwide that it deserves far more attention than I am able to give it here. Being a large company, it has the luxury of being able to experiment with various grapes and blending combinations.

In France, a winery could label its wines after its own name or the village in which the vineyard was located. Penfolds and others did not have that option, due to the diversity of wine they made. To alleviate this minor problem, wines were named after the bin they were stored in - hence names like Bin 389 and Bin 707 that are still in use today. In recent years Penfolds have released two wines of significant importance after extensive experiments - their white Chardonnay, Yattarna, which is otherwise dubbed the white Grange, and the RWT (Red Wine Making Trials), which retails at around A$100. Although, as a publicly-listed company, the focus has now inevitably shifted to profitability, the wines are still very good and appeal across all markets and tastes. The Bin 389 Shiraz is aged in old Grange barrels and is effectively a baby Grange, and but retails for around 15% of the Grange price.

Also based along the Roennfeldt Road is Greenock Creek, a boutique winery of the highest calibre owned by Michael and

ABOVE *At old basket press - many of these are still used today by smaller producers.*

Annabelle Waugh. There is a cellar door here surrounded by decadent old vines, although it is rare for it to be open because the entire range sells out soon after release. When I visited in 2002, a new barrel storage facility was being constructed opposite the winery, which will give the Waugh's room to move. The wines are some of the most lauded in Australia, and receive glowing reviews from around the globe. The flagship wines are known simply as Roennfeldt Road Shiraz and Cabernet Sauvignon. Matured for six years before release and only made when the quality is good enough, and in minuscule quantities, they set a benchmark for super-rich yet elegant wines of an individual nature. The Waughs also demonstrate that terroir does have a place in Australian wines with their individual vineyard bottlings. These wines sell out almost upon release, and this was the only vineyard that I visited that could not let me taste any wines - they simply did not have any. Fortunately I do, so I am able to enjoy them over dinner at home with my family.

A couple of kilometres along the road is a moderately new venture - Torbreck Vintners - which was founded in 1994. Dave Powell makes wines of consistent quality at the upper end of the quality spectrum. He first had the idea of forming a new winery in 1992, when he discovered a selection of old dry-grown vines in a state of disrepair - in fact they were almost dead. He started to nurse the vines back to good health and they duly repaid him with small amounts of excellent fruits. The amount produced, however, was nowhere near the quantity needed for him to make it into a full-time business. Short of money, he pondered

Recommended Producers

Bethany The Bethany family first planted a vineyard in the Barossa in 1852, and today it is run by Geoff and Rob Schrapel, fifth-generation family members. Rob has travelled extensively and has learnt wine-making throughout the world, which is backed up by a formal qualification from Roseworthy Agricultural College.

Charles Cimicky Unusually for the area, this winery makes a very good Sauvignon Blanc - along with good reds that offer value.

Charles Melton Low yields of between 1 and 1.5 tonnes per acre are the norm here. One of the first in the new breed of Rhone Rangers in the mid 1980s, Charles Melton has made the Shiraz and Grenache grapes his own with the seductive Nine Popes blend and straight Shiraz. He also produces an excellent Grenache-based Rose, called Rose of Virginia.

Dutschke Wines A relative newcomer, who has quickly established his name on the Barossa wine scene.

Elderton 70 acres of prime Barossa vineyards planted between 40 and 80 years ago contribute towards the immense quality of the wines from this Estate. The flagship Shiraz Command is outstanding, as too can be their Cabernet - which won the Jimmy Watson Trophy in 1992, their Shiraz being a runner up! Fortunately the Ashmeads, who own the Estate, did not participate in the vine-pull scheme of the early eighties, and consequently have vines that are planted on their own rootstocks.

Glaetzer Glaetzer's Shiraz is grown on a soil unique to the Ebernezer region, which is located in the north west. It is sandy clay loam over a solid limestone pan, and 80-year-old vines and low yields ensure good quality. The owner and winemaker, Colin Glaetzer, created Barossa Valley Estates E & E Black Pepper Shiraz. Previously he had worked in the Hunter, Riverland and France at Beaune.

Grant Burge It seems remarkable that this winery was only set up in 1988. It has since grown into one of the top ten privately owned wine companies in Australia. and has won every major Australian wine award going. There is a very impressive Riesling sourced from fruit grown in the Eden Valley, and the flagship Meshach Shiraz is one of the best examples in the Barossa.

Greenock Creek Owned and operated by Annabelle and Michael Waugh, the wines are some of the most sought after in Australia. From the ultra-premium Roennfeldt Road Shiraz and Cabernet to their Cornerstone Grenache, it is difficult not to be impressed by their wines.

Haan Wines The Merlot is one of the finest wines made here - and so it should be having been made by James Irvine, the region's resident expert.

Heritage Wines Good quality winery which is held in high regard by other local wineries. It also has a nice and cosy cellar door.

Irvine Australia's Merlot expert. Serve it alongside Petrus and Trotanoy and see which you prefer (or which you believe offers better value for money). James Irvine is one of Australia's most experienced winemakers with over 52 years of experience!

Jenke Wines Kym Jenke comes from a long line of winemakers associated with the Barossa. His fore-father started here in the mid 1800s.

how to raise enough to establish himself. After much thought and consideration he decided that "share farming" was the best option. This involves paying the vineyard owner (he had found a great old Shiraz vineyard) a percentage of the grapes' value in return for managing the vineyard and taking all the fruit.

The first harvest was in 1995, from the initial vines that he discovered, and he was able to make around 200 cases of wine from the three tonnes of fruit. Dave had previously lived and worked in Scotland as lumber jack in a forest named Torbreck - the winery had a name.

The wines are based upon the classic Rhone varietals - Shiraz, Grenache and Viognier - with a small amount of white varieties grown also. The flagship wine, Run Rig, is made from the very old, dry-grown vines mentioned earlier, which are located on the north-western boundary of the Barossa. The quality of the fruit is demonstrated by the fact that the wine is matured for 30 months in oak casks, before being blended with a small portion of Viognier to provide extra fragrance. Robert Parker described the first vintage as being Australia's answer to Guigals La Mouline

Langmeil Winery Although occupying a site that was originally planted in the 1840s, it was not until 1996 that the Lindner family established Langmeil. They inherited old machinery from the previous owners and set about cleaning the winery up. The results have been impressive, with their flagship Freedom Shiraz showing very well.

Orlando A large business that is the owner of the Jacobs Creek brand, which helped propel the Barossa name to the world. There are a large range of wines that are all well made and should not disappoint.

Penfolds Perhaps the most internationally-recognised Australian wine company. The range of wines is large, and the majority are made for commercial purposes to a high standard. At the other end of the scale is what is widely considered to be the finest wine in Australia - Grange.

Peter Lehmann A stalwart of the Barossa Valley and the fifth generation of his family to live here. A superb range of wines to match, encompassing most of the varieties grown in the region. The top-of-the-range Stonewell Shiraz is exemplary.

Richmond Grove Excellent wines for the money.

Rockford Dry-grown and basket-pressed, the Shiraz from Rockford, made by Robert O'Callaghan and Chris Ringland of Three Rivers, is spectacular. Also one of the finest sparkling Shirazes in Australia.

St Hallett A large range of well-made wines that are dominated by Shiraz. Look out for the very well priced Old Block Shiraz, which offers a sumptuous array of classic Barossa Shiraz for not a great deal of money.

Three Rivers The most expensive wine in Australia at A$550 on release. Is it worth it? Well it sells out every year without difficulty...

Torbreck Dave Powell and his team have done remarkable things here, since its beginnings in 1994. Although they do not own a large acreage of vineyard themselves they "share farm" around 40% of their total needs. The majority of these are 100+ years old, and produce the fruit for their cult premium wine Run Rig. The Steading, and its unoaked brother Juveniles, are traditional Rhone blends which offer good value.

Trevor Jones The wines bottled under the Trevor Jones label - and most notably the Wild Witch Shiraz - are among the best of the region.

Turkey Flat This hard-to-find Shiraz comes from 150-year-old vines

Veritas Rolf Binder and his sister Christina own and operate this exceptional winery, which makes some of the most under-priced wines in Australia. Top of the range Hanische (pronounced Harrnish) is exceptional, but hard to come by. Its little brother, Heysen, is from the same vines though, and offers a great alternative. Rolf's Cabernet and Grenache wines are also well worth seeking out.

Wolf Blass A name synonymous with the Barossa and now under the control of Beringer Blass.

Yaldara A famous Barossa winery with a large selection of wines on offer from ranges.

Yalumba The Virgilius Viognier is one of the country's finest examples. A very large company that also own the Oxford Landing label.

- one of the finest wines in the world. One notch down from Run Rig is The Descendent, which comes from a vineyard planted with cuttings from the Run Rig vines. It is made in the traditional Cote Rotie manner, by crushing and fermenting the Shiraz with Viognier. The wine is then aged for 18 months in old Run Rig barrels. If anyone believes that young vines cannot produce fine wine, then they really should seek out a bottle of this. The Steading and Juveniles wines are a blend of Grenache, Mataro and Shiraz, the latter being unoaked.

As with the majority of things in life, fash- ions come and go and the wine industry is no exception. In the late 1970s and 80s the fashion in Australia was for cool-climate white wines, and not the full and rich reds from the Barossa. As mentioned before, as result of this the large wineries chose not to purchase grapes from the region, which left the small independent growers with hardly any income. Although Peter Lehmann stepped in, a one man crusade could not save all the precious old vines. Many growers had no option but to pull them out of the ground, with the aid of a Government assistance package. At the time`

ABOVE *The Barossa Valley was first colonised by English settlers in 1840. Its open countryside holds sleepy and charming villages, where the pace of life seems to be the just same as it was 50 years ago.*

the price for Shiraz grapes was A$200 per tonne as opposed to A$1100 today - although this can rise to A$10,000 for dry-grown grapes from very old vines. Times were so bad that it was predicted by a lecturer at Roseworthy, the country's top wine-making college, that the area would not be a major producer by the year 2001. Fortunately he was wrong. From a total of 46,500 tonnes picked across all grape varieties in 1981, the figure had risen to 54,000 by 2002.

When Langmeil Estate was first settled in 1843, it was owned by Christian Auricht and utilised for mixed cottage industries such as orchards, butchery, blacksmiths, cobblers and, of course, a vineyard. It was not until 1932, however, that a winery was established on the site by J S T Hanisch (a name now made famous as the name of Veritas's finest wine). The winery was sold to Bernkastel in 1968 and they ran it for 20 years, before they ceased to operate here and the winery fell into disrepair. It was eight years later, in 1996, that Richard Lindner, Chris Bitter and Carl Lindner took over the property and began renovating all the old equipment. This is not a small winery, and it must have taken some time to make everything operational once again, but they persevered and are now crushing some 750 tonnes of grapes each vintage - mostly for smaller wineries that do not have their own facilities. They do make around 15,000 cases under the Langmeil name, though, of which their Freedom Shiraz heads the list. I had the oppor-

tunity to taste one of the early vintages of this wine from the families' own museum stock whilst I was there. It showed very well and I suspect that the wines from the best vintages will have very good longevity. If you visit the winery, which forms one part of a walk that takes you around four different wineries, then be sure to take a look at the century-old vines on the left as you pass. They really do emphasise just how long Australia has had a wine-making history.

The valley very much knows its importance in the Australian wine scene, and major investment by all the large firms and most smaller ones have made this a user-friendly region to visit. The majority of accommodation is in Nuriootpa, although pub hotels can been found scattered amongst the other small towns. The restaurant to visit is 1918, in Tanunda. As in the rest of the country, food at this level is very good and amazingly inexpensive. Most wineries, apart from the really cult ones, have cellar doors that range from a small tasting room to the Jacobs Creek Visitor Centre, which opened in 2002. This is an impressive piece of architecture, housing a good restaurant and a very good display gallery with plasma screens, offering a full education in the process of making wine. If you have taken the time to visit the Barossa Valley floor, then you must also take a quick drive over to the Eden Valley to see its unspoilt beauty, and to find Henschke and taste through their range of excellent wines.

McLaren Vale

Lovers of big Australian Shiraz the world over will always argue over which is the better region for it, McLaren Vale, or the Barossa Valley two hours to the north and beyond Adelaide. Certainly in the past, most of the world's wine press was focused on the Barossa of the two, as the wines are just so rich, large and bold. McLaren Vale is now receiving a lot of coverage though. Not only is it the perfect location, with the Mount Lofty Ranges to the east, it offers the advantage of having the coast to the west and thus benefiting from a cooling breeze throughout the growing season, which adds a touch more elegance to the wines. Surprisingly, McLaren Vale also crushes more grapes than the Barossa (55,000 tonnes), even though most of the big wine company's headquarters are located in the Barossa.

Up until 1990, McLaren Vale consisted of two towns, Gloucester and Bellevue. In fact the region is still registered under these names. It is a beautiful area, with small independent wineries dominating the landscape with their vineyards, but managing to hide their wineries out of site. The vineyards are also cooled at night by the colder air coming from the Willunga escarpment, which contributes to it being cooler than the Barossa. Very low humidity ensures that pests - apart from Silvereyes and Starlings who have a taste for the ripe grapes - are not a threat and so pesticides and fungicides are used sparingly. There is also very little risk of frost here, which makes it an ideal location for grape-growing. The wines have a little more elegance and structure than those from the Barossa, although they can still compete in terms of sheer weight and size. McLaren Vale also enjoys being on the doorstep of the southern Adelaide suburbs, which have slowly encroached on the Southern Vales over the past few decades. It is still an hour's drive to the centre of Adelaide, but in Australian terms this is only around the corner! Being coastal, the region is as passionate about food as it is about wine. Each year sees the Sea and Vines festival on the June holiday weekend. The majority of wineries put on special menus, with an abundance of shellfish and locally-caught delicacies, whilst the wine flows in celebration of the idyllic location and the end of vintage. It really is the perfect time to visit this region, although do not expect to see the winemaker who will undoubtedly be out enjoying the fruits of his labour.

As is consistent with a substantial part of Australia, lack of water is one of the main problems encountered with viticulture. McLaren Vale is dependent on irrigation from underground sources - the Maslin Sands and Port Willunga Formation aquifers are the main providers here, via rainfall infiltrating the soils. Other sources include streams and inflowing underground water systems, which are found in the basement rocks. As the aquifer is used

ABOVE *It can be hard to believe that the rolling vineyards of McLaren Vale in South Australia are only one hour's drive from the centre of Adelaide.*

Grape Varieties

SHIRAZ - Full bodied and rich with a palate full of blackcurrant, plums and liquorice flavours. Can be quite velvety. Take on a more chocolate and game-like profile as they age. They will usually have seen oak maturation, typically American oak, which can contribute a perceived sweetness to the wine.

CABERNET - Again quite large wines with classic blackcurrant and black fruit flavours. Dark chocolate is often found, as are black olives. mint, cedar, vanilla and leather. These can all show at one time or another on its journey into maturity.

GRENACHE - Some of the finest examples of Grenache in Australia come from here. Full of earthiness, blackcurrants, spice and plum. Can be quite soft and approachable when young, but is usually quite a big wine. Very old vines contribute to the complexity of the wines.

ABOVE *Viognier grapes.*

CHARDONNAY - Typically a large wine that is full flavoured and minerally, with notes of peaches, butter and occasionally ripe melon.

VIOGNIER - McLaren Vale houses more Viognier than any other region in the Southern Hemisphere. The wines are fruit-driven with refreshing acidity.

---

heavily, there is a real danger that saline water may get into the system as the head of fresh water is lowered. Several options are being considered to counteract this problem, which would result in the water being too saline by 2010 for use as irrigation water for vines. One option is to recycle water from a waste water plant, which would be especially useful in the winter months when the vines are dormant. Until a satisfactory solution has been found, it is unlikely that any new plantings will occur.

There are a wide variety of soils in the region, including podzolic of low fertility, fertile red-brown earths, terra rossa, rendzina and dark cracking soils. With such an extensive range of types, along with varying altitudes of between 50 and 100 metres, a rich diversity of wine is made. As is common with all good wine regions the soil is actually very poor, causing the vine to work hard to find water. This has meant that 80% of the area's vineyards need to be drip-irrigated and thus the supply of water to them is controlled very tightly.

The first settlers in McLaren Vale were, unsurprisingly, the British who arrived in the mid 1800s and paved the way for their European counterparts. Most notable were the Italians, who brought olive groves along with them, which flourished in this almost frost-free zone, with its temperate climate and sea breezes coming in from St Vincents Gulf to the west. Vines, however, were first planted before this in 1839 by an enterprising man named John Reynell, presumably at the location of the township which now bears his name (but with

ABOVE *Freshly-picked grapes, waiting to be tipped into the crusher/destemmer. The vines only produce a crop once a year, and take four years to reach maturity.*

an "a" on the end). This is now in the far north of modern-day McLaren Vale, with most of the main wineries located 6-10 miles to the south. Reynell picked a good spot in this vast country, and soon started to make dry red wine in the Bordeaux style, with thick, heavy fortified reds that the British loved so much. The name Reynella continues to this day under the ownership of BRL Hardy, one of Australia's largest wine companies, along with Southcorp, Beringer Blass and Fosters. In Reynell's pursuit of creating a classic style of wine he built an underground cellar, which is still there today and is highly regarded for its place in the history of Australian Viticulture. Another historic event also occurred in McLaren Vale, when Thomas Hardy exported what was perhaps the first-ever delivery of Australian wine to England in 1859. He had previously worked for John Reynell in 1851 and then spent 18 months operating a butchery business near the goldfields. The region continued to flourish, and by the 1950s was producing approximately half of the red wine in Australia.

By 1964, however, things had changed. The enormous amount of grapes available was far in excess of what the wineries wanted, and the grape-growers went through a hard time. It led to grapes being left on the vine to rot, as growers could not get a reasonable price for them. The situation was also fuelled by very restrictive licensing laws that meant cellar doors sales had to be a minimum of two gallons, restaurants in hotels had to impose last orders at 8.00pm, and the bars had to shut at

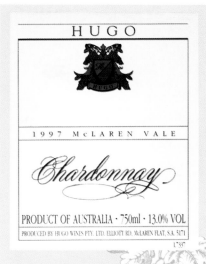

6.00pm. To combat this situation, a Co-operative Winery was set up. It was established along the main road passing through Mclaren Vale, with the intention of making wine from its members grapes to give them extra value (today it is the Tatachilla cellar door). This was not altogether a success, however - these were grape-growers, and not winemakers or marketers. By 1967, with sales not as high as anticipated, they invited all the local winemakers to a tasting. This caused concern among the winemakers, as they believed that the Co-op would effectively undercut them in the market place. They should not have worried though, as the State Prices Commission had set a minimum amount that grape-growers should be

ABOVE *Modern vineyards are planted to take advantage of mechanical harvesting, which can save the pickers from hours of back-breaking work.*

ABOVE *At d'Arenberg Wines, there is a wide range of machinery for different tasks that is powered by electricity - although electric power was only installed here in 1954. Before this, these processes were carried out by hand, which was hard and time-consuming work.*

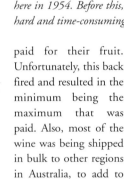

paid for their fruit. Unfortunately, this back fired and resulted in the minimum being the maximum that was paid. Also, most of the wine was being shipped in bulk to other regions in Australia, to add to blended wines. However, this did not detract too much from the event and it was declared a success with a wealth of information being exchanged. The event still continues today, under the guise of the McLaren Vale Wine Show.

As a direct result of this meeting a new association was formed - The McLaren Vale Winemakers Association. The Co-op was sold, as it had run its course and the prices for grapes had stabilised. However, it was not until 1999 that the grape-growers could become members of the Association, after the winemakers realised that it was in their best interests to work closely with the farmers who provided them with the raw materials with which to work. The Association was formed to promote the wines from the region, and regular meetings were held in people's homes or a local restaurant on a voluntary basis. The success of the events that were organised by the

first wave of stalwarts is evident by the fact that they still take place today. The Bushing Festival and Sea and Vines Festival have attracted tens of thousands of visitors, along with countless wine writers and journalists. In 1980 the first paid employee was appointed - Don Hogg. Don had previously been part-time secretary and his promotion to Executive Officer signalled the start of a professional organisation.

By the 1990s the world was waking up in a major way to Australian wines. The region applied for an official GI (Geographic Indicator), which legally defines an area and therefore who can put the name on their wine labels. This was granted in 1997, the same year that the organisation opened the McLaren Vale and Fleurieu Visitor Centre (also involved in this project were the State Government and tourism authorities), which is now also home to the McLaren Vale Winemakers Association. The building is a focus for the region, with information on all the wineries plus its own vineyard, Stump Hill, which helps to finance the centre.

Of the wineries established in the late 1800s and early 1900s, only a handful survive today. Perhaps the most important of these is d'Arenberg, founded by Joseph Osborn - a teetotal director of Thomas Hardy and Son - in 1912. It was continued by his son d'Arry in 1957, who was fortunate to be able to work with electricity - which was only installed in 1954. Today it is run by Chester Osborn, a very likeable and extremely competent man who shows uttermost respect for his family's vineyards and traditions. In recent years, d'Arenberg has been the recipient of many awards and high ratings, especially from American wine critic Robert Parker. Although Chester is quite eccentric (or just a marketing genius), naming wines after tenuous connections or links with the winery such as The Broken Fish Plate Sauvignon Blanc, Hermit Crab Marsanne/Viognier, Dead Arm Shiraz and Last Ditch Viognier, they are all remarkable good and consistent. I can think of no other winemaker in Australia who grows so many varieties to such a high standard. The wines make their presence felt and demand attention and discussion like no others, although this may be due the inevitable dinner table game of trying to guess how the wine derived its name!

ABOVE *Some of the finest grapes are grown on ancient vines at d'Arenberg Wines*

It also helps that this vineyard was originally planted in 1890, and although most vines have long since gone, it is possible to find some original ones hiding away amongst the newer and more productive vines. The wines of d'Arenberg are focused and intense, with an obvious bias towards the classic Rhone varieties of Shiraz, Grenache, Viognier, Marsanne and Rousanne dominating the range. This is predominately Shiraz country - unfortunately McLaren Vale was part of the government vine-pull scheme in the late eighties where vineyard owners were paid to pull up their Grenache vines and plant more popular varieties such as Cabernet and Shiraz. Most of the red varieties flourish here, due to the sandy soils over ironstone subsoils (yes there is a wine called Ironstone Pressings!). The Dead Arm Shiraz is rich and opulent, with lots of fruit and a hint of chocolate to complement the spiciness of the wine, which usually has the ability to age for ten years or more. d'Arenberg's flagship Cabernet Sauvignon is called Coppermine Road, and is made from the fruit of vines grown from cuttings taken from John Reynell's original vineyard. Being 150 years old is not easy for a vine, but it does produce some of the finest fruit available. With a yield of less than one tonne per acre, the fruit is grown up and full of the characteristics need-

ABOVE *At the Woodstock Winery in South Australia, the rows are planted just widely enough apart to allow room for all the equipment that is used for picking. As many of the vineyards in Australia are fairly young, it was easy to allow for such things at the planning stage.*

ed to make a great wine, in an area not known for this variety. The wine is full of leather and cassis, with dry tannins and a very long length. The majority of the vineyards are dry-grown, so the berries are small giving a high skin to pulp ration - essential for the production of fine wine.

Chester still makes wine in a very traditional manner, with each batch vinified separately and crushed in an old Demoisy crusher, which was brought in from Burgundy. It is said that the crushing is so light, with the rollers opened fully, that a vineyard lizard could pass through unscathed! It is the white varieties that are crushed with the rollers wide open, to enable some whole bunches to pass through. These are then pressed straight off the skins in ancient basket presses, to minimise oxidation and make the whole process of extracting flavour and colour a gentle one. The wines are fermented in wax-lined concrete

BELOW *Hand picking at Woodstock Winery. Grapes from the older vines, which are used for quality wines, are often still hand-picked.*

open fermenters, with heading-down boards utilised to keep the cap of grape skins underneath the fermenting juice. The wines are minimally fined and filtered, before bottling after maturation in the cellar.

Clarendon Hills is undoubtedly the finest exponent of Grenache (and Shiraz for that matter) in Australia. I had been warned that Roman Bratasiuk, the owner and winemaker, was a formidable character and a no-nonsense type of man. The no-nonsense part is quite correct, as you would expect from a wine maker of this seriousness. As for formidable, Roman not only gave up a Saturday morning to see me, but on his son's eighteenth birthday as well! He is a inspiration for those not yet converted to the wine philosophy of terroir. This is based on the theory that the flavour of the grapes is influenced by all the elements surrounding them - the soil, weather, aspect etc. Although some new-world producers may refute this theory, it is widely accepted in the Old World and very hard to ignore when faced with Clarendon Hills single vineyard bottlings (which they all are). Roman makes six different Shiraz and four Grenache, all of which can be easily differentiated in a line up. All the wines from each grape variety are made in the exactly the same way, which clearly demonstrates that terroir plays the most significant part in the flavour profile of wines made at this level. This factor is no doubt exaggerated by the fundamental quality of the viticulture and wine-making skills, which are immediately apparent upon entering the vineyard and talking to Roman. It is not feasible to give tasting notes here, as they will almost certainly be out of date fairly quickly. Instead, ask your local

ABOVE *Woodstock Winery in South Australia is named after the town of Woodstock, near Oxford in England - which is where its founder, Arthur Townsend, came from.*

retailer to source these wines for you, and put on a tasting for fellow wine lovers to see exactly what I am referring to.

The Woodstock winery was established in 1850, when Arthur Townsend arrived in McLaren Flat, having travelled from Woodstock, near Oxford in England. Today the winery is owned by the Collett family, with Scott, the middle son, in charge of the winemaking. Woodstock uses modern practices, such as night time harvesting to ensure the grapes arrive cool and thus avoiding oxidation, and purchases dried Swiss yeasts from isolated Rhone Valley cultures, to maximise the characteristics of the grapes during fermentation. Scott produces wines that are well rounded and full in flavour, offering good complexity. Their premium wine The Stocks is made from 100-year-old vines and is always well-structured, balanced and focused. This too can be said for the Grenache, which is made from 90-year-old bush vines.

Hugh Hamilton is a member of the famous Hamilton winemaking family. After establishing his vineyard in 1992, Hugh is making wines that demonstrate why McLaren Vale is such a natural environment for Shiraz - he says that "it grows like a weed down here". Some weed! Hugh, like a few others, is experimenting with different varieties such as Sangiovese, which he dry-grows with great results. Also planted are Tempranillo and Viognier which is unusual for the area. This could be interesting if the latter is co-fermented with Shiraz in the future. Of a more obscure variety is Saperavi, an ancient Georgian grape that produces a wine full of plum characters and has the ability - or indeed demands - to be aged for decades to soften out and develop. It also has excellent blending potential, and this is what Hugh currently utilises it for. Growing all these varieties, in an area known for its Shiraz, is a clue to Hugh's belief that, just as we do not eat the same meal every day, we should try different grape varieties throughout the week. I couldn't agree more.

One of the most likeable and knowledgeable winemakers in the area is Drew Noon from Noon Wines. Drew is in the enviable position of being a Master of Wine a title gained through years of study and tasting. Since the Institute of Masters of Wine was founded in 1953, only 250 people out of the 1900 candidates attempting it have passed. To qualify, one must have completed the Wine & Spirit Education Trust's three prior examinations. Once passed you are eligible to start the MW papers, which is a three-year process. In

ABOVE *Australian wine labels can be far more graphically stimulating and interesting than their classic European counterparts.*

the first year you sit a theory paper, which consists of three parts covering vinification, vitification, the business of wine and contempary issues. If the Board feel you are ready to sit the practical paper you will be invited to sit Part 2 (assuming you pass Part 1). This consists of your organoleptic competencies being examined - or in laymans terms a wine tasting. There are three papers in this part, each of which contains up to 12 wines. You have to

ABOVE *Drew Noon, one of the few winemakers who has achieved the title of Master of Wine.*

Recommended Producers

d'Arenberg Quality excels across the board here and you will rarely be disappointed. Chester Osborn is one of Australia's great winemakers and the entire range is well crafted.

Arrakoon Look out for Sellicks Beach, a Shiraz Grenache blend that is a bargain. The top end Doyen Shiraz is made from fruit sourced from three-year-old vines. This dispels the myth that the older the vine, the better the wine, as it is excellent.

Chapel Hill Along with Sue Hodder from Wynns, Pam Dunsford is considered one of the best female winemakers in Australia. The Vicar Shiraz/Cabernet, which is released in exceptional years, is outstanding.

Clarendon Hills Superlative single vineyard wines, which stand out as being some of the finest in Australia. Roman Bratasiuk, the owner and winemaker is fanatical about quality and this shows across the range. The Grenache range is outstanding and demonstrates the potential of this variety in McLaren Vale.

Coriole Famous for its hard-to-come-by Lloyd Reserve Shiraz, Coriole also produces an interesting Semillon and has a good example of the Italian variety Sangiovese. The blended Redstone also offers fine drinking.

Dennis The Dennis family first occupied this site in 1947 and started making wine in 1971. The mantle was passed over to Peter Dennis in 1979, who has carried on with notable success. They have won over 200 medals, as well as being named as the Bushing Kings. Mead, the honey-based drink is also produced here.

Dowie Doole Established in 1996 by two winemakers in the region, Drew Dowie and Norm Doole. The wines are made off site, but are good efforts.

Edwards and Chaffey Wine has matured in the cellars here for over 140 years. The property is on land that was previously Hope Farm, with a survey address of 353. This has now been commemorated in the name of their premium wines.

Fox Creek Fox Creek received Icon status with the 1998 vintage made by Foxy and Sarah Marquis. As with most of McLaren Vale, the reds really stand out here. It was only founded in 1996, by four medical families who each had their own vineyards. It first release, a 1994 Shiraz, won the Bushing Trophy, which set a precedent for them to follow in subsequent years.

Gemtree A new name in McLaren Vale but one which has been growing grapes for many years and selling them to other wineries. Three wines are made here, a huge Shiraz, a blend called Tally's and a Chardonnay.

Geoff Merrill Quite a large concern now with a good variety to choose from. Look out for the Cabernet and Shiraz from the Reserve range.

Haselgrove Nick Haselgrove, the chief winemaker, is the grandson of Ron Haselgrove who made the famous Mildara wines in the 1950s and 60s. The H series comprises their top wines, which are very good.

Hillstowe A long established name on the wine scene in south Australia, both in McLaren Vale and the Adelaide Hills. Look out for the Buxton range, which can be superb.

Hugh Hamilton Hugh is a great believer in food and wine pairings. Accordingly he grows a multitude of grape varieties to complement different dishes. Alongside the usual suspects he offers Verdelho, Viognier, Tempranillo, Petit Verdot and Saperavi, an ancient Georgian variety which he uses for blending.

Hugo John Hugo and his wife must be the most hardworking people in McLaren Vale. I visited them on a horrific day in June when the rain was so bad that the windscreen wipers in my car could not cope. There were two people outside the winery tending to the manicured gardens. When inside I mentioned how devoted the gardeners must be to be out in that weather. The cellar door lady informed me that it was John and his wife. The wines are impressive enough, especially the Cabernet Sauvignon and Shiraz, which have a touch of sweetness to them, no doubt derived from the American Oak they have been matured in.

Ingoldby Rich and fruity wines from this winery, which can trace its ancestry back over 100 years in the region. Now owned by Beringer Blass.

Kangarilla Road Located at the eastern end of the Valley, this is a newly resurrected operation with a new cellar door, processing plant and 15 acres of new vineyard, to accompany the existing one of the same size that was planted in 1975.

Kay Brothers The top-of-the-range Block 6 Shiraz is a benchmark for the region, coming from ancient vines that are over 100 years old. The winery is steeped in history and tradition.

Maglieri Look out for the Shiraz and Semillon, which can be very full. One of the best known of the region's labels, it is now owned by Beringer Blass.

Maxwell The Reserve Shiraz is a monster and the Lime Cave Cabernet oozes varietal characteristics. Also try the Old Vines Semillon and rich, buttery Chardonnay. A new winery was constructed at the end of the 1990s and you can sample the wines whilst viewing the panoramic view of the vineyards and the winery itself.

Noon Noon is owned and run by Drew Noon, an unassuming man who makes extraordinary wines that can reach alcohol levels in the high teens. Although there is a cellar door, it is very rarely open as the wines sell out upon release. Search out the Solaire Grenache and Eclipse wines. There is also a small amount of Rose made here, which is very rare in McLaren Vale.

Penny's Hill A major new winery and magnificent manor house that is now operating as a guest house. As well as some fine wines the winery also boasts an art gallery, showing works by contempary Australian artists. Ben Riggs is the winemaker and the Shiraz, from narrow planted and low yielding vineyards, is the pick of the bunch.

Perrini Estate Nestled in the foothills of the Southern Mount Lofty Ranges this winery, established in 1997, has spectacular views of the surrounding countryside. The wines are large and intentionally so.

Pertaringa Owned partly by Geoff Hardy of the famous wine-making family, with his business partner Ian Leask, who is an experienced viticultralist. A lot of the grapes are sold on, but a few are made into wine here and sold mainly through the cellar door.

Pirramimma Some interesting grapes grown here, like Cabernet Franc and Petit Verdot, but it is the Cabernet Sauvignon that stands out. The name is aboriginal and means "the moon and the stars".

Scarpantoni Another winery that was started in 1958, after Domenico Scarpantoni had been working at Thomas Hardy and Sons. Some 45 years later, the winery has won over 300 medals at competitions. The family originally hail from Abruzi in central Italy.

Shottesbrooke A small family winery that makes a very good Shiraz. Nick Holmes, the winemaker, used to be the winemaker at Ryecroft.

Simon Hackett Wines Simon has been involved in the world of wine all his life - his father was the managing director of the Barossa Distillery. Today Simon makes wines under his own name, after having worked for Saltram for many years.

Tatachilla Winery Not afraid to experiment and utilises methods from the past as well as modern day practices. It can trace its roots back to the 1990s, granting it its place in history. The Foundation Shiraz is excellent.

Tyrrell's Although based in the Hunter they also have an outpost in McLaren Vale, where their Rufus Stone Shiraz shows the best.

Wirra Wirra Founded in 1893 by state cricketer Robert Strangeways Wigley and restored in 1969 by Greg and Roger Trott. The Church Block Cabernet Shiraz always shows well.

Woodstock The Stocks Shiraz and Grenache from 90-year-old bush vines stand out amongst their impressive range. The original property was established in 1859 by Arthur Townsend, when he built two small cottages and planted vines.

ABOVE *Modern mechanical harvesting in South Australia. The vines are trained to each side of the main stem along wires, so that the harvester can reach the grapes.*

demonstrate that you can identify the provenance of the wine - where it was made - and the grape variety used. You then have to state the production methods, quality level. age, vintage and the commercial positioning of the wine. In the third year you undertake an agreed dissertation. If you are able to pass all components you are awarded with the title Master of Wine. Tough work indeed and only the most knowledgeable succeed. What is even more impressive is that Drew undertook his study in Australia.

Noon Wines is located in a wonderful area - but unfortunately it usually displays a sign informing visitors that the wines are sold out. This is not surprising, given the quality and history of the estate. David Noon, Drew's father, purchased the property in 1976, and it is surrounded by vines that include own-rooted Grenache bushes planted in the 1930s and 40s. Today, Drew makes wines in the same vein as his father, who had no experience in viticulture before taking over and was previously employed as a French teacher. To some the wines are quite controversial, as their alcohol content can reach as high as 18%, but the people who matter (his customers and the author of this book alike) love it. Chatting to Drew it is evident that he loves this area for all the natural beauty and its strong community spirit, especially amongst winemakers, as well as for the quality of wines that are produced.

This spirit is also echoed by Peter and Anthea Hoffmann, of the boutique winery of the same name. They see the people as the making of the area, along with gifted weather conditions and the ability of Shiraz to flourish.

One of the larger wineries in the region is Chapel Hill, who utilise the talents of Pam Dunsford - the first female Australian to graduate as a oenologist in 1973 - as their winemaker. The winery name is taken from an historic ironstone church, built on the property in 1865. The wines are fruit-driven and maintain a balance with the oak. As most wines are consumed within 48 hours of purchase, Chapel Hill purposely makes wines that are approachable early or which can be cellared for the medium term.

Penny's Hill Vineyard has had a new lease of life injected into it by Tony Parkinson and his wife Susie, who are also art lovers. They employ a contract winemaker, so they can focus their attention on the other assets of the business. There is a serious Art Gallery on site, which shows works by contempary Australian artists. This connection follows through onto the labels of the wines, as they are marked with a red dot, which signifies that a painting has been sold.

There is also a Georgian house on the site, which now functions as a luxurious homestead for the weary wine traveller to stay in. I can vouch for this, as I was the second person to stay there after the renovation works had been completed. It is also the ideal place to stay if you wish to dine at the Salopian Inn, a famous McLaren Vale restaurant that is only a couple of minutes away. The wines at Pennys Hill are getting better each year, as Ben Riggs, the contract winemaker, gets accustomed to the fruit that the vineyard yields.

Clare Valley

The Clare Valley, situated one hour away from the Barossa to the north-west, is arguably the finest region in Australia for Riesling and one of the best for Shiraz. When arriving in the Valley for the first time you are struck by its sheer beauty, with rolling green hills and small forgotten-about villages, that seem to be frozen within their own time frame. Surrounding these small centres of population is neat farmland, near-perfect bush and a never-ending pastoral expanse of land to the north. The region has an ideal climate for the growing of grapes and for tourism, as it can reach 36°C during the day, but cools to 16°C by night.

ABOVE *Chardonnay grapes, which are used to make a very full-flavoured and fruity wine.*

As you arrive in the valley, probably having come from the Barossa, the first town you pass through is Auburn, which was originally named "Tateham's Waterhole" in 1849, after its founder. Many of its collection of bluestone buildings are listed on the National Trust register. Auburn is home to a grand total of three wineries, including two world-class ones which I will discuss in further detail later on. As the villages all lie to either side of the main road through the valley, which eventually ends in Darwin in the north of the country, they seem to pass with the bat of an eyelid. A few small wineries are located around the town of Mintaro, which is perhaps the most well preserved in time and seems to have missed out on the new millennium. It is not wine that Mintaro is most famous for though - Martindale Hall was used as the property in the Australian film *Picnic at Hanging Rock*. It

can also lay claim to providing the slate for many of the world's billiard tables; the material can also be seen on numerous houses in the vicinity. Watervale is slightly larger, with eight wineries, and it also has good access to the Riesling Trail, a route that meanders through the villages allowing you stop off and explore the surrounding countryside. It runs for around 17 miles on the old railway line and is not too strenuous; you may either walk or cycle along it. Sevenhill, a few kilometres further on, has 14 wineries including the oldest of them all - Annie's Lane. If you are planning on staying a while then this is a quiet spot with many B&Bs scattered in the bushland, and with many famous cellar doors close by. Clare itself has 13 wineries, including my favourite - Wendouree. It is the largest of the region's towns and has branches of the major banks as well as late-night supermarkets and a good selection of pubs and restaurants.

ABOVE *A view across Clare Valley in South Australia.*

Grape Varieties

RIESLING - These range from mineral and stony examples to lime, grapefruit, lemon and floral, with a good weight. Has a very good ability to age if cellared correctly. It is usually grown specifically on limestone, which gives over 90% of its water to the vine, effectively acting as a reservoir.

SHIRAZ - Almost always tasting of ripe fruit, as is most evident in the wines from Jim Barry, but are very rarely unbalanced. Black pepper can be found easily in good years, as can black fruits, pepper, spice and mint.

CABERNET SAUVIGNON - Can be tight and tannic in some years but usually rather large wines that can take many years to open up fully. Usually displays capsicum, blackcurrant, mint and licorice. Like Shiraz, the "jam" factor is eliminated by the cool nights in the region.

ABOVE *Riesling grapes.*

Yet again it was a European settler who first planted grapes within this region. John Horrocks established Hope Farm in 1840, but his place in history was cemented not by this but by being shot by his camel. How this happened I can only wonder. Not a great deal has been documented about the early years, except that it was mainly agriculture and minerals that kept the community gainfully employed. The mining of minerals only lasted for a couple of years, and wheat quickly became the major crop. Clare soon became a hub for the region, as farming spread further north into the great expanse of land that is Australia. The growing of grapes was spawned by the farm labourers taking part of their wages in wine, in addition to a couple of shillings. This obviously necessitated further plantings to keep up with demand. The first serious attempt at making wine was by the Jesuit priests at Sevenhill, who made it for sacramental purposes. The news about the quality of the wines soon spread, and by the turn of the century some 1500 acres were planted under vine. Sevenhill still exists today, along with the other pioneering wineries of the time, A P Birks (Wendouree) and Quelltaler, which is now known as Annie's Lane.

Annies Lane, or Quelltaler, as it was known then, was first planted on June 15, 1854, by a Cornish farmer named Francis Treloar. The vines bore fruit of sufficient quality to make wine in 1859, which Francis bottled and sold to local people, or used to barter. The property changed hands a couple of times, and in 1889 James Richman, the then owner, sold it to Carl Sobels. whose great-great-great-grandson, Kevin, now owns and run Sobels Wines in the Hunter Valley. For two years the now legendary Australian winemaker, Leo Buring, was a cellar hand here. He, of course, went on to establish himself as one of the all-time great Australian winemakers. Quelltaler's name was documented in history, when in 1937 it became the first Australian wine to be served at the Lord Mayor's banquet held in the House of Commons. Today it is owned by one of the giants of the industry, Beringer Blass. Along with Sue Hodden, Caroline Dunn is one of Australia's finest female winemakers. Whilst studying at Adelaide University she won more wine-making prizes than any other student in history there. In 1999 she went on to be the first woman to win the Jimmy Watson Trophy - a great feat. Not only is Caroline a talented winemaker, she is also a revered judge within the show circuit in Australia. As is common with most Clare wineries, the vineyards are influenced by their own meso-climates and most of the wines are grown on red loam over limestone, which, along with the limited water - give the wines power and intensity.

clos Clare is to the Clare Valley what Zema Estate is to Coonawarra. The vines are hand-harvested and the grapes hand-picked. It is the Riesling from this estate that commands the most attention and acclaim. The best grapes are from the five-acre Florita vineyard, which was made famous by Leo Buring's Watervale Riesling in the mid to late 20th century.

Jeffrey Grosset is the most applauded grower of Riesling in Australia, and would also be placed high up if there were such a thing as a world scale. His really is a specialist operation, which bottles Riesling under two labels, each of which magnificently reflect their own terroir. When I visited Jeffrey he pulled out a map

ABOVE *Jeffrey Grosset, the most lauded grower of Riesling in Australia.*

of the area and went through it, pointing out various contours on the landscape which he thought would be ideal for the growing of Riesling. It was miraculous that he was able to do this, as when I arrived he was experiencing a small crisis due to his filtering machine breaking down at a critical time. I watched nervously as he made minor adjustments to save the vat of wine that was passing through. Although no winery would like to experience a loss of wine, it would be catastrophic here as only 9,000 cases are made each year, of which most are sold before they are made.

The region as a whole varies so much, with its undulating hills and changing climatic conditions, along with varying soils. This means that there are numerous micro-climates at any one time, which results in wines from different vineyards, made in the same way, turning out enormously different. Grosset's Riesling wines from the Watervale, and those from the Polish Hill vineyard demonstrate this well. The Watervale should almost always be approachable from a younger age, with its dry citrus fruits and a mineral edge. The Polish Hill tends to be more austere, and show lime flavours with enormous length. Both will age gracefully, with finesse and balance for many years. Both of these wines are now bottled exclusively with Stelvin Screw caps. Although the purists will always argue that wine should be bottled with a cork closure, this has proved to be an antiquated argument when directed towards Clare Rieslings. I liken it to the arrival of CDs in the early 1980s. All music lovers (including me) far preferred the touch and feel of vinyl, whilst being able to read the inner sleeve. Times change, and now I cannot conceive the idea of having to change sides every 20 minutes, dust the records down and desperately try to avoid scratching them. I am positive the same will happen for wine in the next ten years. The reason for this new type of closure (although it has been around since the 1960s in trial form) is to eliminate the problem of Trichloranisole, which is more commonly known as TCA. It is derived from corks and gives a wine a wet cardboard or corky nose and flavour. The incidence of this occurring is widely speculated, but it is really down to our own ability to pick it up through varying levels of tolerance. Studies have shown it to affect between 2 and 20% of all wines bottled. This is alarmingly high and I can think of no other beverage-based industry that would tolerate

ABOVE **Sunset over the Murray River, South Australia.**

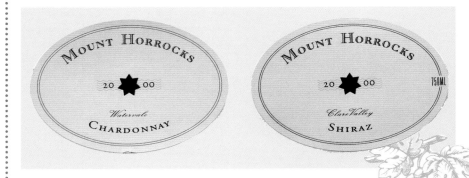

such a high level of spoilage that is only discovered by the paying public. Stelvins have been trialled extensively and perhaps nowhere more so than in the Clare Valley. The district as a whole bottled all of their 2001 production under this closure, through campaigners like Jeffrey Grosset. He is very knowledgeable on the subject, and was one of the early pioneers and trial winemakers in Australia to use it. Its effectiveness is demonstrated by tastings of bottles using both methods. The wines using Stelvin were universally fresher and younger than their cork counterparts. This, in part, is down to the amount of air that is allowed to permeate the wine. Top class corks have a permutation rate of around 0.005, while lower end examples are much higher, causing air to pass through and accelerate the maturation of the wine through aeration.

Jeffrey made headlines again in 2002 when he bottled part of his Bordeaux Blend wine Gaia under Stelvin. This is the first time a premium red wine from Australia had been bottled with this closure, and the event was reported through the wine press globally. Such international attention naturally results in a surge of demand and a influx of devotees to

the cellar door. Much to their disappointment, the wines are usually all gone by the time they arrive in summer - but they can always pop next door to Mount Horrocks, whose owner and winemaker is Jeffrey's long-time partner.

Stephanie Toole limits her production at Mount Horrocks to around 5000 cases per year, which she believes allows her to focus on the intrinsic quality and terroir of the vineyards she owns and purchases fruit from. The most famous of the wines made here is a sweetie known as the Cordon Cut Riesling, which ranks along the finest sweet wines that are made in the country. It is well worth visiting the cellar door here, as it holds its place in history by being the former railway station, which has now been lovingly restored. Only open at the weekends, it caters for the hungry with light lunches.

Wendouree has been described by James Halliday as "a treasure beyond price" - no doubt for its marvellous original buildings along with the wines themselves. This is a relatively hard winery to find, as it is not open to the public at any time and therefore not signposted particularly well. I had almost given up on trying to get an appointment here, as many people had remarked to me that Tony Brady, the owner and winemaker, was a difficult man to get along with. I was determined to try though, as this is, in my opinion, one of the finest wineries in Australia. I eventually had an appointment made for me by the boys at Torbreck in the Barossa, for which I am eternally grateful. I drove up a long and windy driveway with thick-trunked, ancient vines to the right hand side, to be greeted by a delightful Tony Brady. I remarked on the wonderful the old vines that I had passed. "Old vines?" he said, "They are the young ones, only 96 years old!" I was immediately taken back to a bygone age when shown the truly old vines, which are over 100 years old, and the timeless winery the wines are made in. Tony showed me around the cellars and took me into the room where the museum stock was located. It

ABOVE *Vines grafted onto a different rootstock.*

was one of the finest moments of my trip to look at these old bottles, which would continue to develop for years to come. These wines, of all those in Australia, take the longest time to mature - a least a decade is required before they start to show themselves in all their glory. Why this long? Well in my opinion it is due to the intrinsic quality of the fruit, which provides richness and concentration, combined with excellent tannins, and grapes picked when physiologically ripe. Together this makes a very well-balanced wine, which is more than the sum of its parts. It needs time to grow up and settle, and for the fruit to subside a little to allow the finer nuances to show through at their best. This, like top Rhones or Bordeaux, takes years to accomplish - but when it does it really is a privilege to drink.

I was honoured to taste through the entire range, and was mesmerised by the sheer quality of it all. Glancing around the lab I noticed a lot of hand-written data about each wine from various vintages. This information showed that in hot and abundant years, where there had been good rainfall in the dormant season and the yields were rather higher than normal, the wines were far better than those of medium vintages, where yields were low and therefore the grapes more concentrated. When I say higher you have to remember that these are 100-year-old vines, and even in a fine vintage they will struggle to produce two tonnes of fruit per acre.

Skillogalee is a 150-acre property, located to the west of the main road in the district of Penwortham. It is officially in the sub-district of Sevenhill, albeit in the far west extreme of it. The Skillogalee Valley is separated from the main Clare and Polish Hill viticulture districts

ABOVE *The Clare Valley is arguably the finest region in Australia for Riesling and Shiraz.*

by a north-south ridge, and rainfall can be higher at around 700mm per annum. The cellar door here is located within an old stone cottage dating from 1851, which was built by an Cornish miner called John Trestrail. Amazingly, he and his wife had 17 children - which can maybe attributed to the fact that he was religious (one would assume Catholic) and did not approve of alcohol. It was not until the early 1900s that the farm was planted to vines, even though these were only of the currant and sultana varieties. This changed in 1969, when Spencer George took over the property and planted Riesling, Shiraz, Grenache and Crouchen. By the 1980s a grafting programme was implemented, and the Grenache and Crouchen were transformed to Traminer and Cabernet. The vines are planted on steep east-facing slopes at an altitude of around 475 metres, which makes them ripen quite late - sometimes as much as two weeks after the rest of the Clare. In 1989 Dave and Diane Palmer purchased the property, determined to learn the craft of wine-making. Dave had previously

ABOVE *Overall view of mechanical harvesting in the Clare Valley.*

ABOVE *Grapes ripening in the Australian sun.*

been a management consultant for a major accountancy firm so life in the valley was a major change for him - although probably just as stressful. Diane utilised her skills as a newly-qualified chef, having previously been a school teacher, to serve food to those customers visiting the cellar door. This has now evolved into a full-scale restaurant which is thriving with oenaphiles and locals alike. It was over a rather rapid lunch, due to my other commitments later in the day, that I discussed and tasted the wines from Skillogalee. As anticipated, the Riesling shone out with the Shiraz, but the Gewürztraminer also showed well as a food wine. Dave ducked out to the cellar half way through to get a bottle of 1991 Riesling, which was evolved but still had a lovely freshness to it with citrus fruits dominating the nose.

Located just down the road is the Mitchell Winery. Owned and operated by Andrew and

Jane Mitchell since 1975, it has become renowned for some of the best value reds in the region. An old sandstone apple store serves as the cellar door area, which has a homely feel about it. The Riesling is grown on the same famed soil of the Coonawarra district - terra rossa - which gives it a rather more mineralish flavour. Plans for expansion are well underway, with some 70 further acres of vine having been planted and 20 more purchased that are already in production.

The doyen of the area is almost unquestionably Jim Barry, who has the eponymously-named estate situated just north of Clare itself. Having arrived here in 1947, after graduation from the Roseworthy College with a diploma in Oenology, he found it to be the perfect place to practice his new-found skills. It was not until 1959, though, that Jim actually purchased his first property in the area. It formed part of the estate that Edward Gleeson, the founder of Clare, had resided in. Having his thoughts about the quality of the area confirmed, in 1964 he purchased another property on the north-west side of the valley that had belonged to Duncan McRae Wood. This was soon planted with Shiraz, and is now the source for the McRae Wood Shiraz that is the Armagh's (the top wine from the estate) little brother. Jim did not make wine at this time but sold the grapes on, choosing to work at Wendouree for his friend Roly Birk. It took quite some time for him to gain the confidence he needed to bottle a wine under his own name, but that came in 1973 when he established his own winery ready for the 1974 vintage. The wine sold well, and in 1985 he embarked on a project to create one of Australia's very best Shirazes, and the Armagh

ABOVE *South Australia is the premier state in Australia for wine-making and wine tourism.*

ABOVE *These grapes are obviously hand-picked, as they have arrived at the winery in individual baskets, rather than by the tractor-load.*

was born. This wine has received acclaim the world over, and Hugh Johnson describes it as a "Grange Challenger" - not bad for a wine that is a quarter of the price of the country's most famous wine.

Today the family business is run by other members of his family. On the day of my visit it was teaming with rain and getting dark, with the winter about to set in. Peter Barry, the Chief Executive, showed me around the winery, which was far larger than I had anticipated, followed by a tasting of the whole range. Needless to say this impressed, and I had the opportunity to taste a few wines that were for cellar door sales only. Peter then took me out in the 4WD to tour the Armagh vineyards and the rest of the estate. Considering that this vineyard was planted decades ago, it was done so with precision. The vines were planted not in a straight line but in a curve, to follow the natural slope of the hill and to maximise the sunlight that reached the vines. This is impressive stuff, that you do not commonly see in Australia. If you have never tasted the Armagh then you should seek some out, as it is a bench mark for the variety. After the tour Peter took me to the local bar for a quick beer, where we met various other grape-growers and had a good chat. The remarkable thing is that here was the CEO of a good-sized wine business, which is known around the world, drinking in a working mans' bar. It speaks volumes for the people of the district and the work ethic that is naturally installed here. It is far too easy today to think of the people in charge of famous wineries languishing in their leather chair in their plush office. This is simply not the case here, or in most other regions of Australia. The head honchos still see themselves as farmers and are more than approachable.

Knappstein Wines is derived from Tim Knappstein, the previous owner of the business, which is an integral part of the Clare community. Tim could trace back family members connected with the wine trade in Clare to 1895, but the winery only started in its current form in the 1970s. An offer came along from a larger company, Petaluma, in 1992 and to avoid confusion, Tim's name was dropped from the label. Since the acquisition the wines have been transformed by Andrew Hardy, a member of the famous wine-making family, who had previously worked under Brian Crosser at Petaluma. He has put new vigour into the wines resulting in Rieslings with more acidity and elegance. This also fol-

ABOVE *Not a bin number, but a postal address!*

Recommended Producers

Annie's Lane   Great wines across the board especially Semillon, which is unusual for this part of the world.

Claymore Wines   Quite new on the scene and mostly making wines for export. Low yields and dry grown vineyards should mean a good bottle of wine.

clos Clare   Tremendous Riesling and Shiraz. Not a lot made but well worth seeking out. It was once owned by Jim Barry wines, until he gave it to his daughter as a wedding present. It is now owned by Noel Kelly, with the Rieslings made by Jeffrey Grosset and the Shiraz by Dave Powell of Torbreck.

Crabtree Watervale   Good honest wines - the reds particularly.

Grosset   One of the world's best makers of Riesling. Very good Bordeaux blend called Gaia. Also makes a Chardonnay which is easier to find than the other wines.

Jeanneret Wines   One of the only wineries in the valley to have been awarded an "A" organic certification. Not all wines are organic as some fruit is bought in to keep up with demand. Complexity is achieved by purchasing grapes from virtually every area of the valley which is vinified and kept separate until blending begins.

Jim Barry   Old family firm that makes the biggest Shiraz in the region - the Armagh. Hard to find and most expensive in Australia. The McRae wood range is a third of the price and looks like a bargain against the Armagh.

Kilikanoon   The Oracle Shiraz is the one to look for here.

Knappstein Wines   Like so many others in the area, the Riesling is great.

Leasingham Wines   The Bin 7 Riesling is exceptional and has the ability to mature in ideal conditions for many years.

Macaw Creek   A number of wines made organically but uncertified as yet. Located outside of Clare in the Mount Lofty Ranges.

Mitchell Winery   The Shiraz and Cabernet are good value for money.

Mount Horrocks   The Cordon Cut Riesling is one of Australia's greatest pudding wines. The rest of the range is good also.

Old Station   Bill Ireland now owns Old Station, whose Shiraz always impresses. It is con-centrated, focused and offers a good level of complexity. These wine have always show very well when I give them as examples of Clare Shiraz in many of the tastings I have conducted.

ABOVE *Vineyards in South Australia.*

lows through to the reds, making them ideally suited to accompany food.

Demonstrating just how long a tradition the Clare Valley has with winemaking, Leasingham Wines was founded in 1893 and has grown to become one of the largest wineries in the region. It has been through many owners recently, but is now settled within the BRL Hardy portfolio. Making approximately 100,000 cases of wine a year is a tremendous task for a winery of this size, but one which they carry off with skill and commitment to quality. The Rieslings here are every bit as good as others in the Valley, apart perhaps from those made by Grosset. In their red Bin series, Bin 61 and Bin 56 have been the recipients of many trophies and medals in the last ten years, which demonstrates this winery's ability to make serious wines.

Macaw Creek Wines is located in the Gilbert Valley, which comes under the control of the Clare and Gilbert council, so I have included it here although it officially comes

O'Leary Walker Wines Only established in 2001, this is the brain child of David O'Leary and Nick Walker both of whom had previously worked for large wine companies. Between them they have racked up an amazing 300 gold medals, 60 trophies - including a Jimmy Watson - and were twice winners of the International Red Wine Maker of the Year award. With this impressive background they wanted to create their own label and have done so by sourcing fruit from within the valley, mostly from Watervale and David's family vineyards at Oakbank in the Adelaide Hills.

Paulett A beautifully-situated winery that hand-crafts their wines using 100-year-old slate open fermenters and a basket press.

Petaluma Great Clare Riesling is one of the hallmarks of this ever-expanding wine company. It also owns Leasingham, Stonier, Mitchelton and Knappstein wines. Although not based in the region they are included because of their commitment to Riesling in the area.

Sevenhill Cellars The oldest winery in the Valley, having been founded in 1851 by the Jesuits for the making of sacramental wines. This still continues today with 25% of their annual production being sold to religions throughout Australia and Indonesia. The rest of the production is made into table wine, with the Shiraz being the pick of the crop. If visiting you are also able to see the stunning St Aloysius Church, which is one of the area's best kept treasures.

Skillogalee Wines Very good Rieslings that age very well. Also look out for the Traminer and Shiraz. Recent acquisitions should see the production levels go up. If in the area, plan to have lunch here in the restaurant, which offers very good dining at good prices.

Tim Adams Although they do not own their own vineyards they buy grapes from eleven local growers situated throughout the valley, who have a commitment to quality. The wines are reasonably full-bodied and have the ability to age.

Tim Gramp A grandson of the former Managing Director of Orlando wines, Tim studied at Roseworthy and filled various roles within the wine industry until settling with his own label in 1991. A winery was purchased in 1996 where the group is now situated today.

Wendouree One of my favourite wineries in Australia. No other winery produces wines that are so long-lived across the whole range. Very limited quantities that sell via mail order.

under Mount Lofty Ranges. After 15 years experience in the industry, Rod Hooper set up his own winery here in 1995. He was fortunate that the property had been in his family since 1854, at a time when viticulture was starting. In fact at the end of the 18th and beginning of the 19th century, over 400 acres were planted to vine in the area adjacent to his. The majority of these were unfortunately grubbed up during the First World War, to grow much-needed crops such as wheat and barley. It was not until 1995, when Rod started up again, that grape-growing took off again. A number of land owners planted vineyards, and today the vast majority of grapes are sold on to larger companies like Southcorp and BRL Hardy. Not surprisingly the majority of grapes grown are red and most of these are Shiraz.

The soils in the region are quite interesting in that (so Rod tells me), along with the Clare Valley, they have more Terra Rossa than Coonawarra - which is some statement to make. To compliment this they have fertile black loams (Bay of Biscay) similar to that found in the Barossa. Rainfall is quite reliable at 21 inches per year, and Macaw Creek is fortunate to be protected by the Mount Lofty ranges to the east and west.

Production is currently modest at 3000 cases per year, but there are plans to increase this to 20,000 by 2007. These extra sales will be generated by a flourishing export market, where 80% of the wines already end up. One wine of medical note is their Yoolang Shiraz, which is preservative-free. This has enabled them to build up a loyal group of customers who are sulphite-sensitive or asthmatic. It is Rod's aim to gain certification from the Biological Farmers' Association as an organic vineyard in the future. The wines have a flavour profile not dissimilar to the Clare Valley, and this could attract new wineries to the region as the land prices are significantly cheaper. Situated in between the Clare and Barossa, it would also benefit from passing trade making this an area to keep an eye on.

Coonawarra

Coonawarra exists for one purpose and one purpose only - to make some of the finest red wines in Australia. Located in-between Melbourne and Adelaide with a 4.5 hour drive to either major city, it is not somewhere that you make a day trip too. The tourist drive does not even go near here - it follows the splendid coastal route taking in the imaginatively named Great Ocean Road to the south. What brings wine lovers to Coonawarra is a strip of soil 18km long and between 200 metres and 1.5km wide, known as terra rossa or red earth. Underneath this remarkable soil lies a constant table of pure water, which is ideal for the vines to prosper and is also essential as no natural rivers run through the region.

ABOVE *The Coonawarra Region in South Australia is not particularly large.*

This clay soil can be traced back almost one million years, when it was submerged beneath the ocean. The ocean froze during the Ice Age, at a time when the land was gaining an additional altitude of one centimetre per century. When the ice melted 50,000 years later and the ground had risen by five metres, the shoreline had naturally receded and a new limestone ridge was formed. As the limestone was in contact with the air and rainfall containing carbon dioxide, it became slightly acidic. This slowly dissolved the carbonates and left it as a thick surface area that then became the major constituent in the terra rossa soil found today, which is between a couple of centimetres to a metre thick. It derived its colour from iron carried in by strong winds, which oxidised to a beautiful rusty-red. The region is now 60 metres above sea level, surrounded by nothing but empty countryside. Outside the terra rossa strip, to the west, lie black and grey clay soils which are not regarded in the same light. With the introduction of GIs (discussed on page 56) many wineries have fought tenaciously to be included in the Coonawarra boundary, but have failed as their vineyards are outside the area of hallowed soil.

Having such a vibrant-coloured soil might indicate that this region has a very warm in climate, as it is easy to make comparisons with the red centre of Australia. In fact this is a cool region, with a very similar climate to Bordeaux. The daily mean temperature in Coonawarra is 16.5ºC, compared to 16.9ºC in Bordeaux, and perhaps this is why Cabernet Sauvignon excels here. The wines, though, are

ABOVE *The vineyards of Coonawarra produce wines of exceptional finesse and elegance, which are full and upfront with ripe flavours.*

totally different to those of Bordeaux and the two should not be compared like-for-like. Whilst Coonawarra produces wines of exceptional finesse and elegance, like those you would expect to find in Bordeaux, the Australian wines will always be fuller and more upfront, with ripe flavours, as the growing period, although reaching the same mean temperatures, is longer in Coonawarra. This allows the grapes to ripen to a fully physiological state whilst maintaining good acidity, which is essential for these wines. Interestingly, the average rainfall has dropped in the past 30 years. In 1971 to 2000 the average was 663.4mm, in 1981 to 2000 644.2mm, and from 1991 to 2000 604.6mm.

It is quite ironic that the famous old railway station, the very building that enabled Coonawarra to prosper - indeed be there at all - is now not in use. The station not only enabled wineries to sell their wines to the major cities in Australia, but also to send it to the ports for export. This was in 1887, when Europe was plagued by the Phylloxera louse and most of its vineyards were ruined, but the Australians seized the opportunity to introduce their wines to the established world.

Coonawarra was pioneered by a Scot named John Riddoch (c.1827), who came for the gold rush in 1852 after being told by his father that he could make £1,000 in two weeks of hard graft. In the 1860s Riddoch purchased around 35,014 acres of pastoral land in South Australia in an area known as Yallum, with the view of starting townships and creating employment. The first vineyard was the result of a sub-division of the land into 10 acre lots during the 1890s, which were sold at a price of around £100 each through his company, the Coonawarra Fruit Colony. By 1891, 348 acres of vines were planted. The first vintage was made in 1895 in John Riddoch's nursery shed, with not a lot of fuss being made. In 1896 Riddoch employed the services of a winemaker named William Salter, who made a far better wine in his woolshed at the Katnook Estate. This worked admirably and many fruit farmers established themselves and traded well until the advent of the First World War. After this period and before the Second World War, most of the grape juice was distilled, and it was not until Samuel Wynn saw the potential for quality wines that the region re-established itself. He purchased the Riddoch cellars with his son David in 1951, and today Wynns has vineyards that total some 1340 acres.

They are by far the largest operation in the region and yet still manage to make wines of exceptional quality under the supervision of winemaker Sue Hodder. Sue is a charming, hard-working lady who knows her business and is easily one of the best winemakers in the country. How she came into winemaking I do

Grape Varieties

CABERNET SAUVIGNON - It is here that Cabernet Sauvignon reigns supreme and is the most noble variety. The wines exhibit immense varietal character showing mint, blackcurrant, capsicum, plum and prunes when young, developing into earthy, farmyard, chocolate and tobacco flavours when mature.

SHIRAZ - Coonawarra Shiraz is perhaps the most elegant of South Australia's regions. It can be full bodied from the top estates and show blackcurrant, cherry, spice and liquorice whilst young, developing into earthy, farmyard and meaty flavours when mature.

CHARDONNAY - Far less full than other regions and with a touch of elegance. Nuts, citrus, butter, vanilla and melon all appear in the flavour spectrum.

ABOVE *Viognier grapes*

RIESLING - Although not the most widely grown variety in Coonawarra it can produce wines that are a little more immediate than those from the Clare. Typical flavours include lime, mineral and some tropical fruit.

ABOVE *Coonawarra has the famed terra rossa soil, which has proved particularly suitable for the growing of grape vines.*

not know - she grew up in Alice Springs, which is surely one of the most remote towns in the world. Somehow she found herself at Roseworthy College and graduated in 1984 with a degree in Agricultural Science. From here she found work at Penfolds, and then as a Grower Liaison Officer in the Barossa, which involved assessing vineyards and then seeking ways to develop their potential. This gave her the fundamental skills that she utilises today. By continually analysing fruit at all stages of ripeness and how they influenced the final wines, she has built up a considerable knowledge of vineyard management practices. Keen to develop her skills and enter the world of winemaking itself she enrolled in a Graduate Diploma in Winemaking at Roseworthy again, which she graduated from in 1988. After a brief stint in Great Western working at Seppelt she joined the team at Wynns in 1993. After five years she took over the mantle of head winemaker, which she has continued to be ever since, through numerous mergers and acquisitions of the parent company Southcorp.

The top wines that she makes, Michael Shiraz and John Riddoch Cabernet Sauvignon, are world-class and act as benchmarks for the region. Although made in most years from the best barrels of the vintage, there are occasions when it is not produced. The wines can be very long-lived as demonstrated by a recent tasting of a 1960 Cabernet Sauvignon, which had developed into an almost Pinot Noir-like profile, full of farmyard and compost aromas that

were delightful. Although these wines can be approached when young, it is advisable to let them mature for at least ten years in good vintages to show at their best. Going down the scale it is amazing that a winery of this magnitude can produce wines at their base level that are so consistent and delicious. I am referring, of course, to Black Label Cabernet - a tremendous wine given the amount that is produced.

If visiting the region then the Wynns winery acts as a landmark, with its gleaming stainless steel tanks proudly standing tall in this flat landscape. These act as a focal point and also show the direction of the old railway station.

Naturally a lot of change has happened since 1951. Encouraged by the quality of wines being made, a number of people converged on the small nearby township of Penola, to enter the world of winemaking. Amongst those was a certain company called Lindemans. They arrived in 1965 with the purchase of the Rouge Homme Estate, which had 50 acres of land planted to vines out of a total of 395 acres. Today, as you drive north out of Penola along an almost straight road, you are surrounded by vines, which are glorious in their autumn shades. One after the other you pass famous estates such as Bowens, Zema, Parker, Wynns, Balnaves, Majella, Katnook and Petaluma.

Whilst famous for its world-class Cabernet

ABOVE *At Rymill Wines, they make an interesting Bordeaux blend of Merlot, Cabernet and Cabernet Franc, called MC2.*

Sauvignon, which excels here as a low-vigour variety that is only minimally susceptible to disease, berry-splitting and sunburn damage, it is easy to forget that the region was originally known for its Shiraz. It was not until Mildara produced a sensational Cabernet in 1963 that the region discovered its natural affinity for growing Cabernet Sauvignon. Amongst the first to jump onto the winemaking bandwagon in 1967 was the Yunghams family, who purchased the Katnook Estate and planted their first vines in 1969. Today the wines are still made in the same woolshed that William Salter used in 1896, and their Odyssey wine is made to commemorate this. Katnook also commemorates John Riddoch and his association with Coonawarra, with a premium range of wines bottled under the brand name Riddoch. The 1986 Cabernet Shiraz won the famous Jimmy Watson Trophy for the best young wine in Australia.

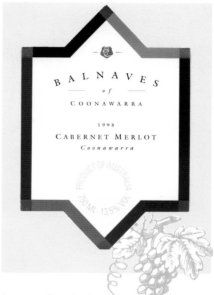

Wayne Stehbens now presides over the wine-making, and has done so since 1980. This long term position has enabled Wayne to develop an encyclopaedic knowledge of the vineyards owned by the Estate and the nuances that they provide to the final wines. He is partnered by Leon Oborn, who is in charge of the vineyards. Oborn utilises vineyard management skills that enable Wayne to show the terroir of the region across the range of wines. They are not afraid to experiment either, which is a trap some old and established wineries can fall into. Whilst there I tasted a Botrytis-affected Chardonnay that was quite unusual - it tasted just like wholemeal bread. Although not a wine that will ever be made in commercial quantities, it is experiments like these that will lead to new discoveries, which may one day prove to be ideal for a region.

Shortly after Katnook was established, the Balnaves family moved into the area. They planted their first vines in 1975 and continued to plant until 1998. Today the family has holdings of 115 acres, most of which are controlled by very sophisticated computer systems that utilise satellite technology to predict current and future weather patterns. This is facilitated by Neutron Probes, which are designed to

ABOVE *The daily mean temperature in Coonawarra is 16.5ºC, and the average rainfall is around 604.6mm, so the growing period is long and the grapes maintain good acidity.*

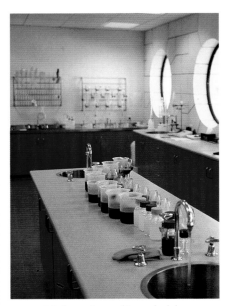

ABOVE *Modern wine-making - the laboratory at Rymill Wines.*

measure volumetric soil moisture content, and gypsum blocks, which measure soil moisture tension in Kilo Pascal (KPa). Readings from these instruments are taken weekly, or before and after a significant weather change. The results are then graphed to show trends in different blocks within the vineyard. The results are combined with localised weather station reports and long-range weather forecasts, to help with decisions on watering or non-watering regimes to suit each block of vines.

The utilisation of modern vineyard management practices carries on throughout the vineyard. Pruning is carried out by one of three mechanical pruners, each one set to best

complement different grape varieties and situations. Once the machines have been through the vineyard a team goes through to finish the pruning by hand, to ensure the correct amount of buds are on each vine. The vines are planted in a north-south direction, which is said to give up to 22% more sunlight through the year. 85% of the vineyard is irrigated, but only a maximum of four times a year, with 40% only once. The soil moisture measuring technology is so advanced it can sub-divide each irrigation area, taking into account the amount of moisture a crop cover will use and the trellising method in place.

The wines' style is one that focuses on gaining complexity and tannin structure as the main profiles. To accomplish this, Balnaves uses techniques that are a little different from the norm. Peter Bissell, their winemaker, encourages the temperature of the ferment to rise up to 32°C as he feels this is the ideal way to extract colour and soft tannins from the skins and seeds. This, coupled with long macerations and maturing the wines on light lees, produces the different style of wines.

A company that still utilises all the traditional methods is Zema Estate, where all the vines are hand-pruned and dry-grown to give the perfect expression of fruit. These wines are rich, intense and long-lived. The Zemas arrived from Italy in 1959, but it was not until 1982 that they purchased a small block of mature Shiraz with a further undeveloped 12 acres, which they planted with Cabernet. These are idiosyncratic wines that are painstakingly made with natural yeasts and naturally-occurring malolactic fermentation. Yields are

ABOVE *The parallel lines of the vines create interesting patterns across the landscape.*

moderate at around 15 tonnes per acre.

One of the newer wineries to gain an international reputation for quality is Penley Estate. The name was concocted by Kym Tolley, the owner and chief winemaker of the estate. Kym himself has a fascinating history, which is full of stories about his family's long association with the wine business. His mother was part of the Penfolds family and this led him to work for Penfolds in 1973 under Max Schubert - the creator of Grange. In 1988, Kym decided to establish his own winery in Coonawarra to carry on his family tradition of wine-making. The Tolleys on his father's side had been a formidable force in Australian wine-making for almost 100 years, with vineyards in the Barossa, Riverland and Padthaway. The first Tolley-made Coonawarra Cabernet was actually exported to the UK in 1910. During the 1960s and 70s this export market was greatly enlarged, due to the problems being experienced in France. Kym wanted to carry on this heritage and formed Penley Estate, creating the name from the first three letters of Penfolds and the last three from Tolley. Kym planted the first 120 acres - out of an eventual 200 - in 1989, and he had to buy fruit in for his first few vintages. This was in a time of recession throughout Australia and most peers thought him mad to embark on such a project. But with 16 years experience at Penfolds, Kym believed that he could make excellent wines and shouted it from the rooftops even before the first vintage was released. He proved himself right, with the 1989 Reserve Cabernet winning the National Bank Trophy for the best dry red at the Adelaide show. It went on to win five gold medals and the die had been cast. Penley Estate has in the past ten years won no less than 672 medals and trophies for its wines, and in 2002 was named as the International Winery of the Year by *Wine & Spirit Magazine* (USA). They say that every cloud has a silver lining and this has proved to be the case at Penley. Soon after planting a new block of vines the heavens opened and the area was consequently flooded. Other vignerons in the region advised Kym to pull the plants up, as they were in far too precarious a location. Kym decided not to follow this advice and today the block produces some of the best fruit they grow, which goes into their Reserve Range of wines. They have named it the Bonus Block for obvious reasons.

The latest plantings at Penley are known as The Steyning Block but they have been unable to register this as a brand name, because Steyning is a registered viticulture region in Sussex, England! This is no doubt due to the Reverend John Penfold, who was the vicar of Steyning and is Kym's great-great-great grandfather. Perhaps he planted vines there all those years ago. If in Coonawarra, it is well worth visiting Penley, for the grounds as much as the wines. They have planted some 500 trees, including 30 indigenous species, which attracts a plethora of birdlife to the area.

In contrast to Penley Estate, who make a multitude of wines, Parker Estate make just two. Both are Cabernet Sauvignon-based and are aimed at the top end of the market. This is reflected in the name of their top wine, First Growth, a direct message to Bordeaux about the quality if ever there was one. The Estate

ABOVE *This aerial view of the Coonawarra region clearly shows the viticulture area, set within acres of empty countryside.*

was founded by John Parker in 1985 and a new cellar door and winery were built in 2002. I was due to meet John Parker in Sydney, but unfortunately he died three days before my arrival. I am sure he will be greatly missed, but his legend will continue through the international success of his wines.

Highbank Wines is owned by Americans Dennis and Bonnie Vice, who returned to Australia in 1985 after a holiday there. They fell in love with the region and started planting vines in 1986, on their newly-acquired ten-acre site. They carefully selected the location for each grape variety on the plot after commissioning a detailed soil survey. This showed subtle differences in both topsoil depth and limestone content so six clones of Cabernet Sauvignon were planted, each ideally matched to their individual plot. A small amount of Chardonnay was also planted, but it proved very difficult to grow as the high rainfall of the south-east made it particularly prone to Powdery Mildew. Although they do not claim to be organic, the Vices certainly believe in low-input sustainable agriculture as being very important to their wines. Dennis keeps the canopy open and is not interested in high yields, preferring to focus on high quality berries. The vineyard floor has been planted with rye grass and fescue, which has proved essential for Apple Moth control. The science behind this is that the moth feeds on broad leaf weeds, which is controlled by having to compete with the shallow root grasses, which only marginally compete with the vines for moisture. The sod is therefore maintained as dense-

ly planted as possible throughout the moth season. Another function of this cover crop is to transpire, pulling excess moisture away from the vine - and when the vines need the moisture they can be cut short. The crop also has another significant benefit, as it helps insulate the vines to cut down potential problems caused by frost. The wines from Highbank naturally fall into the premium sector and have won praise from an international spectrum of wine writers.

Although Cabernet is by far the dominant force in this region, Shiraz, Merlot, Chardonnay and Riesling are all made to a high standard. Ian Hollick, at his eponymously-named vineyard, makes an interesting Riesling full of floral and citrus flavours, which are fuller than those that hail from the Eden Valley area of the Barossa. Riesling vines have to be carefully sprayed to eliminate Botrytis, however, which can be a problem in certain years. Ian first planted vines here in 1975, which resulted in the first commercial release in 1983. Major success was to reward his patience, when in 1985 he won the prestigious Jimmy Watson Trophy for the best young wine in Australia. There are now 178 acres planted to vine, of which around 40% are in Wrattonbully.

Majella's main business is contract grape growing, which grew out of a friendship between George Lynn, who owns the land, and Eric Brand of Brands Coonawarra, the winery. Eric wanted to plant a vineyard on the Lynns' property to sell the grapes to Hardys, so in 1968 he planted six acres of Shiraz. This was

Recommended Producers

Balnaves   As you would expect from Coonawarra, Cabernet dominates the range. Good well-made wines that always please.

Bowen   Doug Bowen runs this impeccable winery which makes rich and ripe wines.

Brands   High quality wines whose quality will be sustained through McWilliam's purchase of the estate.

Hollick   The Wilgha Shiraz and Ravenswood Cabernet complement the tasty Riesling at this Jimmy Watson Trophy-winning estate. Watch out too for the Shiraz/Cabernet blend.

Katnook   The Odyssey Cabernet and Prodigy Shiraz are the two wines to search out for here. Slightly down the scale is the Christmas-pudding-like Shiraz and straight Cabernet. These wines are made to be forward and enjoyed upon release.

Majella   The sparkling Shiraz and Riesling always show well from Majella as does the Cabernet. If you can find any the Malleea is also very good.

Leconfield   A good estate it is especially worthwhile to look out for magnum of the Cabernets.

Penley Estate   Winner of the Winery of the Year award in 2000, given by the American *Wine & Spirit* magazine. The whole range is impressive, especially the Ausvetia Shiraz and the Cabernet Reserve. Standard bottlings of Phoenix Cabernet and Hyland Shiraz are also very good.

Parker Estate   Only two wines are made here, both Cabernet and both exceptional. The founder, John Parker, unfortunately died in May 2002.

Pepper Tree   Part of the same stable as Pepper Tree, in the Hunter Valley, and Audrey Wilkinson, also from the Hunter. Chris Cameron is both the winemaker and Managing Director of the company. The vineyard adjoins the Parker Estate, where Chris also makes the wines.

Rymill   An interesting Bordeaux blend of Merlot, Cabernet and Cabernet Franc called MC2 is worth tasting, alongside their flagship Cabernet and Shiraz.

S Kidman   A small winery at the northern end of the Coonawarra boundary. Good wines are made here, especially the Shiraz, which is spicy, savoury and well balanced with very good length.

St Marys   Although located in the Limestone Coast region it is only ten miles away from Penola so is included here. The estate is mainly a grazing property that was purchased by the Mulligan family in 1937. The vines are planted on an elevated area of terra rossa soil over limestone, which is quite stony. The family utilise small batch ferments, open vats with basket pressing, and barrel maturation in climate-controlled storage for 18 months.

Wynns   Considering the amount of Black Label Cabernet that is produced here, the quality is remarkably high. The Riddoch Cabernet and the Michael Shiraz are both benchmark wines for the area.

Zema   The Cluny Blend and straight Cabernet and Shiraz wines offer an insight into how traditional Coonawarra wines taste.

successful until the late 70s when demand was low and up to 30 tonnes were thrown away from the vineyard, which had by then grown to 70 acres. Since 1980 Majella has sold grapes to Wynns, which has prospered, and now the Estate consists of 150 acres under vine. In 1991, after much persuasion from other growers in the region, the Lynn family decided to bottle a wine under their own name as well. Having no facilities to make it themselves, they rekindled the professional link with Brands - who to this day still make the Majella wines at their facility.

It is perhaps fortunate for the wineries in Coonawarra that Chardonnay seems to prefer the black loam soils to the expensive terra rossa strip. These Chardonnays are not of the rich, ripe, buttery variety that you find in warmer climates, but instead have a refreshing acidity and citrus edge to them.

Adelaide Hills

Adelaide Hills is the one wine region in Australia that you can get totally lost in. Most others are pretty straightforward to find your way around, with just a couple of roads to choose from and vineyards to either side of them. The Adelaide Hills is the opposite - a complete maze. After a visit to one winemaker I asked directions to another and the man concerned was not sure of the exact route even though he had lived in the area for years. In all fairness he could no doubt drive there himself, but giving directions is another thing altogether. The hills stretch for more than 60 miles north to south, and 22 east to west, which takes in the higher sections of the Mount Lofty Ranges that rise to over 400 metres.

If on a wine tour, the Hills are in an ideal position, being flanked by the Barossa and Eden Valleys to the north and McLaren Vale to the south. You could spend weeks going to all the vineyards and never get tired of it.

In terms of setting up a vineyard to meet specific requirements, it is the ideal region due to the plethora of choices available - assuming the land was available for purchase of course. Elevations vary between 400 and 700 metres and you could quite literally choose any point on the compass and find a matching slope. This is one region where micro-climates play a

ABOVE *Chardonnay grapes are one of the three main varieties currently grown here - the other two are Sauvignon Blanc and Pinot Noir.*

significant role in viticulture. Peter Leske of Nepenthe points out that some say there are 150 climates in Burgundy, but if this is so there are 250 in the Adelaide Hills. The climate is broadly Mediterranean, with dry summers and winter dominated by rainfall, although this occurs mainly in the spring and not autumn. The hills are not of an even elevation throughout, but rise sharply on the eastern side of Adelaide and fall away gradually to a plain some 20 miles away. They experience a south-westerly weather pattern, which, along with their topography, cause a rain-shad-

ABOVE *Adelaide Hills. is full of numerous privately-owned vineyards, and there has not yet been serious investment from the larger wine companies.*

ow effect - the wettest and steepest parts are adjacent to Mount Lofty, but as you move away to the east the rains ease as the landscape becomes more gently undulating.

Soils at the base of the hills usually have a deeper structure than those at the top, due to rainfall washing them down. The benefit of this to the vines is that the soils have far greater water retention, although vine vigour can be reduced by avoiding the deep alluvial valleys and planting on the drier, shallower mid slopes, which will also aid the quality. The soils in general are moderately acidic and quite low in nutrients, having been either leached by years of rainfall or previously used for alternative agricultural purposes such as cherry and apple orchards.

All of the above-mentioned factors make site selection a relatively complicated procedure. It is possible that vineyards currently planted with Sauvignon may in fact be more suited to Chardonnay, but only time will tell as experimental plantings come on stream and mature. Peter believes that the greatest benefit of this evolution will be to the red varieties. New varieties are being trialled - with some success - but it would appear that the current three main grapes, Chardonnay, Sauvignon Blanc and Pinot Noir, will dominate. There has not yet been a serious investment from the larger wine companies, which I believe is a good thing. Wines are produced here by them, but not on a hugely commercial basis. This allows the region to show its wares via numerous privately-owned vineyards, who can work on producing wine of an individual character.

Nepenthe is one of the youngest wineries in the Adelaide Hills, having commenced its first vintage in 1997 under the eye of Peter Leske, the chief winemaker. Peter came with 15 years experience and had the good fortune to be able to design the winery to his own specifications.

ABOVE *The Adelaide Hills vary between 400 and 700 metres in elevation.*

It must have been a daunting time for him in the early years to be in a region known for its Sauvignon Blancs and Pinot Noirs - he had never made either before. Like so many others, he graduated from Roseworthy in the early 1980s (his father was a lecturer there for many years) and went to work in the Hunter at the Rothbury Estate under Len Evans. Moving south he worked at Mitchelton for two years, before going to work for Dujac in Burgundy (he must have taken notes on how to make Pinot...). On his return home he worked for Jeffrey Grosset, the king of Riesling - much later, in 1998, becoming the full time winemaker there after other brief interludes in France. In 1992 he had a break from winemaking, and joined the Australian Wine Research Institute advising on all matters vinous to his fellow winemakers.

Being the new boy in a region that has seen the likes of Henschke, Knappstein, Crosser, Weaver and Cootes make a name for themselves is a tough challenge, but he has coped remarkably well and is now considered to be one of the best himself. However, he firmly believes that it is the sum of all the people around him that has contributed to the winery's success - from the Tweddell family's investment in the fine soils and machinery, to the viticultural and winery helpers who are all

ABOVE *Peter Leske, the chief winemaker at Nepenthe*

willing to muck in and do whatever is needed to get the finished result. The range made here is impressive: five white wines and four reds, of which the most interesting to me are the Zinfandel and Tempranillo - not two varieties you would associate with this relatively wet region. Peter has continually made them well, though, and they complement the Sauvignon, Chardonnay and Pinot well.

Paracombe is a small boutique winery in the Adelaide Hills. Paul and Kathy Drogemuller, who own the estate, together established the vineyard and winery in 1983 after the Ash Wednesday bushfires which devastated much of South Australia in February of that year. They had previously been dairy farmers and had no experience in viticulture at all. However, they were convinced they were doing the right thing when they took over a former dairy farm that had been totally destroyed by the bushfire, as they could see the great potential for the property. It is situated 425 metres above sea level, on the edge of the Torrens Valley in the north-eastern Adelaide Hills. This high altitude and cool climate provides them with the ideal environment for producing high-quality fruit, which enables them to show the true expression of the varietals whilst maintaining elegance. At the time the region was undergoing a vine pull scheme, so the locals thought them quite mad. They obviously did a good job, however, as Andrew Garrett soon approached them about supplying grapes to him. The soil type varies from brown sandy loam and ironstone over clay, and quartz rock to brown loam over buckshot gravel and yellow pipe clay. The rainfall per annum is around 35 inches, which falls mainly between April and November. Winters are cold with good rainfalls, spring and autumn often present cool to warm weather, while summers are warm and dry with cool nights and occasional rain. The vineyard is planted to an easterly aspect, to capitalise on the morning sun for optimum fruit ripening. The Drogemullers now have around 35 acres of vines with further plans for expansion. There are currently seven varieties across a total of

ABOVE *View across vineyards in the Adelaide Hills.*

Recommended Producers

Aldgate Ridge   Well worth seeking out as they employ Dave Powell of Torbreck as their consultant winemaker.

Annvers Wines   Wayne and Myriam Keoghan established Annvers in 1998 with the aim of producing wines from the Hills, McLaren Vale and Langhorne Creek. The wines are not overtly oaky, as only barrels that have reached 2-3 years of age are used for the maturation process. Until 2003 no white wine was made here but a "super premium" is due for release.

Ashton Hills   Superb Riesling, Chardonnay and Pinot Noir made by Stephen George.

Barratt   An excellent winery with the Chardonnay and Pinot Noir being made by Jeffrey Grosset. The grapes are sourced from two vineyards in the Piccadilly Valley. The Uley vineyard is one of the oldest in the Hills, having been planted in 1983 after the fires that swept through the valleys.

Bridgewater Mill   Owned and managed by Petaluma

Chain Of Ponds   An eclectic range of wines that are fast becoming the talking point of the region.

Galah   Great value wines made by Stephen George.

Geoff Weaver   A living legend in the Australian wine scene own-label. He used to be the head winemaker for the Hardy group and as such, was at one time responsible for making 10% of all the wine in Australia. One of the pioneers of the region.

Glenara   Good organic wines are made here which tend to age well.

Hillstowe   Located at one of the prettiest villages in the Hills, Hahndorf. If visiting the area then this is a must - its stone cellars date back to the 1800s.

Knappstein Lenswood Vineyards   One of the finest growers in the region, having sold off his estate in the Clare Valley. It is unlikely that any wines from here will disappoint.

Leland Estate   Seek out the Sauvignon Blanc - it can be amongst the finest in the region.

Maximilian's Vineyard   Grant Burge from the Barossa and the Scarpantoni brothers from McLaren Vale make the top wines here, a Chardonnay and Cabernet Sauvignon.

Mount Lofty Ranges Vineyard   The expertise of Peter Leske from Nepenthe is utilised here to craft wines that appeal for everyday drinking.

Nepenthe Vineyards   Peter Leske comes to Nepenthe with a lot of experience and has earned respect very quickly with his exciting range of wines, including Zinfandel.

Paracombe Wines   Search out the Cabernet Franc, which can compete with those from Margaret River.

Petaluma   Headed up by Brian Crosser, one of the figures of the Australian wine scene. Great wines across the range. They very occasionally release a Botrytis wine, which is well worth searching for. The Shiraz is almost as hard to find, but well worth it.

Ravenswood Lane   The idea here is to create wines of European elegance complimented by quality Australian fruit, which go hand in hand with food.

Shaw and Smith   Producers of Australia's finest Sauvignon Blanc. The M3 Chardonnay is engineered to age and the Merlot is full, supple and ripe.

29,250 vines that have been planted since the vineyard was first established in 1983.

The vineyard is carefully managed, with hand-pruning establishing two main canes and further thinning at bud burst to ensure low yields and optimum bunch position. The vines are vertically-shoot-positioned, allowing more sunlight in to the vine, along with greater air-flow around the fruit, thus reducing disease problems. Grapes are carefully hand-picked to further maximise flavour and quality. In 1997 the Drogemullers transplanted around 500, 100-year-old Shiraz vines from another property close by. These old vines were the only remnants left of original local plantings dating back to the late 1800s. There is a history of the grapes from these old vines going in to early vintages from Penfolds Grange and St Henri.

One of the finest places to stop for lunch when visiting this area is the restaurant at the Chain of Ponds cellar door. Its magnificent views offer a spectacular backdrop and in summer you can eat outside on the terrace. The food is special - Italian in influence, because of the Italian origins of the owners, Caj and Genny Amadio. The wines have been subject to a marketing drive of late, with the appointment of Zar Brooks, who used to work at

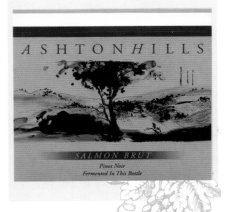

d'Arenberg and enthuses just as much about this business. The wines warrant the exposure that they are getting, with excellent examples of all the classic varieties from the Hills. In fact Chain of Ponds has become the most-awarded winery at the Australian Boutique Wine Competition, with more medals than anyone else. The business is currently undergoing a major expansion, with the planting of substantial new vineyards on a plot heading towards the Barossa. It is on undulating countryside that gives them a range of choices when it comes to site selection. This development should cement their reputations as one of the major players here. They have also secured the services of David Nelson and Eileen O'Regan as consultants, who will take the business to the next stage. He comes with substantial experience, including six years in Georgia, located just a short drive from the Chechnya border. Events there included being surrounded by 25 of the President's guards with AKs, being chased by the police and outrunning them, being shot at, experiencing an earthquake, carrying hand guns, and having four Nivas, three body guards, two Ladas and one threat of kidnapping. These experiences will certainly give him the necessary strength to face any times of adversity in Australia! Chain of Ponds has also taken on Neville Falkenberg as head winemaker. Neville has been in the industry for over 40 years, has held very senior winemaking roles for Penfolds, amongst others, and was instrumental in the development of Yattarna, Penfolds' premium white wine.

Michael Hill Smith was the first person in the Southern Hemisphere to obtain the Master of Wine qualification. He is a direct descendent of the famous wine family of the same name, and set up the Shaw and Smith winery with his brother. It is run meticulously and is spotless, something that is mirrored in the smart appearance of Michael himself. The winery and cellar are impressive, with architecture that would not be out of place in LA. The wines are even more impressive - the whites especially. Michael and his brother have made a conscious decision to make a Chardonnay with the ability to age, which they have named M3. Although it is too early to say if they have achieved their objective, I would be strongly inclined to think they have. They also make Australia's finest Sauvignon Blanc, which exudes fruit and elegance and is miles away from the "in-the-your-face" new Zealand examples. Being an early ripener, Merlot is grown here with a depth that you would not think possible from this region.

Stephen George is something of a legend in my eyes - not only does he excellently craft Pinot Noir for his Ashton Hills label, but he also finds time to consult for Tony Brady at Wendouree (my favourite winery). In addition to this he has another label called Galah, with part of the fruit coming (I believe) from the vineyard planted in 1911 at Wendouree, making these exceptional value for money. Stephen is a true grafter and man of the land. He is at his happiest working outdoors with the vines and wildlife, doing without all the nonsense of the outside world. His Riesling is pure and focused, taking time in bottle to develop the kerosene flavours so often found in mature wines from this grape. The Chardonnays go up to a higher level still, whilst the Pinots are often the finest to be found in the region.

ABOVE *Newly-planted Chardonnay grapevines, with protection from early frosts.*

Southern Australia Other areas

If travelling in a northerly direction from Coonawarra towards Adelaide, you will find the Mount Benson region to the west about one hour away. In the future we may find that it offers Heathcote significant competition as the new "fashionable" region. It is located between the fishing ports of Kingston and Robe, which are famous for their lobsters. With its close proximity to the Great Southern Ocean, vineyards here benefit from a long and cool ripening season, which results in picking around two weeks later than in Coonawarra. The ocean does bring its problems though - strong winds have necessitated the use of trees for wind breaks and shadecloth on edge barriers every five or so rows. The region promotes itself as "Terra Rossa by the Sea", since it has terra rossa soils over limestone. Water is not a problem here, due to an abundance of high-quality underground streams close to the surface to draw from. Mount Bemson is one of the newer regions, having only first been planted in 1989 - mainly with Shiraz, Cabernet and Merlot. Since then the acreage under vine has increased to 500 hectares. As a new region they are still experimenting with various varieties and so far Sauvignon Blanc and Viognier show promise along, I am told, with Cynge Blanc. This is a newly-registered white variety, which is derived from Cabernet Sauvignon. I have not been able to try this yet

ABOVE *Cynge Blanc is a newly-registered white variety derived from Cabernet Sauvignon grapes that is currently exclusive to Mount Benson.*

and it is currently exclusive to Mount Benson.

Perhaps the defining moment that put Mount Benson on the viticultural map was when M. Chapoutier, the esteemed Rhone maestro, decided to locate his Australian operation here in 1998. To my mind this was a very significant move. Mount Benson is away from the main tourist trail (and therefore cellar door sales) but its attributes obviously met all of Chapoutier's criteria better that any other region. For an area that was less than ten years

ABOVE *Banrock Station is a 4,500 acre vineyard in South Australia, which is set in some of the world's most beautiful countryside.*

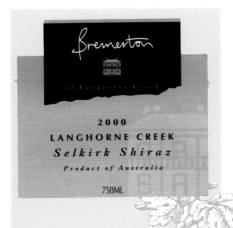

old at the time, it could not wish for a finer seal of approval. Chapoutier's introduction to the area no doubt came from Derek Hooper of Cape Jaffa Wines, who had worked for him in the Rhone. The relationship has continued, and M.Chapoutier's wines are now made at Cape Jaffa.

One of the largest and newest wineries in Mt Benson is Kreglinger, a business established in 1993 with diverse interests. A 2000-tonne production facility has been constructed, with 160 hectares of vineyard. The company also owns the Pipers Brook vineyards in Tasmania. Although it is too early to determine the quality of the wines (2001 was the first vintage) the careful plantings that have taken place and the specific site selection should lead to some excellent wines.

Ralph Fowler has been in the wine industry for 33 years, spending ten years as a winemaker for Tyrrells, ten at Hungerfield Hill and ten as the Director, manager and winemaker for the Leconfield and Hamilton wine groups. Today Ralph is focusing on his own label, Ralph Fowler Wines, which specialises in Shiraz and Viognier. The vines are trellised on a lyre system to maximise fruit exposure, and irrigation is via a new partial root zone drying technology, which reduces water usage and improves sustainability. Ralph's wines are made in the vineyard and the winemaking is traditional, with no SO2 or extended soak times. Only French barriques are used, from Siruque and Remond, which results in elegant and refined wines.

Heading north one passes through Wrattonbully on the way to Padthaway, where you will find Koppamurra Wines - one of only two (along with Bests) that bottles Pinot Meunier as a single variety - although the amount produced is so small that it is sometimes bottled as a dual-vintage wine. This is a

significant growing region, with massive planting by some of the larger firms to meet demand for their South Australian blends. They may also be labelled under the Wrattonbully name, as in some quarters it is being heralded as a finer region than Coonawarra, with its terra rossa soils and warmer climate.

Padthaway, which essentially exists purely to grow grapes, is probably best known (in the UK at least) for Penfolds' Padthaway Chardonnay, which enjoys enormous popularity. It was Seppelt who first planted in the region though, closely followed by the other larger companies. You need to drive through Padthaway to gauge a real sense of size. It feels as though you are surrounded by vines for mile after mile - and you are. It is large and it needs to be, as its grapes are more often than not the backbone behind the mid-priced South Australian wines you find on retailers' shelves.

The engine room of the Australian wine business is further north, however, in Riverland, which extends to the east into Sunraysia and Swan Hill in Victoria. and on to Griffith in NSW. This vineyards has to be seen to be believed. Vines are on the horizon for as far as the eye can see and I estimate it produces around 60 million cases of wine per year. Although its reputation is of a region that produces wine on an industrial scale, there are small patches of old fruit and the overall quality throughout is good.

One of the newest regions is Kangaroo Island, at just 87 miles long and 44 miles wide. Since it is on the same latitude as Margaret River, it looks very promising. Red grapes are dominant here and produce wines that are rich

ABOVE *Many vineyards harvest the grapes at night, to ensure optimum quality.*

ABOVE *Wooden casks at Bleasdale Vineyards, Langhorne Creek.*

ABOVE *Press of red gum wood at Bleasdale, which has a great deal of historic equipment.*

and full. Vine growing started with one vineyard in the early eighties, and it was not until almost a decade later that another four were planted. Currently there are 25 vineyards, with eight producing wines under their own label , which are made at one of the two wineries on the island. The vineyards near the coast enjoy a cooler maritime climate, whilst those inland experience hotter days and cooler nights. There is a large variation in soil types, which contributes to a wide selection of flavour profiles. The main soils in the south are limestone with loam and clay, whilst in the north they are mainly sand/loam over clay. The south is cooler in the summer, due to the south and easterly winds, which results in a longer ripening period.

The arrival of Caj and Genny Amadio from Chain of Ponds was a positive influence on others to set up in the region. Although their holding is only small, it is nevertheless a significant development. The Bay of Shoals vineyard is located just 50 metres from the ocean's edge and they hand-pick and prune all their fruit. The Chardonnay is fruity and the Shiraz shows the classic blackcurrant and pepper characteristics. Cape d'Estaing is one of my tips to watch out for in the future, as is Hazyblur, which has already received very good scores from Robert Parker.

A short drive south from McLaren Vale is Langhorne Creek, another area full of vines with not too many wineries. It is said to be the fastest-growing region in Australia and benefits from a cooling breeze in the afternoon from

Lake Alexandrina, which also acts as a source of irrigation water since this relatively dry area. The soils vary from red sand to heavy black clay and are usually quite deep. There a few wineries of note here, the most important being Bremerton. This was originally founded in 1985 when the Wilson family took over the property, which was erected in 1866. They undertook a large restoration project, which has finally culminated in a new winery being finished in 2002. Craig and Mignonne Wilson's daughter Rebecca is now in charge of wine-making, and her sister Lucy heads up the marketing team. The top wine, Old Adam, has an international following and sells out quickly upon release.

Casa Freschi are the new winery on the block and the future looks good for them with glowing reviews and a good reception from the wine-buying public. Lake Breeze, owned and run by Greg Follett, produces some outstanding Cabernets-based wines from his vineyard, which is located on a farm his family have owned for almost 120 years. Temple Bruer is a champion of organic wines and they offer a wide selection to choose from. Bleasdale Vineyards is one of the most historic in Australia, having been founded in 1850. Inside you can see a wealth of equipment made from Red Gum trees and limestone. The property is owned by Michael Potts and is on the National Heritage Register. The wines are also exemplary across the board, especially the Frank Potts, which is their flagship wine and very deserving of the reputation it has acquired.

Victoria

Victoria is Australia's largest wine producing state and perhaps the most diverse, with many pockets of viticulture located across it. The most celebrated region here is the Yarra Valley, with its sublime Pinot Noirs, Cabernets and Chardonnays. It is a maze of vineyards and sub-regions, producing wines with class and elegance. It is becoming a victim of its own success, though, with Melbournians now moving into the valley to escape the bustle of the city and enjoy a semi-rural life.. The irony of this is that they then complain about the noise of the machinery and traditional farming practices that are intrinsically linked to the wine industry!

One of my most hotly-tipped regions is also located here, Heathcote. This region has all the elements needed to become world class with soils, climate and know-how from people like Ron Laughton at Jasper Hill already in place. This is where Australia's greatest Shiraz will come from in the future.

A selection of the finest sweet wines in the world are made here in Rutherglen. They are totally unique and are not emulated anywhere else on the planet. These really are wines that Australia can lay claim to having produced the finest examples of.

There are many small regions that have developed over the past two decades that show real promise for the future. The majority of these are cool climate and, as such, produce the

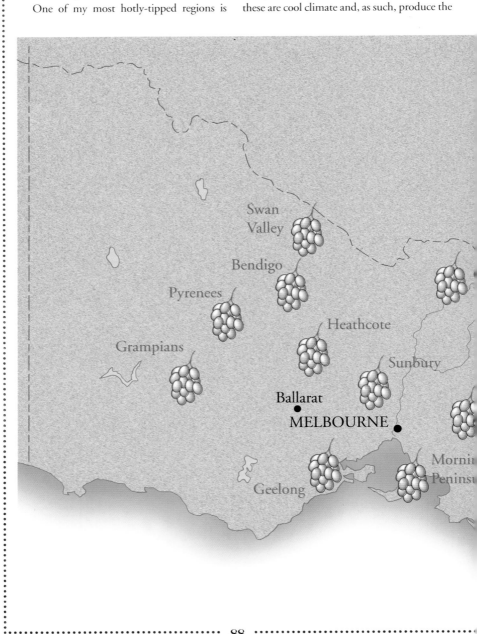

kind of wines of elegance and finesse that can be difficult to find in South Australia. One of the fastest growing of these is the Mornington Peninsula, with its flavoursome Pinot Noir and Chardonnays that are gaining ground with each vintage. It may be that in the next ten years we will see this region being held in the same regard as the Yarra Valley, although there is still some way to go and red tape may get in the way.

The historic inland city of Bendigo has some distinguished wine regions surrounding it, that can produce Shiraz of particular elegance and longevity. It is perhaps the one area that will become more developed in future years, as it is not held so back by planning restrictions as the Mornington Peninsula is. Unlike the Mornington, they are located within traditional farming communities, and as such can operate normal farming practices such as spraying, without fear of the local council imposing restrictions due to town dwellings encroaching upon the area.

Although quite remote, the Grampians are located along the inland road leading into South Australia and this may lead to confident individuals setting up here. The results that have been achieved over the past 150 years demonstrate that this is a region that can produce wines of a world-class quality, and this should act as encouragement.

As a state, Victoria produces a diverse range of wines and is the most similar to Europe of all regions in Australia. If commercially viable, I see no reason why a number of European grape varieties that are not currently grown here could flourish, giving a broader range of wines for us all to choose from.

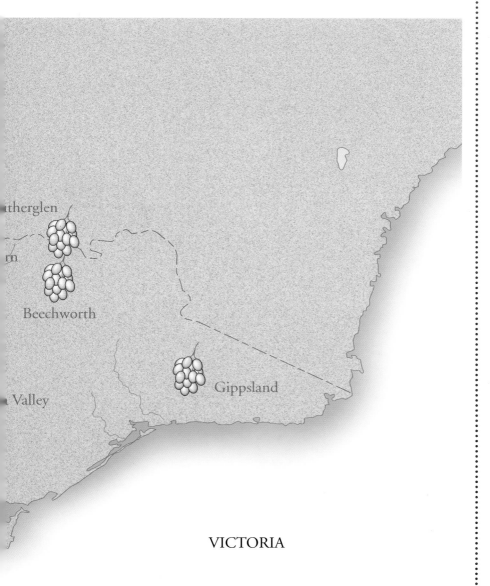

VICTORIA

Yarra Valley

The Yarra Valley, located a short drive east of Melbourne, is perhaps the most akin to a traditional European wine region. It is here that the guardians of the Australian wine industry are based. In an industry filled with young guns who have graduated from Roseworthy and are moulded into the high-alcohol, high-extraction, large-wines mentality (which there is nothing wrong with), it is refreshing to find the old guard making some of the most elegant and refined wines in Australia. It can be a daunting moment when arriving at wineries like Yarra Yering and Yeringberg. You simply do not know what to expect from these legendary wine makers, who in any other life may well have been professors of history or some other similar mentally challenging academic field. Their knowledge of the valley and the history of traditional methods is unsurpassed. Here the wines are crafted like no other. Like the Hunter Valley and Margaret River, it is quite possible that the future will be governed by sales gained through tourism, since the valley is in close proximity to Melbourne. Already the price of land is rising, making the purchase of plots suitable for vineyards very expensive due to the high prices paid for residential development. This brings a Catch-22 situation as well for the new residents - whilst they want to live in an idyllic valley with some of the country's finest vineyards, they object to routine farming practices such as spraying, scare guns, and night-time harvesting. This is, of course, akin to buying a property near an international airport and then complaining about the constant noise of planes. If you do not like it, live elsewhere.

One of the most important factors of the Yarra is its mild climate, which is ideal for vines as it allows the sugars and acids to develop at a steady pace and more evenly. This results in good-quality fruit, which gives the wines from this region their trademark elegance. There are two main types of soil in the region, a grey silty duplex, which is derived from Silurian mudstone and can cause drainage problems, and red volcanic soils, which are mainly found in Seville and Hoddles Creek. Problems can occur with Powdery Mildew and Downy Mildew, but these are overcome by careful spraying and intelligent canopy management. The light brown Apple Moth can also be a nuisance on occasions. In the past people have attempted to plant late-ripening varieties on the south-facing slopes, which have proved almost impossible to bring to full ripeness. Another common mistake has been for newcomers to the world of viticulture to fail to "hill up" their new vines, which has caused them to die of wet feet as the water has been unable to drain away.

The Yarra Valley was first planted in 1838 by William Ryrie, who had travelled from Monaro in New South Wales with his brothers Donald and James the previous year. They had journeyed with a herd of cattle and took up a grazing licence on 43,000 acres, naming the new property Yering. Two varieties were plant-

ABOVE *View of the vineyard at De Bortoli Wines, Yarra Valley*

ed initially, a black cluster of Hamburg, and a white grape called Sweetwater, which is a synonym for Palomino, the Sherry grape. The first vintage was harvested in 1845, after a Swiss vigneron taught William the basics. The Ryries only stayed until 1850, before selling the business to Paul de Castella and Adolphe de Meuron. The latter then sold his share to de Castella in 1853. de Castella embarked upon a period of development for the vineyard and imported 20,000 cuttings from Chateau Lafite in Bordeaux, France, along with machinery purchased in Paris to make the wine. The cuttings were promptly planted and by 1860 over 50 acres were established. As in most other regions, the wine proved excellent and by 1870 the area under vine had grown to 3000 acres. Competition was high amongst wineries even at this early stage. The main competitors for Yering were St Huberts and Yeringberg, which was, and still is, owned by the du Pury family. In 1861 the Yering station vineyard won the Argus Gold Cup for the best Victorian vineyard. Success continued in 1889, when the winery won a Grand Prix at the Paris Exhibition - the only winery in the Southern Hemisphere to do so out of the 14 awarded in total. Meanwhile the St Huberts vineyard, which was owned by Hubert de Castella, brother of Paul, won the accolade of displaying the most "meritorious" exhibit at the Melbourne International Exhibition in 1881. I wonder why it has taken the French so long to wake up to the fact that the Australians were producing excellent wine over 100 years ago. It is not until now in the 21st century that they seem to have realised that they have some serious competition and are doing something about it following the slump in their sales!

Since these jubilant times the valley has been through its share of rough patches, with the arrival of Phylloxera destroying most of Victoria's vineyards (although it did not reach the Yarra), and the Australians' taste for their refined wines changing to heavy port-like wines. The resurrection of the Yarra as we now know it came in the 1960s and 70s, with Dr John Middleton of Mount Mary, Bailey Carrodus at Yarra Yering and Guill de Pury of Yeringberg (who replanted the vineyard after it had fallen by the wayside in 1924). They set about planting the noble varieties of Cabernet Sauvignon, Pinot Noir and Chardonnay, and making them in the classical styles with moderate alcohol and extraction.

I would have loved to have visited Mount Mary on my trip, but I was asked not to by one of their UK importers so I can only say buy

ABOVE *Hand-picking Chardonnay grapes at Hoddles Creek, Yarra Valley, Victoria.*

their wines, as they are world-class across the range - although they can be difficult to understand initially.

Yeringberg is the home of a fascinating electricity free-museum, displaying artefacts of wine-making from a bygone age. It is housed in a fabulous two-storey building, which used to serve as the winery. The grapes were lifted to the upper floor by use of a pulley system, and then transported along the length by carts on rails. They were then crushed and gravity-fed downstairs to the basket presses, where the process was finished. It is enlightening to see the crude instruments used in the winery, and one can only assume that the quality must have been excellent in those days to warrant such labour-intensive methods. The vines are very low-cropping, with minimal irrigation and absolutely no high-tech state-of-the-art equipment. These are wines from the ground, and only fruit from single vineyards is used. Only four wines are made here, a Pinot Noir, a Cabernet/Merlot blend, an interesting Marsanne/Rousanne blend and a Chardonnay. The property is also a working farm, with livestock often herded nearby the museum, which takes you back to when most vineyards in Australia were dual-purpose. It is a terrific sight to see, as well as a great insight into how these business survived in 1800s when all they could rely on for marketing was word of mouth.

Bailey Carrodus of Yarra Yering is a smart and highly intelligent gentleman, who just happens to produce the region's finest Shiraz, along with an assortment of other varieties. Since the labels simply announce the wines as

ABOVE *Riddling racks at Domaine Chandon, Yarra Valley, the Australian outpost of the French company Möet and Chandon*

LEFT *An 140-year-old Shiraz vine, which means it was planted before the American Civil War and before Lincoln became President.*

Dry Red No 1 (Cabernet-based Bordeaux blend) and Dry Red No 2 (Shiraz-based Rhone Blend), and so on, they do not suggest that the wines within are of exceptional quality. I tasted through the range in the immaculate, purpose built storage area, which goes many levels below ground level to maintain optimum storage temperatures. Apart from at Yarra Yarra, I have never seen such attention paid to the cleanliness of the building. If this was a car workshop, it would be McLaren. Bailey has French oak barrels made to his specific specifications from the highest grade oak that is obtainable, which are stored row after row in pristine condition. Great care must be taken when racking the wine, as the amount of stain around the bung hole is minimal.

Ian Maclean and his wife Anne own and preside over the Yarra Yarra vineyard in the Steels Creek section of the valley. This was one of the last great undiscovered vineyards in Australia. This is possibly due to the low production of only 1500 cases, which are only sold through fine restaurants and via a mailing list. As Yarra Yarra is only open by appointment it is not well signposted and as a result is rather hard to find, as it is set back from a dirt track in an isolated position. We obviously approached from the wrong side, as we met a hill that the little car we were driving had difficulty ascending. At one point it actually started to roll backward, which was quite worrying, but luckily my driver, Lynne Cochrane, a friend who runs meetthemakertours.com.au, a tour company, managed to find some grip and get us to the brow. When we arrived I was greeted by Anne and Ian gave me a tour of the barrel room, which was immaculate. Here we tasted through several individual barrels, which highlighted how the different blocks of fruit differed. Afterwards we had a splendid lunch to complement their top wine - a Bordeaux blend. It was one of those wines that just had the "wow" factor - it was so finely oaked with rich fruit and complex aromas developing in the glass as lunch went on. Prior to this we indulged in a bottle of Sauvignon/Semillon, which is made to the same style as a white Bordeaux. If you are beginning to see a pattern forming here, with Bordeaux central to it, it is because Ian has travelled to France to work three vintages at Domaine de Chevalier, one of the top estates. The vineyards here were originally planted in 1979 and 1980 with the classic Bordeaux varieties, with more added in 1996 (including some Shiraz) to make a total of 17 acres. The site is relatively low-vigour, which ensures low yields and grapes that achieve optimum ripeness and concentrated flavours. The Shiraz is made in a Northern Rhone style with a small percentage of Viognier added in to give fragrance and a floral tone to the wine.

The Yering Station winery is located on the original Yering site settled by the Ryrie brothers in 1850. Naturally it has changed considerable since then, especially after the Rathbone family purchased the property in 1996. A period of serious investment has resulted in a newly-extended building, with fabulous panoramic views of the vines in front and hills in the distance from the tasting area and restaurant. The windows are immense, and the roof designed with many curves to eliminate wind noise. You can't help but be impressed as you walk down a gallery of the wines that are currently on offer, showcased like pieces of art,

as you proceed to the viewing platform to peer into the cellars. These too are rather grand, with barrels extending as far as the eye can see and stacked four or five high. This is a clue to the size of the newly-regenerated business, which will become a formidable force in the Yarra. Great care is taken in each aspect of the business and this was evident when I had a private tasting with Darren Rathbone, a director and winemaker. Different Riedel glasses were used for each wine, each glass specifically designed to show the particular nuances of each grape variety fully. We tasted through 12 wines, from the basic Baraks Bridge range through to the Reserve selection. The Pinot Noirs stood out, having strong fruit with a savoury edge, whilst maintaining good acidity.

Almost opposite Yering Station is Domaine Chandon, the Australian outpost of the famous Champagne house Möet et Chandon. As you would expect, they specialise in sparkling wines (no wine that is made out side of Champagne region in France may call itself a champagne), that are made in the traditional method. This is a time-consuming business and terroir is critical for the production of these wines. The three traditional grapes grown for Champagne are Chardonnay, Pinot Noir and Pinot Meunier. In the Champagne region, around the two main cities of Reims and Epernay 145km north-east of Paris, these varieties struggle to ripen fully as they are at the extreme north of the wine-making parallels at 49-50ºN. Not ripening fully, though, is not a problem, as the base wines have a good level of ripe acidity and the wines will go through a secondary fermentation, which gives the wines their bubbles. It is these unique conditions,

ABOVE *Bird netting to protect the grapes at Yerring Station Vineyard, Yarra Valley, Victoria.*

along with specific soil types that are so hard to find elsewhere in the world. Although Domaine Chandon is arguably the finest of the Möet et Chandon subsidiaries I feel that it cannot compete with the real thing. That is not to say that they are bad wines - on the contrary, they are well made, full of fresh fruits and refreshing acidity, and offer a spectrum of flavours through the range. Mine is just a personal preference.

Out of the many boutique wineries in this most spread out of valleys, Diamond Valley stands supreme. Located far from the other wineries at the north-west extreme of the valley, this small production winery makes some of the finest Pinot Noirs to be found in Australia. David, who has a PhD in chemistry, and Cathy Lance had their first vintage here in 1982, and ever since then their wines have been awarded medals and trophies at virtually all the competitions they enter. Their Estate Pinot Noir is regularly named as one of the top ten in the country and also receives international critical acclaim. The buildings and winery, which are not open to the public, are situated on a steep hill with the winery at the bottom. As you reach the crest of the hill you greeted by a plethora of kangaroos and the sight of vines rising majestically from the ground in the valley below. The plot farthest away is the Close Planted block, whose Pinot Noir grapes are made into a wine of the same name. This is arguably their best Pinot of the three produced, the others being White Label and Blue Label. This is not just a Pinot specialist however, Cabernet and Chardonnay all grow well here with the former being blended with Merlot to make a Bordeaux-style blend. David and Cathy's son, James, is now in control of the day-to-day wine-making and shares in all major decisions. His first vintages have proved to be a success, with the style of the wines maintained and respected. Of all the

boutique wineries in Australia, this has to be one of the most active in liaising with its customers. I do not mean this in the cold, harsh way of hard selling, but by writing regular quality newsletters and holding various dinners throughout the year, when old friends and new can sample some of the vintages held back for museum stock, along with fine food.

How Ron Collings at Ridgeback Wine finds time to make wines I do not know, as he is also a pilot for Qantas! Ron purchased the property, which is situated in Panton Hill, during 1990 with his lovely wife Lynne. Originally a gold mining town in the Diamond Creek area, it is situated on mineral-rich hills that overlook the Yarra Valley itself. The area has had a chequered history. It was originally owned by the Howard family, who farmed the land with fruit trees: apples, pears and nashi pears. In the 1950s the land was purchased by Melbourne Water as part of a grand plan to flood the area and create the Watsons Creek Dam. Unfortunately their planning department was rather lacking and had not accounted for the numerous old mine shafts that are scattered around the area. The area proved almost impossible to flood and the estate fell into a state of disrepair, with all the fruit simply falling to the ground. This, of course, was very advantageous for the Collings family, as the ground had had 40 years' worth of organic matter dropping onto it, which greatly enhanced the loam topsoil that overlies a clay base. It was obviously the correct decision to plant here, as James Halliday, the renowned wine author and owner of Coldstream Hills personally selected New Chum Gully (as it was know then) to supply him with fruit from the 1994 vintage onwards. By 1997, Southcorp had purchased Coldstream Hills so Ron made the decision to start bottling wine himself under the name Ridgeback. It was also at this time that the

Collings planted 2000 Pinot Noir vines (MV6) and 2500 Cabernet Sauvignon vines (LC10), to enable them to increase production. Merlot was also planted in 2000, grafted onto American rootstocks. Situated 175m above sea level, the winters are cold in this corner of the Yarra but the spring is milder and the majority of rainfall falls during these two seasons. The labels state that the wines are "robust, full-bodied, yet elegant and refined, exhibiting silky, velvety textures which, with further ageing should mature to become well rounded and enduring". This is also a fine description for their Rhodesian Ridgeback dog, after which the winery is called. The wines are made for short to medium cellaring, which is consistent with most peoples' requirements. Ron believes that the mineral/earth undertone of his Pinot is characteristic of the Diamond Valley sub region. Although a relatively newcomer on the scene, Ron leads the way amongst a group of boutique winemakers, who have formed a collective to promote themselves to the world.

I was fortunate to have a dinner laid on for me during my visit, hosted by the Boutique Wine Makers of Yarra Valley at a local restaurant. After spending all day and the previous days for weeks talking about wine, I had usually had enough by the evening and just wanted to sit down in my hotel room and read or watch a movie. However, the spirit of this group (which included Ron and Lynne Collings) banished my desire to relax, due to their real enthusiasm and belief in the wines they had crafted. They all brought along wines from their estates, so it was a great opportunity to see how these went with food. They

ABOVE *General view, Yarra Valley, Victoria*

worked well, justifying my belief that the Yarra Valley produces some of the most food-friendly wines in Australia. The following day I visited the wineries of a couple of my fellow dinner companions. The most impressive (in terms of buildings) of these was Panton Hills. It was built virtually single-handedly by the owner, Dr Teunis Kwak, a director of a mining company and a geologist. It is a handsome collection of stone buildings, which offer a large tasting area to enjoy the array of wines on offer.

ABOVE *The impressive stone buildings of Panton Hill Vineyard and Winery in Victoria were built virtually single-handedly by the owner.*

My only gripe was that the tasting samples offered were a touch too small but the wines showed well.

A short drive away is Watsons Creek, which has outstanding views of the valley from its commanding high outpost. The winery here was originally an old apple storage building - which is evident from the doors into the self-insulating, above-ground storage rooms. The doors must be close to 12 inches thick and they must have been a complete nightmare to hang! Inside, even on a hot day, the room maintains a cool temperature and this is where we conducted a tasting. The wines were fine, if not out of this world, but this will change as the owner gains more knowledge and experiments. There was a barrel of Cabernet Franc in the corner, which I asked to try and it was superb. It would have been ideal for blending with the Cabernet to round it off.

Perhaps the most impressive wines were those from Strathewen Hills, a winery quite literally in the middle of nowhere. After a 10km drive from the main road along narrow roads that twisted and turned we eventually arrived. The property is the family home of the owners and also offers rather luxurious self-contained rooms for those wishing to stay over. The winery is in an old barn-like building, which does not give any indication that the wines within are some of the best in the area. I was hoping that I would be the first to write about this winery, but Robert Parker has discovered it as well, and he wrote about it in the November 2002 issue of the *Wine Advocate*. He rates the Tribel Elder 2001 at 92-94 points. All of this wine goes to America - although this is not a lot, because only a barrel or two of it is made

Recommended Producers

Ainsworth Estate   The new boy on the block so to speak. Ainsworth opened in 2001 with a spectacular cellar door facility. They specialise in Pinot Noir, Shiraz and Chardonnay. The Reserve Shiraz has done particularly well, receiving numerous awards.

Arthurs Creek   This is a two-wine-only estate, with Chardonnay and Cabernet Sauvignon being grown. It has a chequered history going back to 1976, with the opening and closing of their own winery. The wines, however, have always remained popular locally. They are now made at Yering Station.

Coldstream Hills   Perhaps one of the most recognised names in the Valley. Originally owned and operated by the famed wine author James Halliday, it is now in the hands of Southcorp.

De Bortoli   Another large concern making very good wine in three quality tiers. Naturally the De Bortoli range is the finest of these.

Diamond Valley   One of the finest boutique wineries in Australia. Tremendous Chardonnay and Pinot Noir that continually receive high acclaim. If you can find it, the Close Planted Pinot Noir is exceptional.

Domaine Chandon   The Australian specialists in the production of sparkling wine in terms of quantity and quality together.

Dominique Portet   Wines made by the son of the winery and vineyard manager at Chateau Lafite Rothschild. Dominique is not a young gun, though, and was previously in charge of Taltarni for 20 years.

Elmswood Estate   A small ten-acre vineyard that is located at the southern end of the valley. The Cabernets are showing well coming from 20-year-old vines. Quite fruity wines.

Evelyn County Estate   A vineyard that was once a hay paddock, but this estate employs David Lance of Diamond Valley to make their wines. This should be a good indicator of the quality to expect.

Fergusson   Peter Fergusson has been at the helm here for 20 years now, after his purchase of the vineyard planted in 1968. There is a great restaurant as well, if you are in the area.

Five Oaks   Named after five oak trees that grace the property. They specialise in Cabernet-based wines, but also produce a good Riesling. Good depth of flavour is achieved through low yields and the vines being grown on red volcanic soils.

Gembrook Hill   Ian and June Marks found this site after an extensive four year search. Dwarfed by the Dandenong Ranges and Eucalypt trees, the vineyard is well protected from the harshest of the elements. The Sauvignon is a success for the area, displaying an almost minerally-flavour profile, as opposed to in-your-face gooseberry and passion fruit.

each year.

If you head south from here you will even-tually arrive at the Gembrook sub region of the valley, where Gembrook Hill is located. It is the most southerly and coolest vineyard in the Yarra, which generally means it is the last to be picked - worrying for a winemaker who fears bad weather coming in and ruining the crop. It does have one very distinct advantage though - high acids and very elegant, refined wines. The finest Sauvignon in the Yarra is grown here, along with Chardonnay and Pinot Noir that are more European in style than their counter-parts. As you would expect, the vines are non-irrigated and low-yielding, planted on old red volcanic soil. Ian Marks, the owner, is fairly confident that Gewürtztraminer, Pinot Blanc and Riesling would be well suited to this sub-region due to the climatic conditions, but to

ABOVE *Mechanical harvesting is only used in the younger vineyards.*

Kellybrook Originally a cider maker but now established (well over 20 years ago) as a win-ery as well. You can still buy their specialist ciders for those cold nights in.

Lillydale Vineyards Owned by the large family wine business McWilliams, but the quality still remains.

Long Gully One of the larger family wineries in the region. Great care is taken in the vine-yard and high investment has paid off well. They possess some of the most advanced equip-ment in the region and combine this with hand-pruning and some hand-picking. The Riesling is particularly successful and ages very well.

Lovegrove Vineyard Small production winery in the Diamond Valley region

Metier Wines Although the wines are contract-made, the quality of the fruit shines through and these are impressive wines.

Mount Mary Dr John Middleton makes some of the finest wine in Australia. The Quintet, which is a Bordeaux blend, is exceptionally good.

Oakridge Quite a large range from this growing winery business.

Ridgeback A good quality range all round, the Chardonnay particularly so.

St Huberts An historic estate with connections going back over a century. Now owned by Beringer Blass.

Seville Estate Now owned by Brokenwood in the Hunter Valley, this winery produces top class wines.

Strathewen Hills Tiny production operation that is set to become the Yarra Valleys' cult winery.

Tarrawarra Estate The wines from here are moulded in the Burgundian style and are aged for a minimum of two years before release. Daniel Beson, the founder's son, is now the winemaker here.

Yarra Ridge Another winery in the Beringer Blass portfolio. Since its inception in 1982 by Louis Bialkower, a Melbourne-based lawyer, the winery has received acclaim throughout the country.

Yarra Yarra Ian and Anne Maclean own this immaculately-kept winery. The wines are some of my favourites from the valley and very much made in French mould.

Yarra Yering Dr Bailey Carrodus presides over this internationally-recognised winery. The wines are exemplary and are given as much care and attention as is possible - even down to the barrels, which are specially made for him.

Yeringberg Small winery of the highest calibre - part of the old guard of the Valley.

Yering Station Recent investment has paid dividends in this spectacular winery. A lot of wine is now produced here, but the quality goes all the way to the top. The Reserve Bottling are of note.

his knowledge none have so far been planted. This is perhaps the difference between the other regions in Australia and the Yarra. They are all willing to experiment and have trial blocks of sometimes even the most obscure varieties, but the Yarra stands tall like an elder statesman, unwilling to move from tradition. This is a shame, as variety and experimentation are the corner stones of discovery.

To start a new winery you need money and plenty of it, especially if you wish to establish yourself in an area that is deemed to be one of the finest in Australia. This is a problem for most private individuals, except those who have been very successful in other careers - most notably from the professions - who use the investment to relieve them of part of their tax burden. For them, making money is not essential, but the capital value in the long term is. Although on the face of it this seems to apply to Roger Male, from Evelyn County Estate in the northern part of the valley, in the Shire of Nillumbik, in fact the opposite is true. Although he was formerly a managing partner for Coopers and Lybrand, the global accountancy firm, here it is the wine that counts. Along with his wife Robyn, Roger obviously has an astute head for business as the site selection not only incorporates a fairly unique soil - black volcanic with a high clay and nutrient content at high altitude - it is also, rather conveniently the most accessible vineyard from Melbourne's commercial business district. Robyn realises that wine is not the only method of making money from a vineyard - the ancillary businesses on site contribute to the bottom line, and there is also the attraction of having kangaroos, wallabies, echidnas and a

ABOVE *These days, mechanical help makes the job of wine-making much easier.*

plethora of birdlife all living and roaming around the site. There is a restaurant and art gallery that, combined with the winery, have won the commercial category in the Australian Institute of Architects Awards, Victorian Chapter. The restaurant utilises and promotes fresh Yarra Valley produce, such as cheese, buffalo and yabbies - for which the region is also renowned. Although Robyn has just completed a wine science degree at the Charles Sturt University (where impressively she was awarded the Dean's Award for Academic Excellence for no less than three consecutive years) the wine-making is undertaken by David and James Lance from Diamond Valley Estate, with Robyn giving a helping hand. Vineyard management is strong here, with integrated pest management practices put in place to alleviate the need for most chemical sprays. The

ABOVE *Wine maturing in large oak barrels in an underground cellar.*

ABOVE *The Yarra Valley has a mild climate, which is ideal as it extends the ripening period.*

grapes are hand-picked and the vines hand-pruned. Being newcomers they are not set in their ways and have planted some Tempranillo, the Spanish grape used for Rioja, as an experiment. I shall be very interested to taste this upon release. Another rather unusual wine they make is a Botrytis-affected Chardonnay - I have only come across one other in Australia (although I am sure there are more), which was at Katnook Estate in Coonawarra. The normal range of wines is excellent, with the Chardonnay probably the pick of the crop.

Of the boutique wineries, Long Gully is one of the largest, crushing over 250 tonnes with strong export markets in many countries. Oliver Knapp is the manager here and he holds strong beliefs that Australian boutique wineries are under threat from the big three. Unfortunately this is a commercial reality when achieving a strong share price is the main focus of the company. The large companies are able to subsidise their premium wineries through the immense profits made by their mass-produced brand labels. They are also able to lean on retailers and offer them cash bonuses, free glasses, aprons et al to sell their product lines exclusively. Naturally the small winery cannot compete with this level of marketing, which is made even harder by the fact a new operation opens up every 72 hours in Australia. Aside from their concerns about the above, Long Gully Estate aims to offer a large selection of wines that have sometimes been aged for a few years before release. They grow 13 varieties and the estate is one of only two in Australia that produces an Ice Wine. This is a process where the grapes are left on the vines until well into winter and allowed to freeze. The grapes are then picked and pressed, leav-ing the sweet water particles in the juice. This results in an intensely sweet wine that is a rarity and something to be savoured with a decadent pudding. I have had a eight-year-old Riesling from this estate, which was just starting to develop the paraffin nose so typical of this variety when mature. Not to everyone's taste initially, it soon grows on you and you discover why this grape is often thought of as the most noble of all the white grapes. Long Gully also produces a Shiraz, which is something of a novelty in this corner of Australia. To complement the cool climate fruit they blend it with grapes from Heathcote, to add some body and substance to the finished wine.

Perhaps one of the most distinguished wineries is that of Dominique Portet, whose pedigree goes back nine generations in a family of winemakers. Dominique is the son of André Portet, the vineyard and winery manager at Chateau Lafite Rothschild, one of the most celebrated vineyards in the world. The education that this must have provided is immeasurable, and he combines it with a qualification from Montpellier University of Oenology. Having spent some time in the Napa Valley in California, he took up a position at Taltarni Vineyards in the Pyrenees region. He was the Managing Director there and became firmly established in Australian wine-making circles. It was not until 2000 that he decided on the Yarra Valley as the place to commence his own project, the Dominique Portet label. He felt that this was the region in Australia that was most like his beloved Bordeaux. Although he does not currently own any vineyards, he leases an area within Yering Station. The wines, as you would expect, are defined and focused with a great elegance about them.

Heathcote

Could Heathcote, a few kilometres south of Bendigo to the west and the Goulburn Valley to the east, become regarded as one of the finest wine regions in Australia for Shiraz? Yes and no. Yes for the independent wineries, but maybe not for the big players, who have purchased colossal amounts of land and created "instant vineyards" (to quote Ron Laughton). This has subsequently pushed the land prices up beyond the reach of most private individuals (from A$60 per acre ten years ago to A$6000 today) and virtually no premium land suitable for viticulture is left. A substantial amount of the grapes grown here are selected for everyday commercial wines. Do not let this make you think less highly of the region - it has the potential (and succeeds) to make some of Australia's finest Shiraz wines due to the ideal terroir, of which the most important element is the ancient Cambrian soils. These stretch, sometimes in isolated patches, out some 40 kms in a southerly direction from the centre of the village along the Great Dividing Range. This special soil, unique to Victoria and derived from Cambrian rock 500 million years ago, can be over three metres deep yet only a few hundred metres wide at its maximum and is a friable red-brown ferruginous gravely loam, on well-drained slopes.

The region was first settled in 1838 by farmers who needed to graze their cattle and sheep. This was soon superseded by the discovery of gold at McIvor Creek in 1852. Some 10,000 people descended upon the region to prospect for this most precious of metals. The first vineyards were planted in the mid 1850s, but had a relatively short life due to the advent of Phylloxera in the area during the 1890s. The first commercial plantings came in the 1970s with the Erindale Vineyard, followed by Red Hill (now known as Red Edge) and then Mt Ida, Heathcote Winery and Jasper Hill.

There are only around 25 wineries located in the Heathcote district, which surrounds a sleepy little village where the restaurants seem to open as and when they feel like it.

Perhaps being this way is what attracted Ron Laughton of Jasper Hill to settle here 25 ago, down a long and dusty dirt road that has been the site of many accidents over the years due to careless driving and unexpected large trees. Over lunch in a bizarre restaurant in the

RIGHT *On its first release in 1987, this Shiraz from Hanging Rock won numerous gold medals and was compared with Penfolds' Grange.*

BELOW *Hanging Rock Winery, near the location for the famous Australian film,* Picnic at Hanging Rock.

centre of Heathcote, which was full of pensioners being played old music by an elderly person on an archaic organ (all the smart restaurants were closed), Ron explained that, although he comes from a line of farmers (and this is farming country) the local community looked upon him with deep suspicion when he purchased his property and set to work planting vines. It took some years to be accepted and even then this was partially due to his farming background, which meant that he could talk agriculture as well as the next man. He persevered and today is acknowledged as one of the finest winemakers in Australia which has resulted in a partnership with M. Chapoutier, the famous Rhone doyen. Ron has planted a new vineyard with clones from his Georgia's Paddock vineyard, whilst adjacently Chapoutier has planted clones from his Hermitage vineyard, which have gone through rigorous quarantine examinations. Although it will be a few years before a wine is released, I for one am awaiting it with great eagerness.

I have no hesitation in saying here that the Jasper Hill Georgia's Paddock Shiraz is my favourite red wine in Australia. Why? Because it is hand-crafted with uttermost care from dry-grown, organic vineyards that are planted in the Cambrian soil. The vines are low-yielding, own-rooted and only picked when physiologically ripe. They only see 20% new oak (predominantly American) each vintage, which allows the wine to develop more naturally and preserves natural flavour and balance. Both Georgia's and Emily's Paddock - the other Shiraz from Jasper Hill, which is blended with 5% Cabernet Franc - are named after their daughters, whose names grace the respective vineyards. Both daughters now work in the business and Georgia is making a wine

under her own name. Emily's Paddock differs in that it is located 1km away and has shallower soils and vines that yield around five tonnes per acre, as opposed to 7.5 in Georgia's. It is also aged in French oak, with smaller pores, to give it a more delicate and feminine flavour. Both are world-class and a Nebbiolo planting, which should start producing fruit soon, is an exciting proposition.

In 1983 John and Ann Ellis established the Hanging Rock winery which overlooks Hanging Rock, the location for the famous film. John had previously worked for Tyrrell's as a foundation winemaker and married Ann (a Tyrrell) some years earlier. Between them they decided to set out and create Australia's finest sparkling wine. To accomplish this goal they would need a location that was cool and able to provide Chardonnay and Pinot Noir grapes of sufficient acidity. The mission was to create a wine as close to the style of that of the

ABOVE *Wine tasting at Hanging Rock Winery. Apart from Shiraz, their aim is to create Australia's finest sparkling wine.*

Recommended Producers

Barnadown Run   As one would expect, Shiraz and Cabernet dominate here along with a normal and reserve Chardonnay. Andrew Mills, the owner and winemaker is similar to David Anderson of Wild Duck Creek in that he has a penchant for building things himself and indeed created this winery.

Heathcote Winery   A large range of wines from this comparatively small winery that has resurrected itself in the past few years. The top Mail Coach Shiraz is outstanding and the varietal bottlings of Viognier can be exceptional as well

Huntleigh Vineyards   A long established micro-winery that continues to make quality wines.

Jasper Hill   The most highly regarded winery of the region. Superb Shiraz which is long-lived and grown using organic methods. A jewel in the crown of Australian wineries.

McIvor Creek   The drive up to McIvor Creek is worth it on its own. You ascend the hill with a plethora of wildlife surrounding you and panoramic views of the rolling countryside. The Shiraz is full of plums and spice with a hint of damsons. A large and very good range of table condiments and sauces are also made here and available to buy.

Mount Ida   Now owned by Beringer Blass and one of the top names in their portfolio.

Paul Osicka   This winery will celebrate 50 years in operation in 2005. It is not surprising then, that it has learnt how to make the most of the surrounding soils to create some fine wines.

Red Edge   Very small production Shiraz and Cabernet of the highest quality possible. Fast becoming a benchmark wine for the region.

Wild Duck Creek   David Anderson's wines are crafted to an individual style that you will either love or hate. Personally I am in the former category and look forward to the winter months when I can open a bottle of 17% alc Shiraz and warm myself up.

Champagne houses Bollinger and Krug as possible. The time it takes to age quality sparkling wine doesn't help with the cash flow, however, and so they also made a Sauvignon Blanc called Jim Jim. With its traditional cool climate characteristics of gooseberry, it was a success straight away. The portfolio was missing one important component though - a serious red. John had been making Shiraz for Mt Ida so this seemed the ideal grape to cultivate. The first release was the 1987, which resulted in numerous gold medals with the wine even

ABOVE *Bottled wines in storage. Only the better wines are suitable for long-term storage, others are made for immediate drinking.*

being compared to Grange by the wine Press.

Perhaps the funniest and yet most skilled winemaker in the country is David Anderson of Wild Duck Creek. When I arrived David was just finishing off a runway strip for a new aeroplane he was off to buy that afternoon in NSW - without having seen it! He needs the plane to fly to another vineyard he owns in NSW, as it cuts the journey time down to one and a half hours instead of a four-hour drive. Wild Duck Creek is perhaps most widely known for its super-rich, alcoholic monster of a Shiraz called Duck Muck, to which Robert Parker awarded 99 points (where did he drop 1 point???) for the 1997 vintage. David does not generally socialise with other winemakers (except on wine tours around the world, when he gives lectures after formal dinners and tastings) as he does not wish to be influenced by them but to create wines of a highly individual nature. He believes in drip irrigation to a moderate extent, and argues that irrigation is not the cause of loss of flavour but that over-cropping, and pruning with excessive bud numbers, followed by catch-up watering, is. In other words, if irrigation is used sensibly and the vines cropped well, you still can produce outstanding fruit. Another factor which separates David from the main pack is that his vineyards are not on Cambrian soil but

Alluvial loams, Divonian mudstones, shales and sedimentary clays with quartz, which have a far lower ph rating than the Cambrian soils, which can be as high as 6. David believes that this only assists growth, and that the vines are more vigorous as a result. It also, he argues, does not make a difference to the flavour of the wine - except when over-cropped, when there is a definite weakening of the tannic structure. I have to say that I feel the Cambrian soils give a robust flavour to the wines and a mineral and earthy flavour profile. Duck Muck is exactly what it sets out to achieve - a hugely alcoholic wine at around 17%, but with enough fruit to balance it out. It is unlikely that you will be able to find any though, as only a couple of barrels a year are made from the vineyard adjoining the property. However, it will be comparatively easily accessible if a Reserve Duck Muck is made as planned! In the meantime, search out the straight Springflat Shiraz, or one of the Cabernet bottlings, which you should be able to get from specialist retailers around release.

Red Edge is perhaps the region's best-kept secret. From a vineyard originally planted in the 1970s, Peter Dredge is making formidable Cabernet Sauvignon and Shiraz wines in tiny quantities of around 500 cases in total. Peter's vineyard manages to yield a measly one tonne per acre of fruit, which equates to approximately 75 cases. Great care is taken not to handle the wine too much so that the fruit can show through and develop its natural flavours and nuances unhindered. For this to be possible, Peter uses wild yeasts with gravity pumping and no fining or filtration of the wine. The fruit dominates these wines and the oak is a mere seasoning component in the overall make up of them.

In 2002, Heathcote was granted a legal GI (geographical indicator) from around Corop in the North to Tooborak in the South. This pleased the major players, who have invested heavily in the region over the past few years. In fact in 1998 there were 1000 acres planted, compared with 3000 in 2002. Although some of the initial plantings from the majors are bearing quality fruit (rumour has it that Heathcote fruit may go into Hardy's Eileen Hardy bottling), a lot are at a very infant age and are being subjected to serious amounts of irrigation. At the time of visiting in late May, the nursery vineyards were still showing bright green leaves while leaves on the established, non-irrigated vines had turned brown and were dropping off. The worrying point is that the marketing departments will perhaps start to push these wines when they are still too young, whilst the winemakers are still learning about the area and the fruit that is produced. I hope that the region is treated with the respect it deserves, and that the fruit is primarily used for premium bottlings.

ABOVE *Old hand-dug cellars at Tahbilk, which is a living, working museum. The tasting room is directly above here.*

Goulburn Valley & Macedon

The Goulburn Valley is home to the officially-documented oldest Shiraz vines still in existence in Australia, which were planted in 1860. They belong to Alister Purbrick of Chateau Tahbilk, one of the most respected winemakers and vineyards in the country. As one would expect, Tahbilk (the Chateau has now been dropped) is steeped in history, so much so that Alister has written a book about it. The winery and surrounding buildings put paid to the notion of New World Wine - a phrase that I believe was first penned by the esteemed English author Hugh Johnson. The property contains a magnificent museum of wine-making on the site, from 1860 onward - which is prior to the America Civil War and at a time when Lincoln had not yet been made president. Here you will find original maps, bottles and artefacts that have been carefully stored over the decades for our benefit today. Perhaps this is why, along with the sheer quality of the wines, that Tahbilk receives a phenomenal 80,000 visitors each year to the cellar door, which is located in the original building. The Valley itself is located in the picturesque Nagambie Lakes area, which is an area of outstanding natural beauty. Now it is classified as a unique sub-region of Goulburn, due to its water mass - it is one of only six wine regions in the world where the meso-climate is influenced by a body of inland water. It also has a fairly unique soil type - a red sandy loam with a high ferric-oxide content.

Tahbilk is fortunate to have some 3000 acres of the richest river flats in the area, with 11kms of river frontage. The Purbrick's association with the vineyard can be traced back to 1875, when James Escott Purbrick was

ABOVE *Michelton Wines, Goulburn Valley*

employed to excavate and construct a new cellar. The cellar is still in full use today and is quite magnificent in its splendour. Old vats and cubby holes filled with old, unlabelled wines stored as museum pieces dominate the various tunnels and rooms, which you can actually see from a viewing platform in the museum. Today however, further work has been carried out and the tunnel opened up to the winery to aid fork lift truck access to these perfect storage conditions. The winery utilises up-to-date technology with traditional wine-making techniques to make its array of wines. The whites are the best of the region and include Australia's finest example of Marsanne, which can be cellared with confidence for at least ten years to allow it to really develop its complexities. The vines from which it is made are believed to be the oldest in the world, originally being planted in 1927 from cuttings taken from a Yarra Valley vineyard planted in the 1860s. As expected with such old Shiraz vines, a wine is hand-crafted from them. 1860 Vines Shiraz is a living piece of history, being made from ungrafted, pre-Phylloxera vines that have been hand-picked and fermented in century-old open oak vats. If unable to find this rare treasure, then try to locate the reserve range of wines, which is made from the best casks of the vintage.

Further enhancing the Rhone's influence

ABOVE *Tahbilk, in the Goulburn Valley, has the oldest Shiraz vines still in existence in Australia. They are officially documented as having been planted in 1860.*

on the area, Colin Preece was the founding winemaker at Mitchelton for the first crush in 1973, from vineyards planted in 1969. Preece only completed one vintage here before retirement, and Don Lewis took over in 1974. The site had taken Preece two years to locate on behalf of Ross Shelmerdine, a Melbourne entrepreneur, who had asked him to find the best place in South East Australia for grape growing. The Estate quickly became established, winning its first medal in 1978 for a Riesling, and going on to win both the Jimmy Watson Trophy in 1991 and the title Vineyard of the Year.

Today the winery produces a multitude of wines that use traditional Rhone varietals, along with Don Lewis's famed Riesling and the commercial necessities of Chardonnay, Cabernet and Merlot. Wine-making techniques have evolved over the years, due to Don's 27 years of experience with the fruit from this Estate. They have re-trellised 50% of the vines into an open canopy arrangement, and restricted water to many blocks to encourage the vines to root deeper in search of water and extra mineral content.

The Longleat vineyard was established in 1975 by Peter Schultz (who incidentally arrived in the Barossa during 1942) with the planting of vines on the bank of the Goulburn River. Peter, although passionate about wine was not a vigneron, and enlisted the help of

Recommended Producers

Dalfarras   A winery to watch. This is another property that Alister Purbrick owns but one where he has the freedom to express himself by making wines in a different style to that of Tahbilk. So far they have proved a great success.

David Traegar   You enter David Traegar's cellar via steps leading down from the High Street in Nagambie. David used to be a winemaker at Mitchelton, which shows in the quality of his wines.

Kirwan's Bridge Wines   Unfortunately closed at the time of visiting this Estate has panoramic views of the lakes and is located, as its name would suggest, by Kirwans Bridge, a wooded structure that time has forgotten.

Longleat   Good wines, especially the Shiraz.

Mitchelton   A moderately large estate that is a Rhone specialist. An excellent Riesling is also made.

Monichino Wines   A pudding-wine specialist but also makes the usual variety of dry table wines to a good standard.

Tahbilk   Benchmark wines from the area across the board.

ABOVE *The cellars of Tahbilk date back to 1875, and they are still in full use today - although they have recently been opened up to the winery to allow fork lift truck access.*

Alister Purbrick from Tahbilk. Peter then took over fully and produced a Shiraz, Cabernet and Riesling each year from estate-grown fruit. The business was sold to a group of friends in 1998, who plan to enlarge the area under vine from 22 acres to 31.

Straws Lane, located on the northern slopes of Mt Macedon, may claim to be one of the highest vineyards in the state, at 850 metres. It was originally planted in 1987 with an interesting combination of grape varieties - Pinot Noir and Gewürztraminer. These were sensibly left to mature, before being harvested for the inaugural vintage in 1995. Three wines were made, a light Pinot, a sparkling and of course the Gewürztraminer. Commitment to producing fine wines sometimes means that the Pinot is not released, as the grapes are not of a high enough quality. In these years, I suspect that the juices are used as the base for their sparkling wine, for which they would be perfect. The soils here are rich and volcanic and reach depths of up to five metres.

Bendigo

Bendigo, in contrast to Heathcote, is a sprawling metropolis with wonderful architecture and shops to suit every need. Although not as an important grape growing region as Heathcote, it is nevertheless significant with approximately the same amount of wineries and some seriously good wine being made here. The grape of the area is Shiraz, which is no surprise given that the region has a mean January temperature of 21-22.9°C - the same as the Barossa, Clare and Goulburn Valleys. One of the nicest aspects of the region is the friendliness of the wineries, which are almost all family-owned with no big brand mentality. Here you are likely to meet the winemaker with his sleeves rolled up working hard on the current vintage.

Like Heathcote, the soils are old, deep and

Recommended Producers

Balgownie Estate Now complete with a homestead located alongside the vineyards, this winery continues to make outstanding wine at a modest price.

Blackjack Vineyards Shiraz specialists.

Blanche Barkly Named after a the world's largest gold nugget at the time, found in 1857 underneath what is now the vineyard. The property was owned by Sir Henry Barkly, then governor of Victoria, and his daughter was called Blanche. The wines are moderately low in alcohol and made by maceration-style fermentation with the intention that they will age gracefully for 20 years.

Chateau Dore An historic winery that dates back to the mid 1860s. Unfortunately they have not expanded the business and production remains at a modest level.

Munari Wines Adrian Munari has made an impact over the past ten years with his wines that are produced with his wife Deborah. Multi medal award winners.

ABOVE *Shiraz is the grape of Bendigo region, as it has the same temperature range as Barossa, Clare and Goulburn, which suits this variety.*

mineralised, especially with iron, although not of Cambrian origin. Blanche Barkly Wines report that the soil on their Kingower vineyard extends to a depth of some 20 feet, which should mean that in the relatively hot summers the region experiences, the roots will have to dig deep to find water and nutrients, adding to the complexity of the wines (assuming they are dry-grown).

Like Heathcote, this was originally gold mining country although the region was planted extensively with vineyards. Unfortunately most were scrubbed up in the late 1800s due to the arrival of Phylloxera. The government of the day, presumably in a state of panic, decided that all vineyards should be uprooted and the soil treated to prevent the pest from reaching the state's most prized region, Rutherglen. Unfortunately this did not work and the pest reached Rutherglen anyway.

It was not until almost 1970 that another vine was planted commercially here. Stuart Anderson, a pharmacist, who had presumably seen the vineyards being planted by Doctors in the Yarra Valley just outside of Melbourne, decided to embark on Balgownie Estate, a winery that was to make wines which are now considered a benchmark for the region. My visit coincided with their staffs' 2002 Harvest Supper. I was staying in the luxurious homestead located next to the winery, with sweeping views across the vineyards. Arriving at around 7.00pm after a drive down from Rutherglen, I was welcomed with a sumptuous BBQ and copious amounts of fine wine. Having come from Rutherglen it was nice to enjoy a serious glass of red wine, from around ten open on the table, which included a European favourite - Tignanello. One of the highlights of the evening for me was the chance to taste a 1989 Viognier from the Estate that, although past its prime, was still of fruit and had developed a complex array of secondary flavours. The winery is currently expanding, with the old barrel store now a sophisticated cellar door offering refreshments and one of the finest cheese platters in Australia.

Shortly after Balgownie Estate was established, Water Wheel and Chateau Leamon followed suit and planted their own vineyards. In Chateau Leamon's case, a small farm was purchased, which was then transformed. They released their first wine to rapturous applause in 1977 - just three years after the acquisition of the property. The wine was a Cabernet Sauvignon and it won the Small Wine Makers award at the national wine show in Canberra. Today the winery is run by Ian Leamon, after stints working for Bests, Veuve Cliquot and Rosemount, amongst others.

Rutherglen

This, out of all of Australia's wine producing areas, is perhaps the most special. It creates a totally unique style of wine, which is not emulated successfully anywhere else in the world. This is the land of the "sticky". Even the most basic of examples are an absolute pleasure to drink and the wines at the top end are often described as liquid gold.

Rutherglen is situated at the northern end of Victoria, not too distant from the King Valley, Beechworth and the Goulburn Valley. The town itself, as with most country places in Australia, is very laid back with no real sense of urgency. A ten minute walk would enable you to cover the town centre well, without stopping off at any of the attractions. It is the outskirts, however, that we are most interested in - the outlying vineyards that produce grapes like no others anywhere. Whilst both red and white varieties are planted, it is the Muscat and Tokay that are the essence and backbone of this district. I am not going to go into detail about the different wineries' offerings of these two grapes, as the differences are pretty minimal for each variety. They mostly have the same flavour profiles and textures and are all excellent. I can think of no bad fortified Muscat or Tokay in the region.

Rutherglen was first planted in the early 1850s. coinciding with the gold rush that was sweeping across this part of Australia at the time. One presumes, that - as in other regions

ABOVE *If you do not fancy the wines on offer, you can always have a go at making your own...*

- the workers were paid partly in wine at the end of the week, hence the rapid rise of the region over a decade to become one of the state's leading viticultural areas. Unfortunately the region became a victim of its own success - towards the end of the century, the state government, perhaps thinking they would gain more revenue via taxation, decided to pay every grower £2 for each acre of vines they planted. As you can imagine, this had an immediate effect and soon 1000s of acres were planted by people not qualified to do so. Farmers who previously grew crops converted their land to vines, with very little or no success. This naturally resulted in a lot of very poor wine being made and sold on the open

ABOVE *Vineyards give a very distinctive pattern to the landscape, which can look quite abstract in the right lighting conditions.*

ABOVE *This mechanical harvester operates by shaking the vines, which then drop the ripe bunches onto a conveyor belt. This in turn feeds them into a truck, which takes them to the winery.*

market. Market forces being what they are, the public rejected these wines and the region's reputation was tarnished. Unfortunately this was not the end of Rutherglen's troubles - in the late 1890s Phylloxera, an aphid that feeds of the vine's roots, eventually killing them, was discovered. Rutherglen was not the only region to be affected and serious research was carried out to find a cure. One never materialised (and it still hasn't), but the idea of replanting with resilient rootstocks from California was suggested. This meant uprooting all the vines - a considerable amount of work, but it was the only viable solution to this disaster. Fortunately, a number of the vineyards that were founded in the mid-eighteen hundreds survived this period of gloom and are still flourishing today. Some of the vines replanted in the 1890s are still there.

The climate here is distinctly Continental, being so far inland and protected by the Australian Alps that surround the region. Grape growing is not the easiest of pastimes here though - budburst tends to be rather late and frosts can be a real danger. There are a mixture of soil types, most of which provide excellent drainage. One of the reasons for Rutherglen's dominance with fortified wines lies in the fact that they have large holdings of very old wines in barrel, which they use and then top up. This make the average age of all the stickies quite high. The grapes are picked very late when virtually raisins. They are then crushed, squeezing out what little juice they contain, and fermented.

One of the first wineries to be established, along with Chambers, Morris and All Saints, was Campbells. John Campbell first arrived in Australia in 1857, having come from Scotland on the *Merchant Prince* with so many others who would go on to develop vineyards. He followed the gold rush, which led him to Rutherglen where he bought 79 acres in 1868, adjoining Bobbie Burns' land. Production went well and awards were won, but in 1898 the Phylloxera epidemic set in, which led to less and less wine being made. The vineyard fell into a state of disrepair until John's death in 1909. It was then that a period of rejuvenation began, headed by his son David and daughter-in-law, Isabella. It was a mammoth task, as it would take them 20 years to finish replanting 45 acres. Oh for the technology of today! It was only two years after completing this that the family incurred another set back - David lost his eyesight and Allen, his 15-year-old son, was brought in to help. His father had taught him well and instilled a strong sense of belief in what he was doing. This proved vital when David died two years later in 1933, as Allen was left with a winery heavily in debt with almost 19,000 bottles of wine in stock at a time when the country was in depression. However, he persevered and slightly diversified the business, which resulted in it being saved. Such was his success that an expansion programme was initiated in 1943, with land being purchased that contained ten acres of vines. This was complemented five years later by an additional 24 acres, which was adjacent to the Bobbie Burns vineyard. Once again this proved to have been the right decision to take, and in 1960 a further 200 acres were acquired, which could be irrigated. Two years later Colin and Malcolm Campbell returned to Rutherglen after completing college diplomas.

They initiated the production of bottled wine with labels, which at that stage was still uncommon, and implemented a method to cool the grape must during vinification, which led to white wines of far greater elegance than had previously been possible. This led to the winery being awarded many medals at shows over the following years, with the introduction of new varieties like Trebbiano being particularly successful. They were keen to embrace new ideas and in 1981 decided to purchase a mechanical harvester to relieve some of the hard labour. The machines could also work 24 hours a day. Back then they were very crude and basic - almost everything went into the wine. Today they have changed considerably. They operate by shaking the vines, which then drop the ripe bunches onto a conveyor belt, which in turn feeds them into a truck that takes them to the winery.

During 1999 the Campbells took a study trip to the US and Israel to look at drip-irrigation methods, as opposed to spraying. They obviously found it to be a better method, as it was implemented on their return. Today, Malcolm and Colin have been together for over 30 years at the winery and have continued to win numerous awards around the globe. Their Bobbie Burns Shiraz is regarded as the finest red wine of the region.

I was fortunate to stay with the Chambers, of Chambers Rosewood winery, for two nights when I visited the region. Chambers is perhaps the most successful winery in Rutherglen. Robert Parker rates their "rare" wines at 100 points and James Halliday states that they are

ABOVE *Good quality casks are re-used, adding their own notes to the final wine.*

"on a level of their own - somewhere higher than 5 stars". This is high praise indeed - and it is even rarer that these two wine critics agree!

Chambers was established in the 1850s by a man named Anthony Ruche, but came into the Chambers family during 1891. Bill Chambers and his wife Wendy now run the business - along with their son Stephen, who is largely responsible for the wine-making. Coming from abroad and having read about these winemakers in publications like Robert Parkers' *Wine Advocate*, and knowing that their wines have scored 100 points, you imagine them living a life of decadence and luxury, with the world beating on their door. The latter part is certainly correct, but these Aussies are great - it does not go to their heads and they mostly live like you or me in comfortable surroundings but without all the trappings of wealth. It drives home the point that essentially they are farmers, albeit highly-skilled and specialised ones. To stay with the Chambers was unbelievable and something I shall never forget. They were so friendly and accommodating - and just so happen to make the best wines of their type in the world.

The winery is like a working museum, with ancient old wooden vats that contain countless litres of ageing Muscat and Tokay. The historical aspect of the region, and of Chambers itself, is emphasised even more when a horse and cart arrives with eager wine lovers looking forward to their first taste of the most majestic of wines. Inside they are met with an amazing selection, from the dry whites, reds and fortifieds, to the various Ports and Sherries that are only for the domestic market. To try and describe the Rare Muscat and Tokay is an impossible task - they are simply perfect. Although it is nigh on impossible to find the Rare wines, the Special and Classic wines are a

ABOVE *A young vineyard may yield an average of ten tonnes of fruit per acre.*

Recommended Producers

All Saints Estate   One of the prettiest cellar doors in the country, being housed in an old red brick fortress. The whole range is good, including the table wines. An excellent restaurant is also located here.

Andersons   Howard Anderson owns and operates the Anderson winery, which focuses on table and sparkling wines as opposed to the stickies - which he believes never achieve the money they are worth.

Auldstone   I wrote to Michael Reid, the owner of Auldstone with some questions relating directly to this winery - the reply I received was as follows:- "I find all your questions too daunting. I'm the winemaker, you're the journalist. You do your job and I'll do mine. Either that or you come and do my job whilst I do your research for you". I always thought that speaking to the owner was research?

Bullers Calliope   Amongst the best for fortified wines.

Campbells   As well as excellent fortifieds, the red table wines are also some of the finest of the region. The Bobbie Burns Shiraz is full and flavoursome and Barkly Durif a good alternative to Shiraz and Cabernet.

Chambers Rosewood   Simply the finest sweet wines in the world. The base wine for the Rare Tokay comes from the 1890 vintage.

Cofield   There is a whole mixture of varietals grown here, from Cabernet Franc to Gamay to Chenin Blanc. On the whole they do a good job on wines for everyday consumption.

Morris   Having tasted eight-year-old Shiraz and Cabernet whilst visiting, I can say with confidence that you can comfortably cellar the top reds from this region for ten years plus. The fortified whites are exceptional.

Pfeiffer   The table wines are perhaps of most interest here (and a lovely cellar door). The white wines can age well, as was proved by a 13-year-old Chardonnay sampled, along with an eclectic range of reds, including Merlot, Pinot Noir and Gamay.

St Leonards   In the same stable as All Saints, although the wines here tend to be a bit on the lighter side.

Stanton & Killeen   Another top producer of fortified Muscat and Tokay. Also produce a good range of table wines, which are smooth and some of the finest in the region.

Warrabilla   A lovely Marsanne and a good range of reds including a gripping Durif.

little more obtainable and show the brilliance that can be achieved with the two grapes. This winery must count as being the finest maker of sweet wines in the world, along with Chateau d'Yquem in Sauternes. Bill and Stephen also make numerous dry wines, including a Cinsault, and have a vast array on offer at the cellar door.

Another winery that receives lavish praise from the Press is R.L. Buller & Son, for its wines from their Calliope vineyard. Although they also source fruit from other regions in Victoria, it is from this vineyard in Rutherglen that the finest wines hail. The vineyard was first planted in the 1920s by the present owner's grandfather, Reginald, and is non-irrigated so only musters up an average of one tonne per acre. This is minuscule, but common amongst a number of top wineries throughout the country. Not only does it mean a lot of hard work for not a lot of fruit, but it has strong economic consequences as well. If you take, for example, a relatively

young vineyard that is primarily for the production of a nice everyday table wine, it may yield ten tonnes to the acre. Therefore the winemaker in this vineyard is getting ten times the fruit from the same size vineyard, yet the winemaker getting only one tonne can very rarely sell his wine for ten times the price. This is unfair on the winery but great for us, and is why an expensive bottle can be a bargain. Other costs are also noticeably higher for the Bullers and those like them. Hand-picking is common and there are no real economies of scale. The Winemaker Federation of Australia reports that from a A\$20 bottle of wine, the winery will make a net profit of just 2% whilst the tax man takes 25%. It is therefore imperative to operate a cellar door, as these can bring back an extra 41% of the selling price to the winery, which is the saving on retailers' and distributors' margin. It may sound a lot, but then the cellar door has to be paid for and staffed, not to mention the cost of providing the samples.

Mornington Peninsula

The Mornington Peninsula is one of the most picturesque wine regions in the world. It is bordered by the sea on three sides and contains some of the finest golf courses to be found. It is a relatively new region, having only been established since 1975, but it is increasingly growing in importance. As the area develops and becomes known internationally, I am certain that it will be held in the same regard as other regions in the state.

Miceli, owned by Anthony Miceli, is located in the Main Ridge area of the Mornington Peninsular, which is at the southern end, making it higher and cooler. This means that their harvest dates are some 4-5 weeks later than their northern counterparts. The soils here are mainly kraznozem, which is a red, deep and well-drained medium clay, and a volcanic-derived mildly acidic soil. Due to their height of 250 metres they do experience some problems with wind, and regularly have broken canes. To avoid this, trellis structures have been modified and windbreaks of natural species have been planted. Anthony has three blocks each measuring around two and a half acres, which he has planted with each variety of Pinot Noir, Chardonnay and Pinot Grigio to develop complexity in the wines. There are also multiple clones for each variety, to extend this even further. The making of the Pinot Noir is very complex and involves a portion receiving prolonged maceration prior to fermentation for one week, followed by a wild yeast ferment, a portion of which is fermented at a relatively cool 26ºC and pressed just at dryness. Another portion is fermented at a higher temperature of 32ºC, and part of this is drained for barrel-ferment, with another portion remaining on lees for an additional two weeks post-ferment in contact with the skins. I am pleased that he knows what he is doing.

Paringa Estate is one of, if not the, finest winery in the Mornington Peninsula. It was established by former teacher Lindsay McCall in 1984, who decided to take a gamble and plant the vineyard in the hope that one day it would become commercially viable. If success and recognition are anything to go by, he has achieved this aim easily. The son of a dairy farmer, Lindsay was experienced in working on the land and this helped him considerably, as he possessed some of the basic skills needed. The area under vine has now grown to ten acres, with a further 25 under lease nearby. Like Cullens in Margaret River, Paringa installed a Lyre Trellis System around 1990, to improve fruit quality.

Stumpy Gully Vineyard was established in 1989 by the Zantvoort family, in the Moorooduc region of the Peninsula. They are notable due to the many grape varieties grown, which makes a break from the norm. The first vines were planted in 1989, partly on historic dairy land unused for half a century, and partly on virgin bush soil. These unspoiled Moorooduc soils and the cool climate of the

ABOVE *Turramurra Estate has been established for 15 years, and its first vintage, in 1996, sold out on release. Since then it has gone from strength to strength.*

ABOVE *A selection of wines from Stumpy Gully Vineyard, which grows a wide variety of grapes. The red varieties have only been available since 2001.*

Mornington Peninsula, along with the unique meso-climate between two bays, contribute to the complexity of the wine. The modern viticultural techniques practiced by Frank and Michael Zantvoort, and the expertise of three winemakers (including Victoria's only mother/daughter team) also add to the unique quality of the produce from this vineyard. Further plantings during the 1990s have led to a total of 27 acres under vine, and the establishment of ten varieties under the Stumpy Gully label. The more unusual Pinot Grigio and Marsanne are amongst the lesser known varieties grown here, along with Sangiovese. A further 50 acres of red varieties, from a new site on Stumpy Gully Road, came on line from 2001. Perhaps the finest wine they make here is the Sauvignon Blanc, which seems to have excelled in this warm pocket of the Peninsula. They produce wines in the style of New Zealand, with passion fruit being a common descriptor.

Tuck's Ridge is owned by Peter Hollick, a distant relative of the Hollicks in Coonawarra. To date, the greatest achievement this vineyard has made is winning the Jimmy Watson Trophy in 1995 with their 1994 Pinot Noir. This is not altogether surprising, as they specialise in the variety and have seven clones of it. They have recently released their first single vineyard bottling. Peter Kittle joined the team in 2001 as senior winemaker, having worked at Leeuwin Estate and Stoniers, which gives him a great pedigree to continue Tucks Ridge's rise in fame and critical acclaim. If in the area at the right time, it is an ideal place to visit if you wish to enhance your knowledge of winemaking as they run a grape stomping day called Pinot Rustica, on which you can pick grapes and help in making the Pinot. They

have, along with other vineyards in the region, been going through an experimental period to discover what grows best and where. So far, they have found that the Semillon and Cabernet were not particularly successful, so these have been grubbed up from vineyards equal in area to those they have in production today. Simon Napthine, the general manager, points out that a number of the vineyards planted today will have disappeared in ten years time, as they are simply planted in the wrong spots. It is unlikely that these areas will be used for agriculture again, as the city folk from Melbourne are moving into this idyllic spot, with its magnificent views, golf courses and restaurants.

There are two white grape varieties grown here in small quantities that, as they gain in stature and reputation, may become the hallmarks of the region. These are Pinot Gris and Albarino, the Spanish variety. However, site selection will be of paramount importance.

ABOVE *Chardonnay is an early ripening variety.*

At the Turramurra Estate, Paula Leslie describes herself and her husband David as "has beens" - not due to the wine they make, but because of the time of life that they entered the wine business. They had originally been micro-propagating orchards and needed more land. They eventually ended up with far more than they required, so they decided to start a vineyard. David went back to university to study oenology for six years on a part-time basis whilst Paula, in her own words "worked her butt off" to set up the vineyard. They built a winery in 1995, and their 1996 vintage sold out on release.

Phil Kerny is in charge at Willow Creek and wines are made with terroir in mind, from the vineyard planted in 1989. To this end, a programme of repositioning is currently taking place to put all the vines on a Vertical Shoot Positioning system, with plans to crop at below two tonnes per acre.

Main Ridge Estate was the first to be established on the Peninsula in 1975 and they only use grapes from their own vineyards, which provides them with just 1000 cases per year. Small production indeed, but these wines are of the highest quality. Nat White, the owner, has no doubt proved to be an inspiration to all other vignerons in the area, giving them the confidence to start their own operations based upon his success. Originally Nat was a civil engineer, but he completed a degree at Charles Sturt in wine science and made his first vintage in 1980.

Although Main Ridge was the first to be established on the Peninsula, Moorooduc Estate was the first to venture into the Moorooduc sub-region in 1982, with 12 acres under vine. It is a north-facing hillside property situated about 100 metres above sea level. The topsoil here is very sandy and the subsoil is a sandy clay. Through the years it has become evident to Richard McIntyre - and most others in the region - that the early ripening varieties of Chardonnay and Pinot Noir are most suited. Richard also points out that his wine-making over the years has become more defined through experimentation, research and reflection. In 1996 he started experimenting with indigenous yeasts that were naturally present in the vineyard, relying on these to effect the primary fermentation since they tended to give less fruit but richer and more complex wines. This proved to work well, and now all wines are made in this fashion. Their top wine, Moorooduc, is made with fruit from their Derril Road vineyard, which they feel demonstrates the finest possible quality that they can achieve at the site.

The Vale Vineyard is just over one mile from the water and at a very low elevation, meaning that it is somewhat warmer and moderate (no frosts) than the higher elevation of Main Ridge or Red Hill (at 300 metres). Contrary to what I have written above, John Vale has had success in ripening Merlot and Cabernet Sauvignon, as bud burst on these lower areas can be up to two weeks before the higher sites. It also helps that his soil is a sandy grey loam of only 30cm depth over a gravel and clay base - quite different from the deep and rich volcanic ones of the higher areas. Traditional sulphur and copper sprays are used to control Powdery and Downy Mildew, which are ever-present in this cooler area. They have not had too much problem with Botrytis to date, but did suffer an attack of Bunch Rot in 2001, when eight inches of rain fell on their ripe Cabernet grapes over 48 hours! John is another vigneron who is experimenting with Albarino and some Tempranillo, in an effort to make his wines stand out and offer something different to Shiraz. He has also been very bold and planted some Durif, which he intends to use in his Cabernets to give it a boost.

Brian Stonier presides over Stonier Wines, which are at the forefront of wine-making in the region. Brian established the business at Merricks in 1977, with his wife Noel, at a time when he says "the region was better known for caravan parks than vineyards". The vineyards were first planted in 1978 with just 600 vines, but over the course of ten years this expanded to cover an area of 15 acres. The business has grown in line with the popularity the area has gained, and today some 50 acres are planted, mainly to Chardonnay and Pinot Noir. Fruit is also bought-in from growers under the direct control of Stoniers, to ensure quality and consistency. The emphasis of the wines is on ele-

Recommended Producers

Dromana Estate   Gary Crittenden is one of the pioneers and one of the most enthusiastic promoters of this region. A large range of wines are made under three labels, including some excellent Italian varietals made from fruit in the King Valley. As with most others here, it is the Chardonnay and Pinot Noir to go for, which are elegant and finely balanced.

Eldridge Estate   Although once known for its Cabernet, the new owners have grubbed them all up and now focus on Pinot Noir and Chardonnay with impressive results.

Elgee Park   One of the warmer sites on the Peninsula, producing flavoursome wines that are now made off site.

Main Ridge Estate   The finest estate in the region.

Miceli   Good focused wines.

Montalto Vineyards   Good wines across the range on offer.

Moorooduc   Experimentation with Pinot Noir and Chardonnay has resulted in these wines now being the ones to look out for.

Paringa Estate   A real Pinot Noir specialist. Winner of a multitude of medals.

Port Phillip Estate   The Port Phillip Estate was established in 1987 with the planting of 15 acres in the heart of the Peninsula by Jeff Sher QC. Today the property is under the ownership of Giorgio and Dianne Gjergja who purchased it in February 2000.

Red Hill Estate   Vines were first planted in 1989 by Sir Peter and Lady Derham, who had originally purchased the property in 1979 with a view to retirement. Obviously this did not happen and since then a top-class restaurant has been incorporated into the business. The range of wines on offer is numerous and includes a good sparkling offering. They have won a multitude of awards and seem to be gaining momentum each year.

Stonier Wines   Stonier's reputation precedes it. They have recently launched a sparkling win to commemorate 15 years in business.

Stumpy Gully   A large range of wines, which give an insight into how the region may develop in the long term.

T'Gallant   A winery always on the move with new names and labels each year. The Pinot Gris is one of finest in Australia

Tuck's Ridge   Pinot Noir specialists and winners of the Jimmy Watson Trophy.

Turramurra Estate   Having been established for 13 years, Turramurra is now really coming into its own. A winery to watch in the future.

Ten Minutes by Tractor   Imaginatively-named, as this business is owned by three families, all owning vineyards that are ten minutes by tractor from each other! The Wallis vineyard is north-facing and slightly warmer than the other two. The McCutcheon vineyard is on an easterly aspect and the Judd vineyard is north-westerly. All are managed in the same manner and the results so far have been very encouraging.

gance, complexity and power, which is achieved by vinifying each variety from each block separately, and limiting crop levels to three tonnes per acre. This has not come easily, though, due to the deep Alluvial soils that retain much of the moisture from the rains, causing vigorous vine growth at the expense of the grapes. Different systems have been tried to overcome this problem in experimental rows - for instance close-planting of the vines as is done in Burgundy, but the grapes just did not ripen fully. The solution was found to be using two trellis systems (Lyre and Scott Henry), which control vigour by opening the fruit and leaves to the air and sunlight.

Stonier has become renowned for its Reserve range of wines, especially the Pinot Noir, which are all made by Tod Dexter using a Demoisy crusher from Burgundy and a Willmes airbag press from Germany. The Pinot is pure and focused - probably due to it only seeing 30% new oak, which allows the natural flavours to dominate, making this one of the benchmark wines of the region.

The Port Phillip Estate was established in 1987 with the planting of 15 acres in the heart of the Peninsula by Jeff Sher QC. Today the property is under the ownership of Giorgio and Dianne Gjergja, who purchased it in February 2000. Lindsay McCall has been the winemaker since 1995 and his use of traditional methods has resulted in the estate being awarded many medals at the competitions they enter.

Beechworth

If you are wondering why I have written so much on Beechworth - a region that has only five wineries of note - it is because of the potential it holds and because, despite this, it is unlikely that the major players will buy land here. Why? Because the ground is far too rocky and needs serious amounts of ground preparation to make it viable. The yields are also measly, so they would not return a sufficient profit for a publicly-listed company.

It was the famous explorer Hamilton Hume who first discovered the area, on his expedition with William Hovell to Port Phillip from Sydney in 1824. It took until 1838, though, for the area to be settled by William and George Faithful, who had come in the opposite direction and were heading south - they set up businesses in the Ovens district. Their residence here was cut short by attacks from Aboriginals, who massacred all but two of the 19 strong population. After this, Dr G E McKay, who had planned on heading south, decided instead to settle at Warrowly, until he too was ousted by Aboriginals, who killed 2993 of his herd of 3000 cattle. He set off once again, and became the first to set eyes on what is now Beechworth. The area soon became better known due to the discovery of gold, which brought in many miners and was an integral factor in bringing people to the region. By 1847 it was recorded that 1279 miners were gainfully employed, but this had decreased to only 144 a century later. The name Beechworth is now synonymous with gold in Australia, as it is probably the best-preserved historic mining area. There are numerous buildings of significance, with many being recognised by the National Trust. In addition, Ned Kelly, the famous Australian outlaw, appeared many times at the local courthouse from the age of 16 onwards. In fact the train that his gang tried to derail, which led to his capture, was on its way to Beechworth. Today you can visit the cell he was detained in.

Vines were first planted in or around 1856, by a Mr Rochlitz in Havelock Road, who had purchased an astonishing 95 different grape varieties in Adelaide. These were to be planted in his vineyard, which until then was still wild bush land. He also helped the propagation of vines by providing rare vine and fruit trees to the wider community. The quality must have been acceptable, as a number of vineyards evolved over the following years. Francois Bertrand planted Shiraz on a four-acre site in Newtown, on a northerly slope facing the waterfalls. Louis Chevalier also had a vineyard at Newton, as did Alexander Dubois. Ambrose Grandjoux sold his stock of wine in 1865, which gives us a good insight into the wines produced. His 1200 gallons consisted of Brown Muscatel, Colonial Claret, Malbec, Muscatel Alexandri, Riesling, Gold Chassala and Tokay. A German, by the name of John August Zimmerman, established a winery of ten acres in 1863, which had grown to 20 acres within two years. His wines sold well and became known under the name of Alexandra Vineyard. At the same time he took out a Colonial Wine Licence and sold a good selection by the glass or bottle. The 1860s were a buoyant time, with major plantings (for the time) bringing the total area under vine up to 90 acres.

ABOVE *The soil in Beechworth is rocky and needs serious preparation before vines will do well.*

The wines were not always well-received abroad though. The *Ovens and Murray Advertiser* reported in its October 16, 1867 edition that:- "There seems to be an impression abroad that good wine cannot be made in the immediate vicinity of Beechworth. That impression is most decidedly a wrong one. There is exceedingly good wine made at more than one winery around Beechworth. We tasted several samples of two year old wine the other day, and they were generally excellent. The Shiraz and Tokay were especially good, and a cask of Verdelho, although rather sweet at present will make a very strong, full bodied and well flavoured wine if kept for five or six years - we were surprised at the excellent quality of wine in his cellar, and we have no doubt that there are others that would go to remove that impression that Beechworth is too high for wine growing". Although the region never gained the reputation of South Australia and was fighting against the odds, the almost cottage industry continued and six wine licences were granted in Beechworth by 1968. This fuelled other industries like coopers, retailers and auctioneers to sell the wines. It would be easy to dismiss these associated businesses with so few wineries but the region did produce over 90,000 bottles per year, which was no doubt sufficient to keep them alive.

The dreaded vine louse, Phylloxera, probably caused the area to diminish substantially in 1910, by two thirds to just 33 acres. Although it is not certain that this was the cause, it is the most probably since it was discovered in nearby Rutherglen in 1899. The decline continued, until eventually the only plantings that remained were for personal use.

It was in 1945 that the appropriately named Vin Capriotti planted five acres of vines, from cuttings taken at Chateau Tahbilk. These were soon purchased in 1950 by Brown Brothers, who increased the acreage to 40. It did not prove to be profitable, due to the low yields, and they pulled out of the region. Hardly any of these vines remain today.

The modern resurrection of the region can be put down to Rick Kinzbrunner from Giaconda, whose vineyards at Everton Hills and Beechworth produce one of - perhaps even the - finest Chardonnay in Australia. The sheer quality of these wines has resulted in major plantings recently, with 163 acres now under vine. Giaconda's first vintage was in 1985, and their success has been partly due to traditional farming methods. Only natural yeasts are used and the wines are unfiltered,

ABOVE *The Viognier grape is one of those trial planted in this region.*

allowing the true terroir to show. Minimal chemicals and no fertilizer, along with low-yield and hand-picking, also add dimension to the wines. Shiraz has also been planted recently, and looks as if it will produce quality fruit to equal the Pinot Noir and Chardonnay. When planting, consideration is given to the aspect of the vineyard and soil type to ensure a perfect match for the selected rootstock. Rick uses Schwarzmann for wetter areas and either Richter 99 or Paulsen 1103 for the drier ones.

As an area, it is somewhat behind the mainstream ones, as pointed out by Julian Castagna of Castagna. By this he means that they do not necessarily know which grape varieties, apart from Chardonnay and Pinot Noir, are most suited to the soils and climate. A number of trial plantings are in place, including Nebbiolo, Viognier and Sangiovese. I find these interesting choices in terms of commercial viability, but then wines from this region will never be mass-produced bottlings, but small amounts for the real wine enthusiast to seek out and enjoy. Castagna wines are gaining a good reputation, with positive reviews from journalists like Robert Parker and those at the top of the literary profession in Australia. Like Giaconda, a hands-off approach is used, along with bio-dynamic farming systems. The result is wines of a savoury character that have rich fruit and a nice texture, combined with balance and finesse. In fact the 1999 Genesis was placed first in a blind tasting of wines from Australia and France by Ewineexchange. Jancis Robinson also wrote on her website, www.jancisrobinson.com, that Beechworth was "home to three of the world's most remarkable wine producers" and included Julian. This is high praise and these terroir-driven wines are sure to make a large impact on the international wine scene in the coming years.

Victoria Other Areas

Geelong

Geelong is just a short boat ride from the Mornington Peninsula, or a pleasant drive, taking around two hours at a leisurely pace, from Melbourne. The views from here are magnificent, especially if you visit Scotchmans Hill or attend one of their many concerts throughout the year. Although a relatively small region it is blessed with a number of wineries, producing wines of a high quality. There are four distinct sub-regions - Anakie, Moorabool Valley, Waurn Ponds and the Bellarine Peninsula. The difference between them is that Anakie and Moorabool Valley are affected by a rain shadow and have a larger diurnal temperature range, which produces wines that have greater structure and colour than Waurn Ponds and Bellarine, whose wines are generally prettier and more fragrant.

Curlewis is one of the finest proponents of Pinot Noir in the country. This is not totally surprising given that their vines, which cover only four acres, are 19 years old, placing them amongst the oldest 10% in Australia. The vineyard sold its fruit to Scotchmans Hill until 1997, when Rainer Breit and Wendy Oliver became the new owners. It has always been their intention to focus on wines that showed well on the middle-to-back palate, rather than those with up-front primary flavours. They are helped naturally in this by the low-cropping vines (1.5 tonnes per acre), and by the addition of a small winery built in 1998, giving them total control. Some fruit is bought in from other vineyards, to enable them to make small amounts of Shiraz and Chardonnay, but the total production still is a very modest 1500 cases. The great thing about these wines is their consistency. They have been placed third equal in the Concours des Vins du Victoria run by the French Chamber of Commerce for the past two years. This is a tremendous achievement given the amount of Pinot produced in the state. Their Shiraz also shows well, which is possibly due to the favourable climatic conditions experienced in the region. Although it has a maritime influence it is small hot pocket in what is otherwise a cool climate region, allowing the grapes to ripen easily whilst retaining varietal definition.

Lethbridge Wines in Geelong was founded by three scientists, Ray Nadeson, Maree Collis and Adrian Thomas, who recognise the importance of terroir in the production of dis-

ABOVE *Scotchmans Hill wines are becoming increasingly well known internationally.*

ABOVE *The views in Geelong are magnificent and Scotchmans Hill winery also hosts concerts.*

Recommended Producers

Bannockburn   Gary Farr produces some of the most complex and intriguing wines of the region.

Curlewis Winery   Pinot Noir that shows some of the Old World how it should be done.

Del Rios Vineyard   Good Shiraz from this Spanish family.

Jindalee Estate   Scott Ireland, the head winemaker here, makes a range of very supple Shiraz and refreshing Chardonnay that echo citrus and peach flavours. The Pinot Noir has good colour and depth, achieved through making the wine carefully in small batches.

Lethbridge Wines   Organic wines made by three scientists. Their aim is to consistently demonstrate the terroir of the land the vines are grown on. They have been successful in doing so thus far.

Prince Albert   True Pinot Noir specialists making exceptional hand crafted wines.

Provenance Wines   Small production winery with wines being made by Scott Ireland, which should guarantee their quality.

Scotchmans Hill   A major operation in Geelong with wines that are becoming increasingly well known internationally. Tremendous views and events held throughout the year in the grounds.

Shadowfax   Founded in 2000 within the grounds of the magnificent Werribee Park estate, they are already making wines that demand attention. Striking packaging and wines to match.

ABOVE *A view of Spray Farm, which is part of the Scotchmans Hill operation.*

tinctive wines. In the development of the vineyard they have followed organic principles and used traditional wine-making techniques, to allow the wines to show the unique character of the site.

One stumbling block on their quest to create wine in a traditional manner was how to store the wine. They came up with an ingenious solution - a straw bale winery. Its design allows them to recreate the controlled environment that so many European wineries have in their cellars. It is also a very environmentally-friendly building, fitting in with their belief in environmental sustainability. Both Maree Collis and Ray Nadeson were initially trained as research scientists and hold PhD degrees in chemistry and medicine respectively. Although they maintain that they find their scientific careers both challenging and stimulating, they share a love of wine. Ray believes that wine-making is not really that

different to science, both are creative and both involve 99% perspiration, 1% inspiration. They have both also graduated from Charles Sturt with degrees in wine-making. Although they acknowledge that this has been a learning experience and that they have taken a lot from the course, they also really want to understand more about the scientific aspect. For instance, they would like to know more about exactly what goes on during wild yeast ferments, pre and post-fermentation maceration and extended lees contact. By gaining this understanding, they will be able to apply decisions authoritatively and intelligently to best bring out the terroir.

Prince Albert was the first vineyard in Australia to plant Pinot Noir exclusively. It is located in an ideal position, with rolling countryside surrounding it. Five acres are planted on a north-facing slope on highly-valued terra rossa soils, which are 60 cm deep. The entire

ABOVE *Grapes from the Prince Albert Vineyard, where they specialise in Pinot Noir.*

production, from growing to bottling, is completed on site, with the majority of the work being done by hand. The wines are certified as being organic and the grapes are crushed and then treated by pigeage (the cap is only hand-plunged) in open wax-lined concrete fermenters. The wine is then aged in French barriques for ten months, prior to being bottled. Bruce Hyett, the owner, works very hard to make his Pinot one of the finest in the country so it always sells out very quickly.

The most recent new entrant to the area is Shadowfax, who entered with a big splash in 1998. Although a boutique winery making around 15,000 cases, it is run as if it is a major concern with strong marketing and a keen eye for detail. Matt Harrop is in charge of wine-making and he sources fruit from their own and other vineyards around Australia. These include Heathcote, from where they are able to acquire Shiraz fruit from 20-year-old vines, and Geelong, where they source Pinot Noir. Sauvignon Blanc comes from the Adelaide

Hills and further Shiraz from McLaren Vale. From their own vineyards in Tallarook they have more Shiraz and Viognier. As you can tell from the many regions that they source the fruit from, the idea here is to provide a portfolio of wines that is not restricted by the geographic limitations of the area that they are based in. This is not necessarily easy though, so it is fortunate that Matt has previously worked at Brokenwood in the Hunter Valley - a specialist in this kind of production - which has given him the required skills.

The actual cellar door of Shadowfax is located within Werribee Park, which holds Victoria's grandest house and is home to many high-profile events, including polo. The wines have showed well since their first release, receiving acclaim from most critics who have tasted them.

Gippsland

Gippsland is the largest of all the wine growing regions in Australia, at 280 miles long and 93 miles wide, and is almost the most southerly one. It totally negates the prospect of labelling each Geographical Indicator in Australia with its own regional flavour descriptors, because for a start there are at least ten different climates contained within Gippsland, with enormous variation in the wines. It is unlikely that the region will be broken down into smaller GIs either, as each sub-region produces less than the 500 tonnes of fruit per vintage that is needed to qualify. With the region being cool, damp and with rainfall of 1000mm per annum, it the business of grape growing is a very difficult one, and it

ABOVE *Cabernet Sauvignon grapes grow well in several areas of Victoria.*

only attracts the most diehard enthusiasts.

Phillip Jones started Bass Phillip in 1979 with the intention of making the Australian equivalent of the French Chateau Ducru Beaucaillou. This cannot have worked, as in the early 1980s he scrubbed up most of the vineyard and restarted from new with Pinot Noir, the first releases being in 1991. Today Phillip produces seven varieties of Pinot, making Bass Phillip, along with Prince Albert in Geelong, the country's experts with this grape. Phillip has four vineyards separated by 6-12 miles, which allows him to express the terroir of each in his individual wines. This desire is also fuelled by his Buddhism, to which he was introduced by his Thai wife, as it installs a total respect for nature and a reluctance to change it in any way. For Australia, the vines are planted very densely at 9000 vines per 2.5 acres. They yield a measly one tonne per acre, which really focuses the flavours in the fruit. The top wine here, the Reserve, is made in very small countries and I understand that as few as 18 bottles reach the UK in some years.

The Cannibal Creek vineyard is owned by the Hardiker family and was first planted in 1997, with five acres each of Chardonnay and Pinot Noir. The earth here has been deeply weathered and on the gentle slopes there are deep soils with a high proportion of gravel. Surface soils are generally sandy clay loams with bleached sub-surfaces. The sunshine hours are more than adequate for the early grape varieties and they have been able to ripen Merlot and Cabernet Sauvignon without difficulty. Yields are currently two tonnes per acre, and only French barriques with a fine grain are used for maturation. The vineyard follows organic practices, which is consistent with their membership of Landcare. Although its name might engender wild speculation, it is in fact named after a plot of pastoral land that was called the Connabul run - the spelling over the years has been corrupted. The first vintage in 1999 saw a small amount of Chardonnay being made, while subsequent vintages also included Sauvignon Blanc, Merlot and Cabernet Sauvignon.

Nicholson River is owned by Ken and Juliet Eckersley. They have deservedly won a world-wide reputation for quality from their small production operation. Although 12 wines are made in various styles, each vintage leads to only 50-200 cases of each, making them highly sought after. One of the reasons that the Chardonnay is so highly sought after is its long ripening period - which can last for between 170-180 days, giving it more depth of

ABOVE *When Chardonnay grapes are ripened for longer periods, the wines can be richer and have more tropical flavours.*

flavour and body.

Located in the south west of Gippsland is the Gurdies Winery, which was planted in 1982 by Frank Cutler as a hobby vineyard. It was some years before Frank could actually harvest any grapes, though, due to the extreme climatic conditions and the rather large appetite of the native birds, who took to this new-found food source rather like a wine lover to Romanee Conti! Netting was soon installed to alleviate this problem, and in line with some other good vintages in the late 1980s, some wine was produced. The business was sold in the early 1990s, and Peter Kozik is now at the helm and in charge of the wine-making. Plantings have been increased to 15 acres, which produce around 40 tonnes of fruit, but this is enough to keep him busy. Interestingly, there are a number of varieties planted here, including Verdelho and Merlot, which could be quite interesting alongside their Shiraz - of which another four acres have been planted.

Grampians

I have to confess that two of my favourite wineries are in the Grampians - Bests and Mount Langi Ghiran. Driving through this region you might have no idea that it was grape-growing country - only a few small signs point you towards a cellar door here and there. What captures you about this region is its natural beauty and presence, which is dominated by the Grampians National Park with its twisting roads and commanding views for miles around. The National Park itself is situated around four areas, the Wartook Valley, Halls Gap, Pomonal and Dunkeld, all of which are inhabited sections of this 167,000 acre park. The park has an unbelievable one third of all Australia's plant species contained within it. This area is also famous for its "crag-rock" climbing, attracting a mammoth 1.4 million visitors per year. The region has a long history of producing elegant, powerful and long-lived wines. The first vines were planted here in the 1860s, and by 1887 it was reported in the local *Ararat Advertiser* that wines from the region had "won honours all over the world".

As in all regions, the soils play an integral part in the making of fine wine and the most desired type in the Grampians is a red clay loam. This is usually peppered with ironstone nodules and can be gravelly, and usually overlies rocky parent material. As you would expect, variations do occur - when granite outcrops surface, their erosion results in sandy clay loam topsoils, often with gritty sand layers below.

Bests is one of the most historic vineyards in this region - and in Australia - with its history of producing wines continuously for over 125 years. In all this time it has only been in the ownership of two families - the Bests originally and the Thompsons since 1920. The jewel in the crown is the Concongella vineyard, which was planted in 1866 by Henry Best - who at the time knew little about wine but was an ambitious fellow with a strong work ethic, which saw him through the initial stages. His commitment paid off and although perhaps he never made great wines, he stayed in business until his death in 1920. His son sold the business to Frederick Thompson, an experienced vigneron. The Thompson family had first settled in the area in 1892 - when Frederick's father purchased the St Andrews vineyard at Great Western - but poor trading meant that in 1927 he was forced to sell. By this time his son had already purchased Bests and his own desire to make wine was still burning, so he bought a small holding in the warmer Victorian district of Lake Boga and called it St Andrews. These two vineyards are still owned and run by the Thompsons today, with Viv and his wife at the helm. Fruit from the Concongella vineyard goes into their Great Western Range and fruit from their St Andrews vineyard goes into the Victoria Range. They have also recently planted a new vineyard, which is imaginatively called the No Name Vineyard. The wines from Concongella are always elegant and this can be put down to the ideal conditions that it experiences. The land along the creek where the vineyard is situated is very flat, with a powdery, limey loam overlaying a deep clay sub-soil. The ripening period is long and slow, which allows the grapes to ripen physiologically. In the finest years a Thompson Family Reserve is made, which is often ranked by a prominent Australian author as the finest in the country. In vintages which are not perfect, this wine is downgraded to one called FHT, and as a result is effectively a great bargain.

I was fortunate to stay with the Thompsons during my latest trip and this proved to be a wonderful experience. Dinner was a particular highlight, as we drank Riesling 1977, Pinot Meunier 1969, and Shiraz 1976 and 1972. All these wines, although mature, still had a youthfulness about them that took me by surprise. It is a great credit to Viv that the 1969 Pinot Meunier was only the third vintage that he was solely responsible for, having taken over from his father in 1967 after travelling around Kenya and Europe. There the emphasis was on wine-making, as opposed to grapes, so Viv decided to find someone to come in and take over the viticultural responsibilities. That person was Trevor Mast, who joined the team in

Cliff Edge
2000
MOUNT LANGI GHIRAN
Shiraz
14.0% vol. PRODUCE OF AUSTRALIA 750 ML

ABOVE *Lots of vineyard owners have the good fortune to live on their estate and can keep a constant eye on their vines.*

1972 and continued until 1988, when he joined Mount Langi Ghiran.

Mount Langi Ghiran is located to the east of Ararat on the eastern foothills of the mountain it takes its name from. The vineyards have been planted at an elevation of 450 metres, and for the prized Shiraz vines they use a Air Mass Protection System, which is an ingenious method of reducing the wind factor whilst allowing the sunlight to penetrate quite normally. Although quite technical it works like a wave, allowing the air to roll over the top of it. Trevor Mast, now winemaker here, purchased a half-share in the property in 1997, having been the winemaker for several years.

Vineyard management is taken very seriously here and many clones have been trialled to find the perfect match to the soil type. The

original vineyard was planted in 1969, with cuttings from Great Western, which has proved to be a good move. Since soil plays such a major part in influencing wine, the sandy loam topsoils, with their gritty, sandy layers overlaying red clay loam, are important parts of the Langi style. The wine-making here also fashions the wines, with open fermentors for oxidation fermentation since the grapes have high acid levels but also a good malic:tartaric ratio. No SO2 is added and native yeasts start the fermentation around 4-5 days after the grapes have been crushed. However, the native yeasts begin to struggle halfway through the crush, so cultured ones are added - which also prevents the native yeast giving off H2S. The results are very impressive, with the Shiraz regularly considered to be one of Australia's finest, along with Bests.

The third great winery in the Grampians is Seppelt Great Western, one of the most historic wine making centres in the country. Seppelt is blessed with marvellous underground cellars that hint at this winery's speciality - sparkling wines. They are perhaps the most well-known and loved sparkling wines in Australia, as they fall in all price brackets and compete well with all competition. In fact they have won seven times more medals in competition than their nearest rivals. Located along the damp and dark corridors are millions of bottles of varying ages, which are just begging to be opened. All are made in the traditional method, although instead of having to be turned by hand they are now done by machine. The Australian Prime Minister is always offered the opportunity to store his own

ABOVE *Millions of natural yeasts are present on grape skins.*

wines in one of the vaults here, along with other highly important people in the community. If visiting, do make time to take the tour as it goes into detail about wine-making and takes you down into the cellars, which are very reminiscent of those in Champagne.

Pyrenees

The Pyrenees lies at the heart of the Victorian gold country - or it did during the gold rush days of the 1850s. The early settlers must have been kicking themselves as it is recorded that vines were first planted in Avoca in 1848, by a man named MacKereth, to supply the local miners. They must have been quite angry at not having discovered gold whilst preparing the vineyards!

Although one of the oldest regions in Australia, this is also one of the smallest, having only around 12 commercial producers of varying size. It is not hard to see why - although viticulturally it is well placed, being north of the Great Dividing Range and with a continental climate, it just does not attract a real tourist market, thus making cellar door sales quite difficult. This is beginning to change, with some large vineyards being planted (land prices are still affordable here), but this may cause another problem - water is scarce here so it is going to be a major challenge to harvest enough grapes.

Peerick is one of the least accessible wineries in the Pyrenees, being at the end of a 6km gravel road called Wild Dog Track. It is well worth a visit though, as the wines are made under contract by Trevor Mast from Mount Langi Ghiran. Unusually, but perhaps starting a new trend, Peerick specialises in Viognier, which was first planted in 1992. The variety would seem ideal, as its historical home is the Rhone Valley in France, along with the Shiraz that the region is well-known for. Both varieties tend to ripen at the same time and it will be interesting to see if a Cote Rotie-style wine is made in future years by co-fermenting the two varieties.

Taltarni (which means Red Earth) was established in 1972 by American John Goelet and it was one of the founding wineries in the Pyrenees. It is located in a sheltered amphitheatre at the top of a valley, in the northern foothills of the ranges, 200km north-west of Melbourne. The site was selected after a worldwide search of the finest growing regions that would complement John's knowledge of traditional wine-making skills and state-of-the-art

ABOVE *Taltarni Vineyard in the Pyrenees has sold more than 2.5 million bottles of its sparkling wine, which is made in the methode champenoise, although it is also very well-known for its premium red wines.*

ABOVE *Pumping over Shiraz juice in a stainless steel fermentation vat - the skins float to the top to form a cap, so this process rolls the wine over, breaking the cap up and adding more flavour.*

technology. John's relationship with wine is a long one. He is a direct descendent of Daniel Guestier, who established the Bordeaux wine negociants Barton & Guestier at the end of the 18th century. His cousin, Guy Schyler, introduced him to Dominique Portet whose father was the regisseur of Chateau Lafite Rothschild in Bordeaux. Dominique headed up the Australian operation and built it to a significant size, winning many medals along the way. Although known for its premium red wines, Taltarni has sold more than 2.5 million bottles of its sparkling wine, which is made in the methode champenoise. In 1986 the business expanded into Tasmania, with its purchase of the Clover Hill Estate, which is devoted to the production of sparkling wine. The 1994 was selected as Australia's Best Sparkling Wine by the Penguin *Good Australian Wine Guide* 1997/8.

Jane Holt, the winemaker at Berrys Bridge has been very successful and regularly produces one of the finest Shiraz in Australia. She achieves this primarily by having excellent fruit, but then hand-picks to enable her to select all the grapes at a maturity level of her choice, which is simply not possible with a machine harvester. The vineyard is also easily manageable, being 16 acres in the northern foothills of the Pyrenees. The wines produced are individualistic, with the Shiraz having a smoky, mint and berry nose and the Cabernet notes of leather, cassis and cherries.

One of the largest producers here is Dalwhinnie, which was founded by an architect, Ewan Jones, in 1973. He originally purchased the property with a view to clearing it and then building a house with perhaps a few

vines, as a weekend retreat. However, like many before him, he became seduced by the idea of making wine from his own grapes. The first wine to be made here was in 1979, and was a blend of Shiraz and Cabernet which was transported to the Yellowglen winery where eight cases were made by Gary Farr. By 1984 production had risen to 800 cases, but then Yellowglen was purchased by Mildara so the relationship had to end. In 1983, Ewan's son David had moved to the area, having lost interest in his apprenticeship as a joiner. He soon hooked up with Keith Farnsworth, a retired viticulturist, who was working part time in the vineyard. For four years Keith passed on his knowledge to David, until the latter became the vineyard manager.

The business he took on was in a very bad way - at the time banks were not at all keen to lend money to vineyards and the stock had built up to some 3000 cases. A solution was found by opening a cellar door in 1985, at a time when the wines had some bottle age and the economy was starting to pick up again. By 1990 they had struck a deal with Mitchelton to make their wine as well, which proved to be a very good decision. With winemaker Don Lewis's skill and Dalwhinnie fruit, some excellent wines were made - and a Mitchelton wine that used 50% of Dalwhinnie's fruit won the Jimmy Watson Trophy. This success has continued and today the Dalwhinnie winery is considered to be one of the finest in Australia, although production is still relatively small.

The other wineries in this region that also command a mention are Mount Avoca, Blue Pyrenees and Sumerfield. All are worth a visit if you are in the area.

Sunbury

This small cool-climate viticultural area is located between the Bendigo region and the Yarra Valley, but is far closer to the latter and only 20 minutes from Melbourne. The soils are predominantly volcanic with black basalt and red clays over scoria. There are a few wineries here, the most important of which are Goona Warra and Craiglee.

Goona Warra, meaning "resting place of Black Swan" was named in 1863 when the winery was founded by the Hon James Goodall Francis, who arrived in Australia at the age of 16 and went on to make a small fortune in land before entering Parliament. Interestingly, he set up the compulsory state education system that still is in place today. He planted the vineyard at a cost of £150 per acre

- which was extraordinarily high at the time - and employed an Italian winemaker. By the 1870s the area was flourishing and seven other vineyards were in operation, including Craiglee, which is located opposite Goona Warra and was also owned by a politician. Like so many others in the state, trade was seriously affected by the onset of Phylloxera and the Government-sponsored vine pull scheme, which meant the vineyard found itself in a period of demise. It was not until John Barnier, a partner in a large law firm, and his wife Elizabeth, an architect, purchased the property in 1983 that it was restored to its former glory. This was a big gamble on their part, as they had only taken a wine appreciation course and obviously got a little carried away! As one can imagine, times were not easy to begin with as they had to replant the vineyard and restore the derelict property. Although they almost starved in doing so, they accomplished their goal and re-established the Goona Warra name. Shiraz, which is synonymous with the region, is the main focus but recent success has been found with Cabernet Franc and latterly Pinot Noir.

Craiglee is presided over by Patrick Carmody, and like Goona Warra is steeped in history - one wine was honoured with the title of the best wine at the Vienna show in 1875. Unfortunately it too fell into a state of disre-

ABOVE *Goona Warra in the Sunbury region, which was founded by the Hon James Goodall Francis in 1863. In the 1890s the area was affected by Phylloxera and the vineyard began to fall into disrepair. It was rescued by John Barnier and his wife, Elizabeth, who have replanted the vineyard and restored the property.*

ABOVE *A beautiful sunset over Sunbury, which mirrors the red clays of the region.*

the variety is unknown. Since all the miners were largely of European descent, there was a strong market for wine and the industry thrived for 30 years. It is reported that Phylloxera was not responsible for the demise of this region, as it did not reach the Yandoit Creek area where much of the production was then based. Instead the downturn was caused by the economic crisis, which loomed not only in Australia but also in England, which was a large importer of the wine. This also coincided with the end of the Italian Civil War, which meant many natives returned there, and the government-sponsored vine pull scheme (for some reason they also had a vine planting levy running at the same time!) The region re-established itself around 35 years ago and now has a number of wineries of note. The most highly regarded of these is Virgin Hills, now owned by Michael Hope, of Hope Estate in the Hunter Valley. This is a very focused winery with only one wine being made - a blend of Cabernet Sauvignon, Shiraz and Merlot. Being able to focus all of their attention on just one wine per year enables them to make it the best it can possibly be.

Ellender Estate was established and planted in 1995 by Graham Ellender, an academic who has held posts at many universities. Their focus is on producing sparkling wine, along with plantings of the usual varieties.

Andrew Peace Wines rank in the top 20 for crush and packaged sales in Australia, although they are far removed from the South Australian industrial vineyards that are scattered across the countryside. Andrew Peace is situated in the Swan District of Victoria along the Murray River, where the temperature can fluctuate wildly from 45ºC to -5ºC in the winter. Some of Andrew's success with placing wines from this region into supermarkets must come from the favourable vines he has access too - they are low-cropping, own-rooted and up to 60 years old, producing fruit with intense flavours. Good low-salt water from the Murray also helps when irrigation is needed in this dry location.

The township of Yea, located in a valley at the juncture of the Yea and Goulburn rivers, 60 miles north-east of Melbourne, is home to Cheviot Bridge. This is a relatively new business and is owned by a team of very experienced wine industry professionals, who each owned vineyards in the Victorian High Country and decided to make their own wine with the best parcels of fruit - the remainder being sold on. This has resulted in a new label which promises good things.

pair, but was painstakingly restored by Patrick in 1976. As is consistent with most small boutique winemakers, Patrick is often to be found working in the vineyard rather than stuck behind a desk, which means that the cellar door is only open on Sundays and public holidays. The demand for Patrick's wines is so great, though, that they generally sell out very quickly. When I visited, Patrick pointed out to me how critical the selection of land for viticulture is here. Near the creek running at the bottom of the property, the ph level of the soil is 5.5 - but just 150 metres further up it has become a more neutral 7. The ripening times here are also vastly different from the Yarra, with some varieties needing an extra four weeks to reach full physiological ripeness. Although some Cabernet is made, it is the Shiraz and Pinot which are of real interest - the Shiraz particularly. Both wines benefit tremendously from around five years bottle age.

The Macedon Ranges cover an area from Daylesford in the west, Guilford in the north, Kilmore to the east and Gisborne in the south. Most of the viticultural emphasis has been on the easterly area, ignoring the old gold fields of the west. In the early days this was a popular location for Swiss and Italian gold prospectors, who planted between two and five acres each - some of which can still be found here although

New South Wales

New South Wales is perhaps the least well known of the states, in wine-making terms, outside of Australia. It is most akin to Western Australia, with one major region dominating (the Hunter Valley) and a splattering of others, some established and others newly founded. Perhaps more than any other state, new viticultural areas are being found and developed in this vast region, which offers so much potential. The Lower Hunter is a tourist Mecca, with many Sydneysiders flocking there for the weekend. It is as much a leisure area as a wine-growing one. The Shiraz here is leathery and the Semillon, when made and aged in the traditional manner, totally unique and full of honeysuckle. The Upper Hunter is totally different in its appeal. It contains some large farms and a few cellar doors, making it more of a work horse area than the Lower Hunter.

To the west of the Hunter Valley, over the mountains, lies the larger but even less well-known region of Mudgee, which has not yet become a tourist hot spot. It is also one of the oldest wine regions in Australia. The wines are quite "large" and the grapes often acknowledged to be finer than those of the Hunter.

Orange has had its future as a wine-growing region cemented by the arrival of Rosemount, who have extensive plantings in the region. The Reynolds winery make some of the finest wines here, although they now

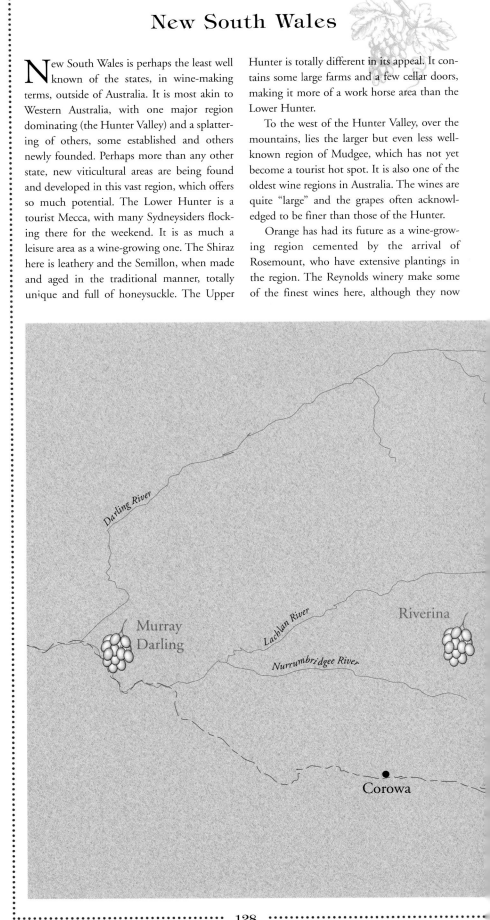

have some competition coming in from Canobolas-Smith, Bloodwood and Brangayne of Orange. The Reynolds Little Boomey wines are widely available and offer a good insight into the region at a prices that don't break the bank. Moving up the ladder, their Yarraman wines can be exceptional.

Cowra and Hilltops to the South offer a large area for the bigger companies to grow grapes. The days are warm and nights cool, which is a good combination. Chardonnay is the main variety grown successfully here, although others also perform to a good commercial standard.

After the Hunter Valley, Canberra is the most quality-orientated region in the state. The likes of Lark Hill and Clonakilla have shown the way, and revealed to the outside world what the capital territory is capable of.

There are not a lot of wineries, but the potential for the future - especially with recent large investments - should pave the way for great things to come.

Riverina is a huge area, where you can see vines for mile after mile. It has often been thought of as the backroom of the Australian wine industry, but this belies the fact that some serious wines are made here. Perhaps the most famous of all is the De Bortoli Botrytis Semillons, which have taken the world by storm. These are seriously good and made other producers in the region wake up to the fact that premium-bottling could also be commercially made.

Botrytis is a fungus which is reponsible for the development of Noble Rot. This causes the grapes to shrivel, with the juice becoming sweeter, whilst the yeasts diminish.

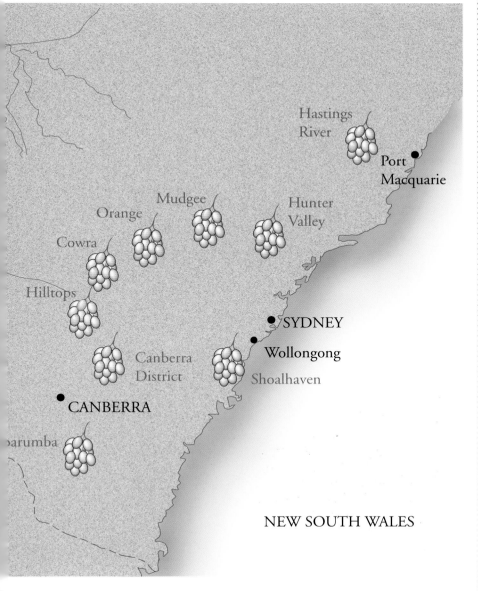

NEW SOUTH WALES

Hunter Valley

The Hunter Valley is the Sydneysiders preferred weekend retreat venue. Just two hours north of the city, it has over the past ten years grown into a tourist Mecca with an abundance of vineyards and golf courses, providing the ideal location to get away from all the hustle and bustle of Sydney. This has led to a number of people investing in wineries throughout the region, with the sole purpose of making cellar door sales and filling their on-site restaurants. With virtually all-year-round sunshine this is not a problem. The Hunter is also famous for being the first region to boast a boutique winery, now commonplace throughout the country. The mean temperature from October to April is 21-22ºC. While maximum growth is achieved at an average of 23-25ºC, the optimum temperature for flavour is 20-22ºC. There are four main types of soil in the region: the majority of the old red vines are planted on doleritic soil from Fordwich that extends to the sub-regions of Broke and Bulga. The river flats, with their deep alluvial soils that can be as deep as seven metres in places, contain the majority of new plantings. The third type is dark sandy loam that provides excellent drainage for the vines, and finally there are weathered conglomeratic soils from Triassic sediments overlying the Permian coal-bearing strata that is exposed throughout the Hunter Valley.

ABOVE *Hand-picking grapes at Tyrrells. This kind of work is back-breaking, but it means that the bunches of grapes can be individually selected for optimum ripeness.*

The Hunter Valley is Australia's oldest wine growing region with vines first planted here in the 1820s by the forefather of Australian wine, James Busby. Busby's connection with the area happened through a meeting with William Kelman, who had travelled to Australia with him on board the ship *Triton*. Kelman went on to marry James Busby's sister, which led to him using Busby's vines in his plot.

Later on, in the mid 1930s, George Wyndham grew vines on his Dalwood vineyard completing the first vintage in 1935.

ABOVE *A magnificent view across the rolling hills of the Hunter Valley.*

Grape Varieties

SEMILLON - The finest area in Australia for this grape. Whilst young the wines can be very tight and difficult to understand, sometimes being almost devoid of flavour, or showing straw, lime, talc and herbaceous notes. They develop weight and complexity after eight years or so in bottle, showing honeysuckle and fig flavours.

CHARDONNAY - The Chardonnays here can exhibit a multitude of flavours that are synonymous with the grape, from melon and butter to pineapple, fruit salad and pear. When developed and after malolactic fermentation, there can be signs of butterscotch and caramel.

VERDELHO - Best drunk when young, it has an abundance of exotic fruit that bursts out at you. From sweet rock melon, apple, honeysuckle, ripe pineapple and peach to exotic floral scents.

SHIRAZ - When young the wines display plum, mulberry, spice, pepper, boiled sweets and blackcurrant flavours. After a few years they develop into a signature leather character.

ABOVE *Semillon grapes.*

CABERNET SAUVIGNON - A lot of Cabernets from the Hunter utilise bought-in fruit from South Australia. The finest example of 100% Hunter fruit is from Lakes Folly, whose wines show great varietal flavour of blackcurrants, violets, plums and a hint of mint.

BARBERA - Although not widely grown across the whole valley, there are around six vineyards in the Broke Fordwich region that are having success with this variety. Most notably is Mt Broke Wines who plant the it on river banks for the clay and water retention properties that they give.

Word soon spread about the potential of the region and by 1850 some 500 acres had been planted. One of the growers to arrive in Hunter during this early period was James King, who started correspondence with a famous German chemist called Baron J von Liebig. Through this connection King travelled to Europe and was able to take a wine to the 1855 Exhibition in Paris, which resulted in a medal. Although the region has been through its ups and downs since then, it is now back on track making wines worthy of the praise that have been lavished upon them.

It is a sprawling region, based around four districts. The main town is Cessnock, a thriving community that is the gateway to the Valleys when travelling from Sydney. From here it is an easy drive of up to 45km to reach all of the 100+ wineries in the region. Other towns that you may choose to base yourself in are Broke and Kurrin Kurri in the Lower Hunter and Muswellbrook in the Upper Hunter. The area is picturesque and one cannot fail to be impressed by the autumnal colours in May throughout the vineyards. The

ABOVE *The Lower Hunter Valley is very geared up to the tourist industry.*

1999
BROKENWOOD
cricket pitch

2000
BROKENWOOD
harlequin
shiraz, cabernet franc
cabernet sauvignon

Lower Hunter is geared up for the tourist industry, with cellar door sales and a plethora of restaurants and hotels to choose from. Some might argue that the drive to attract tourists, with impressive wineries and restaurants being constructed, has detracted from the core business of making wine in the region. In the last decade or so, though, the Lower Hunter has been back on track and is now once again one of the world's premium wine growing regions.

Semillon is probably what the Lower Hunter Valley does best and what it is most widely known for. Traditional Semillons, when young, can be very tight and closed and really not very inspiring at all. However, after a few years in the bottle it starts to develop wonderful honeysuckle and mineral flavours and deepens in its flavour. This does take patience, however, as it usually takes ten years plus to reach this stage. Unfortunately, as most wine purchased in the 21st Century is consumed within 48 hours of purchase, there is a move away from this style and into making a wine

that is ready for drinking immediately upon release. This is made in much the same as Chardonnay, with the grapes being picked at a riper level and barrel-fermented, which produces a wine that is far more popular with the younger consumers.

The finest examples of traditional Semillon hail from the light sandy soils of the dry creek beds located around the valley. Severe hailstorms around harvest time in the late fifties and early sixties ruined crops, and so the winemaker decided to pick the fruit earlier. Since the fruit had not reached full phenolic ripeness, the acid components were more predominant than the fruit. This acts as a preservative for the wine and the freshness is maintained for longer, while allowing the full flavours to develop in the bottle, as chemical changes occur over time. The toasty and honeysuckle flavours really start to develop at this stage. The most prolific exponent of Semillon in the Lower Hunter is Tyrrells, who have grown it for over 100 years, although it was

ABOVE *Vines were first planted in the Hunter Valley in the 1820s and one of the early vintages won a prize at the 1855 Exhibition in Paris.*

not until the release in 1963 of their dry-grown Vat 1 Semillon that a benchmark style was created. Their Vat 1 is still the flagship of the range and is complimented by no less than four other bottlings to meet the requirements of virtually all aficionados. The HVD comes from an historic vineyard called the Hunter Valley Distillery, which consistently produces fruit of exceptional quality. Only a small amount of this wine is made. The Stevens Reserve fruit is sourced from the 40 to 80-year-old vineyards owned by Neil Stevens. Tyrrells make the wine and age it for four years before release, compared to the five years age-ing the Vat 1 receives. Also in the range, although less serious wines, are the Lost Block (named after the 1993 vintage when the fruit was mistakenly allowed to ripen longer than usual) and the Old Winery Semillon, which is their everyday branded wine.

The earlier-drinking Semillons we have today are thanks to Iain Riggs of Brokenwood, who in 1983, one year after his arrival at the winery, made a wine that was more accessible at a young age. This caught on and has resulted in the style commonly found today. They possess more fresh lemony and herbaceous flavours, whilst having a certain oiliness about them. In the Upper Hunter it is far more likely that the wines will have received some form of oak treatment, whether it be through fermentation or ageing before release. The wines do not generally age as well as their counterparts from the Lower Hunter and should be enjoyed in the first five years after the vintage.

For me, Verdelho is the most exciting of the grape varieties grown in the Lower Hunter. It is currently undergoing a surge of populari-ty with most wineries releasing an example of it. In the past it was used to beef up the Semillons, until Wyndhams released a 100% Verdelho as recently as 1989. The grape bursts

ABOVE *Here the vines have been planted in rows following the contours of the slopes.*

out with fruit and creates a multitude of flavours in your mouth. Traditionally it is a grape used in the production of Madeira but has found a new home here in Australia. For everyday enjoyment it is hard to beat with its cocktail of tropical fruit flavours and refreshing acidity, backed up with just the slightest hint of sweetness.

Chardonnay, following the trend in most of Australia, is the most widely-planted variety across both valleys, although most is grown in the Upper Hunter. From there, it tends to develop rather more quickly and is best drunk within three years of the vintage. Due to this, most of the wineries in the Upper Hunter are very large, producing wines for commercial bottlings, as opposed to small production wineries. As with most generalisations there are exceptions and Rosemount's Roxburgh is amongst these. Although not in the absolute top tier of Australian Chardonnay, it is almost there with its very rich, creamy and toasty flavours and long length. The Lower Hunter can claim to have released the first commercial bottling of Chardonnay in Australia with Tyrrells Vat 47. Winemakers in other regions discovered the richness and agreeable flavours generated from the Chardonnay grape and started to grow their own. This was a tremendous success and resulted in the variety being one of the most planted in Australia. Naturally not all could copy (or would want to) the richness from the Hunter, so we are left with a wide diversity of styles to accommodate all tastes.

Although different styles of Chardonnay are grown throughout the country, you only have to look at single vineyards that own various different plots to see the differences in flavours that are achieved as a direct result of terroir and wine-making techniques. A great example of this is Hope Estate, based near Broke, who commenced their first vintage in 1997 under the watchful eye of pharmacist Michael Hope, who had purchased the vineyards some years earlier. Here the grapes are picked from up to ten separate blocks with each one being vinified differently. Some are whole-bunched pressed, whilst others are fermented with their own wild yeasts. The result of this, and different barrel selections, gives the winery ten totally unique wines that can be blended together to create the best example for the vintage. It is a tremendous advantage to have so many different components at your disposal, from the elegant flavours created from cold-pressed grapes aged in tightly grained French oak barrels, to the huge pear-like flavours that are the result of wild yeasts

ABOVE *The scenery in Hunter Valley can be spectacular, with its backdrop of mountains.*

and American oak. Chardonnay continues to be one of the most prolific varieties in the region, as is proved by the 252,000 tonnes of it that were crushed to make approximately 16.5 million cases in 2002.

Shiraz performs well in the Lower Hunter Valley and is considered equal to Semillon as the most natural variety for the region. I would suggest that Verdelho should also be included here. One of the finest exponents of the variety is Mark Davidson, from the Tamburlaine Vineyard. He writes in a piece entitled "Bridesmaid Revisited", that Verdelho often lies dormant on wine shop shelves, as the Chardonnays, Semillons and even Pinot Grigios are sold. He, like me, does not understand this at all. The first cuttings of Verdelho were planted in 1816 in NSW, after being bought over from the Atlantic coast of Southern Europe (where the variety is the principal one in Madeira). They were sustained throughout the journey by being inserted into potatoes. However, it was a long time before the first commercial release of the wine, which was around 1973. The region is viticulturally ideal for Verdelho - it is mainly grown on alluvial soils, when the yields can be in excess of five tonnes per acre whilst still proving a quality wine. To produce the best examples the grapes need to be fully ripened.

ABOVE *The Hunter Valley contains more than 100 wineries, which are an easy driving distance from each other. The area is picturesque, and well geared up for tourism.*

Cabernet Sauvignon, along with Semillon, can age gracefully for 20 years or more. When fully-developed the wine shows wonderful old leather aromas with a hint of compost, whilst when young they display an array of fresh blackcurrants, vanilla, and toffee characteristics, along with their signature earthy and savoury flavours.

Although the Hunter cannot lay claim to making the finest examples of Cabernet to be found in Australia (they can lack structure due to the warm climate), there are some exceedingly good ones and amongst these are wines from Lake's Folly. Max Lake arrived in 1963 with the luxury of being able to choose the perfect site for his vineyard. He came across a rare combination of a volcanic hill, alluvial creek flat and a south-easterly aspect - ideal for viticulture. Max gathered his friends from food and wine societies, along with a plethora of students, to plant the vineyard, which he named Lake's Folly. The first variety to be grown was Cabernet Sauvignon, followed by Chardonnay some six years later in 1969. Great care was taken in the planting of the vineyards, with particular thought given to the logistics of transporting the grapes to the winery in the shortest possible time. The answer was simple - Max built the winery in the middle of the vineyard where it still stands today.

Max's philosophy was that great wine was

ABOVE *Young vines in the Hunter Valley.*

made in the vineyard, and the winemaker is only there to facilitate this. By following this view, and combining it with excellent wine-making skills, the winery soon began to gain recognition and importance in the wine world. This was fuelled by critics such as Len Evans, Hugh Johnson and Michael Broadbent, who praised the high quality of the wines, and by winning a multitude of awards over many years. The Cabernet even found its way onto the wine list of the Ritz Hotel in London's Piccadilly.

In 2000 the ownership of Lake's Folly changed to Peter Fogarty, with Rodney Kempe appointed as winemaker. The same traditions

ABOVE *Some areas of the Hunter Valley have rich, red weathered doleritic soil, which is ideal for growing the old red vines.*

Recommended Producers

Allandale Bill Sneddon makes an excellent Chardonnay from Hunter fruit, along with a selection of other varieties that have been bought in from Mudgee, McLaren Vale and the Hilltops area of NSW.

Allanmere A good range, of which the Durham Chardonnay stands out - along with the Cabernet Sauvignon. The Shiraz can also be good.

Baintons Mail Based in Broke Fordwich the oldest vines on this estate date back to 1923, when soldiers were granted land on their return from the First World War.

Beaumont Estate A newly-established vineyard that was first planted in 1999. Usually it takes five years or so for vines to produce good fruit, but this is an exception. The initial release was a 2001 Semillon, which has been awarded numerous medals at wine shows. They believe that their instant success was due to the organic viticulture being practiced, along with revolutionary "New Soil" being trialled by Boral Limited.

Broke Estate The Ryan family operate this estate, which has an outstanding Chardonnay and was established in 1987.

Brokenwood Started as a hobby in 1970, Brokenwood has evolved into one of New South Wales greatest wineries with the help of Iain Riggs, who joined in 1992. A lot of grapes are sourced from South Australia to complement their range from the Hunter. The Graveyard Shiraz is the finest in the region.

Briar Ridge Intensely flavoured, medal-winning wines that are distinctively Hunter in character. Adrian Lockhart, the winemaker, told me about his time working in a Romanian vineyard. He was told to expect a lot of foliage when the fruit arrived at the crush as the pickers were prisoners who were not allowed knives - they literally had to rip the grapes from the vine! The vineyards here are located high on the slopes of Mount View at the southern tip of the Hunter viticultural area. The yields are are low at 2.5 tons per acre and the vines are green-harvested. The result is wines exhibiting varietal character and flavours.

Calais Estate Originally a cattle farm, the focus was changed to viticulture in 1971. In 2000 the Bradley family purchased the property and breathed new life into it. Some interesting varietals including Zinfandel, Chambourcin and Marsanne are now grown with some success.

Catherine Vale Bill and Wendy Lawson started here in 1997 and every wine they have released so far has been a medal-winner. Keen on Italian varietals, Dolcetto and Barbera were released in the early part of the 21st century.

Cockfighters Ghost Part of Pooles Rock wines, which aims to produce wines from the top regions in Australia. Each wine is made by a different winemaker who is a specialist in the grape variety in question.

Fairview Although dismissed as being in the wrong location by locals when first established, this estate has won nine medals and one trophy since the 2000 vintage, proving their critics wrong. The trophy was won for a 2001 Shiraz, which was declared the best currently available red at the St George Hunter Valley wine show. There is a block of Barbera growing that should be interesting. No Cabernet is produced here as it ripens after the rainfalls begin in March.

Hope Estate Prolific winery set up by pharmacist David Hope in 1994. Produces excellent Chardonnay and Cabernet Sauvignon. Virgin Hills in Coonawarra is also under the same ownership.

Hunter Valley Elements This is a collaboration of Ross McDonald of Macquariedale and Joss De Iuliis of De Iuliis Wines. The label is aimed at an international market and fruit is drawn from the partner's own vineyards, some of which were planted in the 1970s. A new winery has been built, which can handle 600 tonnes of fruit, so expect to see more of this winery in the near future.

Ivanhoe A small winery owned and operated by Stephen and Tracey Drayton. The vineyards stretch up onto the Brockenback Range. Classic Hunter wines, especially the Shiraz.

Jacksons Hill Located in the Mount View region, Mike Winborne believes that his vineyard is located on the best soils of the Lower Hunter and is blessed with an exceptional micro-climate. A specialist in Cabernet Franc and the first person in the region to bottle it as a single varietal. Mike also informed me that Petit Verdot may be a variety that could excel in the Mount View area or the foothills of Pokolbin due to the better soils. Also makes outstanding chocolates on site!

Keith Tulloch Wines   A member of the famous Tulloch wine family, Keith also is the winemaker at the Evans Family Estate and created his own label in 1997. The Semillon, as you might expect, is sensational in most years.

Kevin Sobels Wines   Kevin can trace his family's association with wine-making back to 1847, when his great-great-grandfather arrived in the Barossa having worked in Germany and Champagne previously. Kevin told me that the history books state that he was a consultant responsible for training all the early pioneer wine companies. Each and every year since then, a member of the family has been responsible for making wine in either the Barossa, Clare or Hunter Valleys. The wines are made at the winery under very hygienic conditions with minimal use of chemicals and anti-oxidants.

Lake's Folly   Only two wines are made here, a Chardonnay and a Cabernet Blend. Both are excellent examples of what the region has to offer. The first boutique winery in Australia.

Macquariedale Estate   One of the newer wineries in the region, Macquariedale is quickly establishing a reputation and attempting to go organic - which is not easy in this region due to the climate. Their flagship vineyard Four Winds was planted 34 years ago on old creek beds with deep well-drained sandy loam soil, which has proved ideal for Semillon. The roots of the vines here go down almost ten metres to find the water table.

Margan   Andrew Margan is quickly becoming established as one of the great winemakers in Broke Fordwich and the Lower Hunter Valley. 30 years wine-making experience in both Australia and Europe have enabled him to build a true understanding of vines and indeed what customers want. As such, his wines are made to drink upon release, which is consistent with a society that usually consumes their wine within 48 hours of purchase. Multiple awards and medals in the past few years.

Meerea Park   Rhys Eather, the winemaker, travelled to France in 1998 to work the vintage with M. Chapoutier, the world-famous Rhone winemaker. This shows in his Viognier and Shiraz wines, which are exemplary.

Mount Eyre Vineyard   Located in the Broke Fordwich sub-region the wines are from estate-grown fruit, apart from the Shiraz whose grapes come from McLaren Vale. The vines are all aged between 89 and 32 years with annual production running at 800 cases.

Mt Broke Wines. Only established in 1997 this winery is already making a name for itself, with Shiraz, Verdelho and Barbera being the wines to search out. Named after the highest peak in the Hunter Valley.

Pendarves Estate   Owned by Dr Philip Norrie, the acclaimed author and expert on wine and health matters. Verdelho is the wine to buy from here.

Penmara Wines   A new entrant in the Hunter Wine scene. It is the joint effort of five families who have established vineyards in the region. It looks as though they have ambitious plans, with 400 acres of vineyard and the potential to crush 1600 tonnes.

Pepper Tree   Like a number of wineries in region, grapes are bought in to complement the range on offer. A particular success is their Sauvignon/Semillon blend.

Razina Park. This is a very historic property, since the first boat to explore the Hunter River in 1801 stopped here. They did not stop for very long however, soon returning to Sydney.

Scarborough   A Chardonnay specialist whose wines age well. The Scarboroughs have recently purchased a 100-acre plot of land that used to be owned by Lindermans. Here they will experiment with different varieties and build a storage area to mature the wines in.

Tamburlaine   High quality wines that are only available through the cellar door and their mailing list. It is one of the 50 largest wineries in Australia. Trials with Chambourcin are being made as they believe the climate could be ideal for this French hybrid. The vineyards are going through a period of change at the moment, as they move towards a more organic farming model.

Tyrells   Historic winery with a great range of Semillons.

Wattlebrook Vineyard   Although most grapes are sold to larger companies, in the best years they bottle a little under their own name. Most of the reds are made using fruit from their own vineyards in Mudgee.

ABOVE *Hill of Hope vineyard in the Hunter Valley.*

are carried on in the vineyard, with the vines pruned heavily to maximise the quality of fruit. Being a boutique winemaker and therefore small, they are able to pick each individual block of grapes at optimum ripeness and transport them to the winery quickly. Once here the reds are treated very gently to give soft tannins and make the wines approachable at an early age. They are aged in small 100% French barrels for one year before bottling. The Chardonnay, which is equally revered, is barrel-fermented and kept on its lees (dead yeast cells) for a few months in small new French oak barriques. The wines do not go through a secondary malolactic fermentation. The winery only makes a total, of around 4500 cases per year, divided between Cabernet and Chardonnay. The Cabernet always exudes elegance with a fine texture that will develop for many years.

It is often said that going the extra distance on your journey can pay off with new discoveries. This is certainly the case at Broke Fordwich. The first European settler to acquire land here was John Blaxland in 1807, who had 8000 acres. He originated from Fordwich in Kent, which is very close to my own home. Moving on a century, soldiers returning from the First World War were granted ten acres each under the "Fordwich Soldiers Settlement Purchase Area", which were planted to vine. This did not last long, however, as in 1929, after a horrific hail storm, they departed. The Tulloch family took over the vineyards and sold the fruit to larger companies in Pokolbin. Today there are around 50 vineyards and eight cellar doors operating here and it is now officially designated as a sub-region of the Hunter.

The Bainton family has been growing grapes here since 1982, when they took over a vineyard that had previously been owned by Len Evans, amongst others. The estate had a long tradition of supplying all its grapes to the larger companies in the area, until in 1999 the family decided to bottle a proportion under the Bainton Family Wines label. Although still in its infancy as a label, the Estate has some very good fruit to work with - including Semillon coming from vines planted in 1923.

Also in this expanding sub-region are Mt Broke wines. They are blessed with three different types of soil - red weathered doleritic, which most of the old red vines are planted on, Fordwich sill, which extends north-west to south-east from Bulga to Broke, and dark sandy loams that provide excellent drainage. Some other plantings are on weathered conglomeratic soils, from Triassic sediments that overlay the Permian coal-bearing strata exposed throughout the valley. Budburst here is some two weeks later than the main Hunter Valley and they tend to get less rain, apart from at the end of the summer - which can cause problems with late-ripening varieties such as Cabernet Sauvignon. They have found that young vines on red soil do not do as well as those on river beds, due to the clay content and water retention of the former.

One of the newer wineries in the region, Macquariedale is quickly establishing a reputation and attempting to go organic, which is not easy in this region due to the climate. Their flagship vineyard Four Winds was planted 34 years ago on old creek beds, with deep well-drained sandy loam soil, which has proved ideal for Semillon. The roots of the vines here go down almost ten metres to find the water table.

Canberra

Canberra is an unusual place that exists solely because Melbourne and Sydney were unable to decide which should be made into Australia's capital city. After many years quarrelling a solution was found - build a brand new city. Due to a rather bizarre piece of planning, Canberra is one of the most inconvenient places to get to in Australia. Although it lies between Sydney and Melbourne, it is some 40 minutes away from the main highway that links the two cities. Coming from Sydney there are two exits for the capital, which are at least a one hour drive apart from each other - which is quite disconcerting for the weary traveller who had been instructed to take the second turning!

Canberra is not known for its long history of wine-making, in fact the industry has only been in existence here since the 1970s, when Doctor John Kirk planted a vineyard that he named Clonakilla near Murrumbateman, some ten miles from the city centre. Around the same time Dr Edgar Riek planted a vineyard at the site of Lake George, and these became the first in a small line of professionals who took up hobby wine-making here. There are still only around 20 wineries in the region, making it very small. In fact there is only one winery in all of the ACT - BRL Hardy. One of the primary reasons for this is that all the land in the area is under lease for 99 years from the Federal Government, so the prospect of developing a vineyard - which would have a lifespan of 30 years plus - with an imposed short term lease, (although renewable), would be suicidal.

Grape Varieties

CABERNET - Blackcurrant and mint.

MERLOT - Plum and mint.

SHIRAZ - Pepper, spice and dark chocolate.

PINOT NOIR - Spice, plum and strawberries.

CHARDONNAY - Melon, peach and fig.

RIESLING - Floral, mineral and citrus.

ABOVE *Chardonnay grapes*

It does have one distinct benefit though - a Federal constitution requires that "fair and proper" compensation be paid by the Government for improvements to the land. Today there are 29 wineries operating in the Canberra District, which are mostly within a 25 minute drive of the city centre.

One company that has decided to go out on a limb here is BRL Hardy - a heavy weight amongst all the wine companies in Australia.

ABOVE *A stunning sunset in New South Wales. Apart from the Hunter Valley, the state is not as well known for wine-making outside Australia as some other states.*

Presumably Hardy's has obtained some sort of guarantee from the Federal Government that they will not be ousted, given the substantial amount of investment in the region that they have made and the employment they have created. 2002 is the first year that the vines cropped sufficiently to enable the company to make a wine, so there is as yet little information on their quality. The eventual production will be large, with 600 acres planted that will produce around 500,000-1,000,000 cases per year, depending on yields.

Not much has been written about this region in the past. Australian wine books of the 1980s barely devoted a paragraph to it, such was its insignificance in the larger scheme of things. Today is a different matter though, with at least three wineries making wines of a world-class level. The landscape ranges from 550-870 metres in altitude and the higher vineyards are generally accepted to be suited to the earlier-ripening varieties, such as Pinot Noir, Riesling and Chardonnay, whilst at Murrumbateman (at 620 metres), varieties such as Shiraz, Merlot, Cabernet Sauvignon, Riesling and Chardonnay can be successfully grown. Rainfall is spread evenly throughout the year, at around 600mm.

The most prominent winery in the region was also one of the first planted - Clonakilla Estate. Tim now runs the winery and owns vineyards adjoining the property. It is here that the most Cote Rotie-like wine in Australia is made. Over lunch with Tim, a man devoted to the art of wine-making and totally passionate about wines from around the world, I was dumbfounded by the sheer quality of the 2001 Shiraz (a wine many months away from being released), which had been blended, as is the norm at Clonakilla, with 7% Viognier. Never have I been so despondent at the prospect of having to drive south towards Melbourne - I just wanted to stay all afternoon to sip and savour this extraordinary wine, which has since been named as the Penguin Wine of the Year. As with European wines, it is designed to go with food as opposed to being a blockbuster. Prior to this we had indulged in a bottle of straight Viognier, which was intensely perfumed and was a clue as to just how good the red would be. After lunch we drove back up to the winery, to have a look around and taste some barrel samples.

Wimbaliri Estate is ideally located between Clonakilla to the east and Doonkuna to the west, which - although no guarantee of quali-

ABOVE *Unfortunately birds also love ripe grapes, so the vines have to be protected with bird netting to make sure there is going to be something left to harvest.*

ABOVE *Taking a sample - the wine-making team will taste through each individual batch to determine the final blend before the wine is bottled.*

ty - should give it a favourable advantage over others in the region. John and Margaret Anderson established the estate in 1998, when the building of their house and the planting of vines was completed. Currently it is relatively small, with only 5.5 acres planted to Cabernet Sauvignon, Merlot, Shiraz, Cabernet Franc, Pinot Noir and Chardonnay. The vines are vertically-trellised to enable the light to penetrate to the fruit on each side of the narrow rows, and are planted on a north-easterly facing slope, which has decomposed granite-based soils and gravels. You also find sandy-clay loams and gravels in the area. John looks after all aspects of the business, from vineyard management right through to bottling, but in recent years has been helped by Margaret, who looks after the packaging and marketing side of the business.

Brindabella Hills is situated 15 miles to the north-west of Canberra, on the escarpment of the Murrumbidgee River, which is 100 metres below the vineyard. It sits in a natural, albeit large, amphitheatre with the Brindabella Mountain Range to the west and hills to the south. This helps the vineyard take advantage of a relatively warm site in a cool district. The vineyard is owned and managed by Roger Harris, a lifetime lover of fine wine. His travels throughout Europe inspired him to purchase this plot of land, which was selected for its climatic similarities with Rioja, Tuscany, the Rhone Valley, Adelaide Hills and the Clare Valley. The soil offers good drainage, due to its gravely, light volcanic structure.

Milimani Estate is located 820 metres above sea level, near the town of Bungendore,

a few kilometres outside Canberra. The philosophy here is to make wines of the highest quality. Founded by Dr Peter Preston in 1988, after a year's sabbatical in Cognac, France, this was a originally a run-down farm that his inquisitive wife Rosemary insisted they look at after seeing a "For Sale" board outside. A dream was born and the first vines were planted in 1989. Initially these were Chardonnay, Cabernet Franc and Merlot but this expanded to Pinot Noir and Sauvignon Blanc in the early 1990s. More recently, they have experimented with Traminer, Shiraz and Malbec which should prove to be interesting.

ABOVE *Kangaroos are more welcome, as they do not damage the vines.*

Recommended Producers

Brindabella Hills   Dr Roger Harris presides over this winery, which makes wines to a very high standard.

Clonakilla   Stunning Shiraz/Viognier blend that was awarded Red Wine of the Year for the year 2001 by Huon Hooke in the Penguin wine guide to Australia.

Doonkuna   Good everyday wines that are improving year-on-year.

Helm   Consistent quality throughout the range.

Jeir Creek   More plantings here should lead to wider availability of these wines. Rob Howell is the owner/winemaker and his passion shows through in the wines. Either he or one of the team is always willing to discuss wine-making with you, if you pop into the cellar door. Interestingly, after purchasing the land in 1984 and developing the vineyards and winery, Rob discovered that his paternal grandmother had been born in "Jeir" about a mile from the winery in 1892. His great-great-great-uncle had also developed a winery at Rye Park, which is around 40 miles away, in the 1860s.

Kyeema Estate   Limited quantities which have a cult following. Good, solid quality.

Lake George Winery   An interesting small winery that was established in 1971. Traditional methods hold true here - the wines are processed at a rate of one tonne per day and are crushed by foot. The wines then ferment on their own wild yeasts, before being pressed in a basket press and then aged in old and new French barrels for up to two years. Unusually, the wines are not racked during this period.

Lark Hill   Splendid Pinot Noir and Chardonnay - world class.

Milimani   Planting began here in 1989 so the vines are now mature. More recently Shiraz, Malbec and Traminer have been added, which could be interesting.

Mount Majura Wines   Dr Roger Harris of Brindabella is the winemaker and consultant here. Tiny quantities of wine are made to a high standard. The Pinot Noir fruit used to be sold to Lark Hill, but is now released under their own label.

Pankhurst   Like many of the region's vineyards the wines are made by the Carpenters at Lark Hill, which may explain why they can be so good. The quality of fruit also helps of course.

Wimbaliri Wines   Another micro vineyard producing less than 1000 cases per year. Ideal location next door to Clonakilla should ensure the quality of the wines.

ABOVE *Wine is for sale everywhere here!*

One of the finest Pinot Noirs in Australia is made by David and Sue Carpenter at Lark Hill. They established their winery in 1978 to realise their dream to make wines in a cool climate region of Australia, which were typical of those produced in Europe. At this stage, though, it was only a part-time operation. David had originally come from England, where he gained an Honours Degree in Physics and a Masters in Optics at the University of Reading. This led him to Australia, where he worked as an oceanographer and met Sue who was a research statistician. As the urge for further education became stronger, David left his position to study for a Doctorate in Physical Sciences at the Australian National University. After the completion of this course he continued at the University as a research fellow until, in 1986, he decided to leave academia behind to focus on Lark Hill. Sue joined him full-time one year later in 1987, after leaving her position at

ABOVE *Sunrise in New South Wales. This is a vast state with a great deal of potential in wine-making terms, so look out for some even greater things from here at some time in the future.*

CSIRO. She, too, had led an academic life with a BSc in Maths, BSc Hons in Statistics, a Teaching Diploma, Master of Statistics and finally a degree in Wine Science. This is one amazing array of qualifications, and I am in a way pleased that they were not there when I visited, as I am a most un-academic person!

The vineyard is probably one of the highest in the county at an elevation of 860m with the winery set just below this. This altitude means that it is seriously cool climate here - so much so that snow has even been known to settle during winter. It is also in an area of outstanding natural beauty, with rolling hills and a plethora of wildlife roaming through the vineyard, including an abundance of birds to be seen all year round.

Like so many other wineries of this size, they have been the recipients of numerous awards and accolades for their highly-prized wines. Are they all justified? Yes because of the international praise they have also received away from the Australian show circuit. Jancis Robinson (who incidentally is my favourite wine writer) speaks highly of them and rates the wines well. Their two Pinot Noirs both won silver medals at the International Wine Challenge in London, out of a total of eight medals awarded to Australian wineries for this grape. The Carpenters have also been instrumental in the promotion and establishment of the Canberra region, by travelling and making wine for various other local wineries.

Ken Helm who runs Helm Wines, situated 18 miles from the city centre, is a stalwart of the region. Responsible for pioneering the development of the National Wine Show, as well as numerous other shows and events, he can lay claim to being one of the region's most ardent promoters. We have all heard about child prodigies and parents who give up everything to enable their offspring to achieve sporting greatness - well here Stephanie Helm, Ken's daughter, made her first wine at the grand age of nine! Now this does not sound like a hardship to me - more like a decade's-worth of presents rolled into one! The wine she made was entered into a regional show and was awarded a bronze medal. The ironic thing is that she was not allowed to enter the judging area to pick up her medal because of her tender years. Remember her name for the future - she is sure to go onto great things.

ABOVE *The winemaker has taken some wine from a barrel with this instrument, to enable him to evaluate it.*

Mudgee

Mudgee has more grapes planted than the Hunter Valley and is one of the oldest regions in the country, having first been planted in 1821. By the gold rush of the 1850s it is recorded that around 20-30 wineries were in operation here. As in many other grape-growing areas, the vineyards then declined due to the depression around the 1890s. They did not really revive again until the founding of Botobolar, the first serious organic vineyard in Australia, and Huntington Estate, both of which began in the early 1970s. However, Poets Corner, which is now owned by Orlando-Wyndhamm, has been in continual production since 1856. Mudgee is located in the Central Ranges and varies in altitude from 450-650 metres. The climate is warm with sunny days and clear cool nights.

There are currently around 30 cellar door outlets, a number of which use one of the 13 wineries currently in the region to make their wines for them. The growers here have always been quality-conscious and in the 1970s they started an Appellation program to ensure that the quality levels of the area were adhered to, and to certify the authenticity of the wines. This was abandoned after the Label Integrity Programme came into force in 1990. This programme was developed by the Australian Wine and Brandy Corporation at the request of vineyard owners nationwide. Its purpose is to guarantee that what is printed on the label is truthful and can be traced via an audit trail to its origins. To enable an audit, a wealth of

ABOVE *A helpful indication for visitors that Shiraz grapes are grown here.*

information is recorded that must be available for inspection, upon request by the relevant authorities.

Tim and Connie Stevens purchased the Abercorn Estate when it was a second-rate vineyard, selling fruit to Rosemount. The attraction for the Stevens was the vines' age and historical importance, as they can be traced back to the original cuttings that were imported by James Busby in 1832. Those cuttings were originally planted in the Craigmoor vineyard, from where the cuttings for Abercorn were taken. The vision the Stevens had required a lot of hard graft - it is never an easy task to take a run-down vineyard and

ABOVE *After pressing, the rotary press has to be carefully cleaned.*

Recommended Producers

Abercorn   Another winery that can trace its Chardonnay clones back to the Busby cuttings. The Reserve A range, although made in limited quantities, is very good.

Andrew Harris   Established in 1991 on an old sheep farm, this property benefits from rich clay soils and limestone. Interesting varieties such as Zinfandel have been planted recently, which should prove interesting.

Blue Wren   The wines here are made from two vineyards, the high-altitude Stoney Creek and Bombira, which is well suited to red varieties. The estate was purchased in 1998 by James and Diana Anderson who hand-pick from the dry-grown vines.

Botobolar   This is Australia's oldest organic vineyard, having been planted in 1971. There is a free BBQ if you are visiting.

Burnbrae   This winery is particularly on form at the moment, with a succession of good wines and medals.

Elliot Rocke Estate   The vineyards here were established as long ago as 1858 on the other side of a hill to the homestead, so it was referred to as the "Seldom Seen" vineyard. Today the wines are made by Simon Gilbert, the famous Hunter Valley vigneron.

Farmer's Daughter Wines   This is a moderately new venture that is already doing well on the show circuit. They also offer accommodation in the centre of the vines.

Frog Rock   This has been in business for over thirty years but it is only since 1997 that wines have been made under the name. Most wines are crafted for early drinking although they do make a reserve range, which has the ability to age.

High Valley Wines   Located in the north of the region, the majority of grapes are sold on but a small proportion is kept and bottled. The wines have shown well.

Huntington Estate   The red wines here are big, strong and full-flavoured and come from a vineyard that was planted in 1969. Some of the finest wines in the region.

Lawson's Hill   This label is under new ownership and it looks as if developments made could be very interesting.

Miramar   Ian MacRae runs this winery, which not only contract-grows for others but releases some fine wines under its own label. The Riesling shows consistently well and the current Cabernet Sauvignon was the runner-up for the best wine of the show out of 2000 at the Cowra wine show. Ian is also very successful with Sauvignon Blanc, which can be something of a rarity outside the Adelaide Hills.

Mountilford Vineyard   Makes wines from varieties such as Sylvaner and Pinot Gris.

Poets Corner   The wines at this historic winery are great when young, and can age well in good years.

Rosemount   The Rosemount Mountain Blue Shiraz Cabernet always impresses and works as a benchmark for the region.

Seldom Seen Vineyards   Ever-improving wines.

Simon Gilbert Wines   The Gilbert family has been making wine for over 160 years and Simon has been awarded over 1200 medals in his career so far. A new cellar door facility has recently opened.

rejuvenate it. Along with a lot of work on the vines, weeds had to be eradicated and a functional and efficient irrigation system installed. Success came in 1997, with their Shiraz receiving critical acclaim. Since then they have gone from strength to strength, with magazines and critics around the world applauding the wines.

The Elliot Rocke Estate vineyards were established as long ago as 1858, on the other side of the hill the homestead was located on - and so were referred to as the "Seldom Seen" vineyards. Today the wines are made by Simon Gilbert, the famous Hunter Valley vigneron.

ABOVE *Many Chardonnay clones have come from original cuttings imported in 1832.*

New South Wales Other Areas

Orange is one of those towns that seems to offer something for everyone who wishes to escape the frantic pace of big city life for a smaller more friendly habitat. With a population of around 100,000, it has all the facilities one would expect, including three eighteen hole golf courses and a plethora of restaurants. If visiting, there are many historic villages located nearby with a wealth of attractions to keep you occupied. The name would suggest that this was prime orchard country, but this was many years so most have long disappeared.

As a wine region it is relatively new, having only been established in 1983. So far over 60 varieties of grape have been planted, so we will probably have to wait to see the finest that can

ABOVE *Two wines from Reynolds, whose range appeals to a wide cross-section of the market.*

Recommended Producers

Bloodwood   Bloodwood was the pioneer in Orange, having first planted in 1983 at time when there were no other commercial vineyards here. The site selected was on a north-east facing slope on calcareous silt stone, greywake and limestone breccia soils, which lie on top of friable red clay. The winter-dominated rainfall is around 750mm and they regularly experience snow fall. Minimal intervention is applied in the vineyard and also in the wine-making. To this extent no insecticides have ever been used and all pruning and picking is done personally by the hands of Stephen Doyle the owner. Irrigation is only used in the very driest of circumstances. Cabernet Sauvignon and Chardonnay are the dominant varieties but there are also Shiraz, Riesling, Merlot and Pinot Noir. You can be confident in all the wines from here and it is interesting to taste one of the Chardonnays, which come from vines that originated in Montrachet.

Brangayne of Orange   Don and Pamela Hoskins contract-out their wine-making to Simon Gilbert, which has proved to be a great success. They are Pinot Noir and Chardonnay specialists and both varieties seem ideally suited to their land.

Canobolas-Smith   One of the newest wineries in the region and also one of the most promising.

Highland Heritage   The premium range of wines from this estate is called Mt Canobolas, after the highest point between Orange and Perth.

Ibis   Although Ibis wines are made by Phil Stevenson with basic equipment, they are of an acceptable quality. This is one of only a handful of producers who bottle a varietal Cabernet Franc. The wines naturally have cool climate characteristics and are complemented by maturation in oak barriques.

Indigo Ridge   This winery easily demonstrates why Sauvignon Blanc is becoming synonymous with the region. I particularly like the label designs.

Logan   Peter Logan, a thirty-something graduate in Oenology of Adelaide University, presides over the wine-making at this family estate. Striking labels with focused marketing has ensured quick success. It also helps that the wines are good!

Reynolds   Reynolds have high ambitions to put themselves within the top five wine companies in Australia. This will not be an easy task to achieve, but will be made easier by their Little Boomey range of wines, which appeal to a wide cross-section of customers. An interesting statistic is that the company have some 1800 miles of vines comprising 1.15 million vines. Jon Reynolds is the chief winemaker and naturally has a wealth of experience, including a long period at Wyndham as Group Chief winemaker.

be made. The vineyards are located at an altitude of between 600-1000 metres, making it one of the highest regions in Australia. It is also one of the coldest.

The Hastings River region is located in the north of the state and north-east of Hunter Valley. There is only one winery of significance here - Cassegrain who have made quite an impact since John Cassegrain and his wife Eva purchased the property from their parents in 2001. John is a graduate of Roseworthy and firmly believes that all fine wine is primarily based in the quality of fruit from the vineyards. As well as sourcing grapes from their own considerable acreage they have started to buy in grapes from other areas whose growers share their philosophy. The results should prove to very impressive across their range of five labels.

The Tumbarumba region is widely recognised for its quality sparkling wines. This can be attributed to the cool climate, which is perfect for a slow, long ripening period of the classic Chardonnay and Pinot Noir grapes. There are a couple of wineries here, most notably Excelsior Park, which was the first to plant vines in 1980. They do not possess the finances of the larger wine companies with vineyards here, from which they utilise the grapes for blending.

The Shoalhaven region lies right on the coast near the town of Nowra, with magnificent beaches up to seven miles long, that stretch for 600 in total. Wollongong, Australia's eighth largest city, is also a short drive away. One of the newer wineries here is Seven Mile Vineyard, which releases a Chambourcin, Verdelho and Chardonnay, with a Petit Verdot to come on stream in the future. It has not been easy for Eric and Joan Swarbrick, the owners. After beginning to plant in 1997, they suffered serious droughts in the region and this has led to some major decisions being made. Is it better to save water for when the fruit is developing and after it has been picked, which will give essential carbohydrates to the vine, or to water later to give the next season's crop a boost? They elected to water before budburst and allow vine growth, with the option later of cropping, to allow what moisture there was to go to fewer grapes. One of the most historical sites in Shoalhaven and Australia also happens to be a vineyard - Coolangatta. The site was the first in NSW to have a European settlement built upon it, which was started by Alexander Berry in 1822. The estate also comprises a golf course, hotel and conference facilities. The label has been the recipient of many awards, which is no surprise because of the standards of viticulture and since the wine is contract-made by Tyrells.

The McWilliams Barwang Vineyard produces some of the finest wines from the Hilltops region, which lies in the shadow of the Great Dividing Range. It is located some 90 miles north-west of Canberra and 120 miles south of the Hunter. Like other regions here viticulture is not easy, with snowfall, heavy frosts and large rainfall to contend with. Barwang has faced these challenges and triumphed for over 30 years, helped by the deep red granite clays with basalt soil, which aid the drainage of the vineyards. The wines are naturally cool-climate and full-bodied with a large spectrum of flavours, good acidity and ripe tannins in the red wines. There is also a certain elegance about the wines, and if from the finest vintages they can mature happily for ten years. McWilliams Barwang enjoyed little competition for many years but now there are a handful of winemakers in the region who are starting to rise to the challenge. Although I have not tasted Hansen Hilltops wines, they are reputed to be excellent and made from vines ten years older than Barwangs. Another winery grabbing the headlines is Chalkers Crossing, which was planted by in 1998 by Ted and Wendy Ambler at Rockleigh near Young (most famous for its cherries). The year 2000 saw the completion of a state-of-the-art winery just in time for the vintage. Due to climatic and physical constraints, some grapes are bought in from other areas to supplement the wines. This has no doubt helped Celine Rousseau, the winemaker, in obtaining a medal for each wine she has made here. Celine is one of the rising stars of the Australian wine scene and it is predicted that she will go on to reach the upper echelons of the industry in the not too distant future.

ABOVE *A cork in a barrel. For bottles, many Australian winemakers prefer the Stelvin, a form of screw cap.*

Tasmania

Tasmania is often the forgotten Australian state. Even the Olympic committee famously forgot to include it on the map of Australia produced specially for the Games in Sydney 2000. Although it does get its fair share of visitors, numbers are nothing like those that visit even the remoter mainland regions whilst they are touring the major cities. It does not deserve to be left out in the cold, though, as it produces some of the finest Pinot Noir and Chardonnay in Australia.

Located south of Victoria, the island is divided into two areas viticulturally - north and south - with the main wine-growing region in the north. It can lay claim to having vines planted some 20 years before the earliest in South Australia and Victoria. They were planted by Bartholomew Broughton in the early 1820s, with wines offered for sale in 1827. This is by far the smallest region in Australia (and the coolest) containing around 1% of the country's vineyards - even though plantings increased by over 20% at the beginning of this century. Growing grapes here is not an easy business, due to the cool climate and the plethora of boutique wineries - some of whose owners are not fully acquainted with the intricacies of vine growing or of wine-making. Where they sometimes fail though, there are others who excel and make extraordinary Pinot Noirs that can rival the finest that the so-called "Old World" can offer. Site selection is paramount, with Riesling and Chardonnay being suited to the Piper River sub-region in northern Tasmania, and the Derwent and Huon Valleys in the south. Pinot Noir, Cabernet and full-bodied Chardonnay are more suited to the Tamar Valley in the North, and Coal River and East Coast in the South. The vines originally cultivated here in the 1820s did not develop into a thriving industry due to the harsh climate and the growers' lack of expertise in coping with these conditions. However, as European settlers arrived in Tasmania during the 1950s the industry was resurrected. They brought with them the necessary and much-valued skills that were needed, and a determination to emulate their families' small vineyards, which they had grown up on so many years previously.

The relative success of these early vineyards encouraged further would-be growers to embark on a career in viticulture, and the industry grew from a minute status to one that could be termed a cottage industry. In 2002

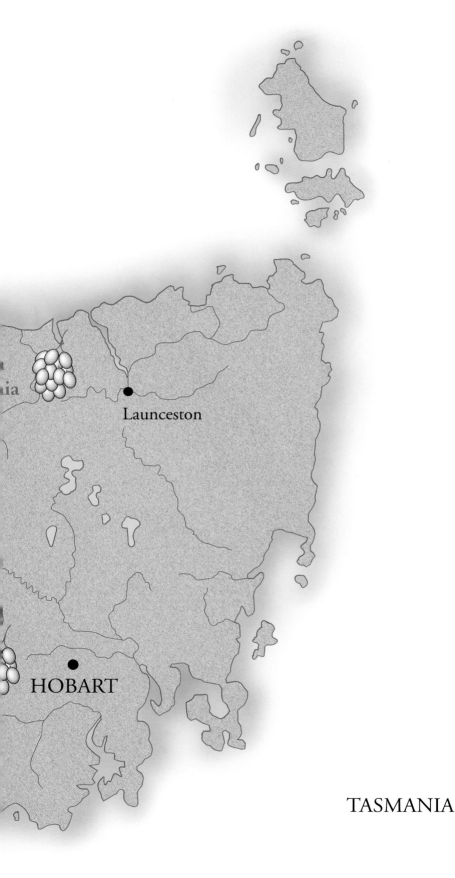

Launceston

HOBART

TASMANIA

there were 119 vineyards in Tasmania, although many of them do not have their own winery and the wines are contract-made. Andrew Hood of Hood Wines provides this service to 40 of the growers, which allows them to preserve their vineyard's idiosyncrasies and not show the winery's stamp. The growth in the industry here has been phenomenal, and it still continues - it is forecast that by 2007 it will have doubled in size. This interest has been fuelled by the quality of the wines made here, especially the Pinot Noirs, Chardonnay and sparkling wines. In fact five out of Australia's top ten sparklers are made here - Pirie, Arras, Jansz, Clover Hill and Radenti. The larger companies have also gained interests here, which cements the belief that this is prime viticultural land.

As well as site selection, pest management is crucial here. The light brown Apple Moth, which is controlled by the use of pheromones, can be a problem for some, whilst others are affected by birds (silvereyes, starlings, black-birds and crows) and European wasps, which all need extensive netting to combat.

The pre-eminent winery on the island is Pipers Brook, located in the Piper River sub-region, who produce almost one quarter of all the wines made here. It was founded by Dr Andrew Pirie with his brother David in 1974, following extensive research to find the ideal site. Prior to this Dr Pirie had studied at the university of Sydney, and gained a PhD in vine physiology. A period was spent working in European vineyards, where he was able to gain an invaluable insight into viticulture and the process of making wine. Each variety here has been planted with the purpose of expressing the terroir of Piper Brook, whilst maintaining the classic characters found in their respective European homeland. The Piries were one of the first vine growers to establish close-planted

ABOVE *Hand-picking Chardonnay grapes, which is time-consuming and expensive, but is also essential for the best quality.*

Vertical Shoot Positioning (VSP) vineyard, which are now widespread throughout the country. This system allows the canopy to be positioned in such a way to allow the sun to penetrate further, giving maximum photosynthesis and helping the grapes to gain physiological ripeness - which is helped by the high humidity levels in the Piper River region. The soils are similar to Coonawarra region being Kraznozems, which are deep and friable, as opposed to the more gravely basalt on an ironstone and clay base, as found in the Tamar River located to the south nearer Launceston. The wines, as you would expect, are impressive and the winery is currently looking at bottling single vineyard wines.

Grey Sands Vineyard is appropriately named after the soils it is situated on - grey sand on clay. The vineyard is located in the Tamar Valley on a north-east facing slope and specialises in Pinot Gris and Merlot. Robert

ESTABLISHED BY THE PIRIE FAMILY IN 1974

PIPERS BROOK VINEYARD

1999 RIESLING

Tasmania

ESTABLISHED BY THE PIRIE FAMILY IN 1974

PIPERS BROOK VINEYARD

1998 SUMMIT CHARDONNAY

Tasmania

Richter, the owner, is very keen to maximise the flavour within his wines and as such has chosen not to irrigate the vines, which are planted on their own rootstocks. Planting is at a very high density of 8800 vines per hectare, with a single vertical trellis supporting one arched cane of 6 buds per vine. To aid the complexity that Robert strives for in Pinot Gris, the juice handling is unprotected and it undergoes malolactic fermentation with an extended lees contact. This is in much the same way that the variety is handled in Alsace, France, and leads to a Pinot Gris that is possibly Australia's finest in good years. The Merlot is made to be full and dry.

The oldest established vineyard in Tasmania is Providence Vineyard, which was first planted in 1956 by a Frenchman named Jean Miguet. Jean was a 5th generation wine-maker from Provence in France, who leased the vineyard for seven years before purchasing it in 1963 for £2300. When they originally took on the lease Jean decided to go ahead purely on the soil analysis, without actually looking at the house that would become their home for the next 20 years. Jean's is a story of ambition and passion. The local residents soon threw up all manner of objections when they learned of his plans. His vines (which had been brought over illegally from France) were sprayed with weed-killer, as were the wind-break trees. Even their goat was poisoned. Undeterred he persevered, and built a winery

ABOVE *The colourful and eye-catching sign for Marion's Vineyard.*

with basket presses and wax-lined concrete fermenters. The vines were painstakingly tended, with the bark being removed each winter by hand to deter the insect pests from feeding off them. During this period no legislation existed in Tasmania to allow Jean to sell his wine, so heartbreakingly he had to sell it to a wholesaler at first. He campaigned for years to change this, but it was only after his death in 1975 that legislation was brought in to allow the sale of wine from a vineyard.

The vineyard was then purchased in 1980 by the Bryce family, with the wine-making

ABOVE *In this vineyard the vines are low-growing bushes, which means the grapes will have to be harvested by hand.*

ABOVE *Pushing the cap down into the fermenting juice with a paddle, to give the red wine its colour and extraction.*

vineyard. It was planted in 1987 by Dr Bertel Sundstrup and Anne Sundstrup, and has increased its plantings year-on-year to its current size of 22 acres. It is located in the Pipers Brook region, with vines planted in a north-easterly direction on sloping hills overlooking the picturesque seascape of the Bass Strait. Dr Sundstrup and Anne were fortunate to secure the services of Dominique Portet, then of Taltarni, to help in the search for the perfect site. Dominique, who is written about in more detail in the Yarra Valley chapter, is a stickler for detail and meticulous in his research so from the outset they knew that the site was capable of making serious wine. The vineyard still has to be managed effectively though, and to this end studies of the basaltic soil covering a bed of clay are made each year, to aid the fertilisation programmes. Close planting is the norm here, with 1.95m between the rows and 1.1m between the vines, which are trellised with the Scott Henry system.

The first vintage of Pinot Noir and Chardonnay were made in 1991 under contract, but the completion of a winery on site in 1997 enabled Dr Sundstrum to undertake the wine-making himself. This brought instant success and his first wine, a 1996 Pinot Noir was ranked the best Australian Pinot in a tasting organised for *Winewise* magazine. His 1998 Sauvignon Blanc received the highest score in its class at a tasting for the "Top 100" held by the *Adelaide Advertiser*.

being conducted at Heemskerk. Management changes in 1993 saw this relationship dissipate, and Andrew Hood, a contract winemaker, was employed, as he is to this day. Changes have now been made in the vineyard, with unsuccessful varieties grafted over to Chardonnay and new trellising systems implemented. The wines made today are in strong demand and this has led to the acquisition of a new vineyard close by, which will be planted with Pinot Noir. The Pinots here display a myriad of flavours, going through rich cherry, black plum, violets, forest floor and game.

A number of the vineyards on the island started out as fruit farms and have diversified into grape growing. Dalrymple is one such

One of the smaller labels in the north is Golders Vineyard, which is tucked away behind larger vineyards with no cellar door. It was first planted in 1989 with Pinot Noir, which is still the speciality, although another vineyard has since been purchased on the other side of the brook. This has been planted 50/50

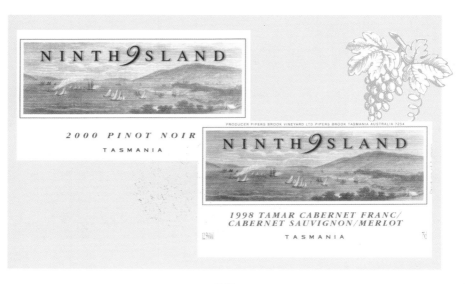

Recommended Wineries

Apsley Gorge   Pinot and Chardonnay specialists.

Clover Hill   Quality sparkling wine producer.

Coal Valley Vineyard   Hand-picking, vinification by Andrew Hood and the minimal use of chemicals all contribute to Coal Valley's success.

Coombend Estate   Cabernet Sauvignon, Sauvignon Blanc and Riesling are grown here on north-facing slopes that maximise the fruit's quality.

Dalrymple   Every wine that Dalrymple has entered into a show has won a medal, which is a remarkable achievement.

Delamere Vineyard   Classic Pinot Noir and Chardonnay made from vines planted in 1986.

Domaine A   Winemaker Peter Althaus leads a competent team to make these distinctive estate wines.

East Arm Vineyard   Tasmania's Riesling experts.

Elsewhere Vineyard   Dry-grown vines and leaf-picking during the growing season all contribute to the success of this vineyard.

Freycinet   Outstanding Pinot Noir.

Golders Vineyard   Small producer fine Pinot Noir - well worth seeking out if you can find some.

Grey Sands   A big Merlot and a flavoursome Pinot Gris made in the French style are specialities of this estate.

Hawley Vineyard   All on its own by Hawley Beach, the wines are made under contract by Andrew Pirie. The Pinot is highly recommended.

Herons Rise   Herons Rise overlooks the D'Entrecasteaux Channel and Bruny Island. It was first planted in 1984, with the first wines being produced in 1991. Interestingly, they make a Muller Thurgau, which is also successful in England.

Holm Oak   As well as the Chardonnay and Pinot Noir, Holm Oak competently produces Cabernet Sauvignon and an interesting Rose.

Kelly's Creek   Award-winning wines made in small quantities.

Meadowbank   One of the oldest vineyards on the island and close to Hobart. Integrated Pest Management is utilised here, which monitors pests and diseases and cuts down on spraying by moving away from regular spraying to when the vines actually need treating.

Moorilla   The birthplace of the modern Tasmanian wine industry, with vines planted in 1955 by Claudio Alcorso. Has been revitalised since 1990, when the current owners took over. Outstanding wines.

Ninth Island   Facilities are shared with Pipers Brook, although wines are made in their own right here. Good quality.

No Regrets   Imaginatively named after Eric and Jette Phillips sold Elsewhere Vineyard and moved into this one. They will be focusing on tiny amounts of Pinot Noir.

Panorama   Another producer of superb Pinot Noir.

Pipers Brook   Tasmania's largest and justifiably most famous name. Exemplary wine-making.

Providence   An old established vineyard that is one of Tasmania's finest.

Sharmans   A winery to look out for in the future. Can produce great Riesling.

Silk Hill   Only Pinot Noir is made from this vineyard, which overlooks the Tamar River at Deviot.

Stefano Lubiana   A business that has gained momentum and offers a good range at fair prices.

Tamar Ridge   Owned by business supremo Joe Chromy, investment in Tamar Ridge has not been lacking. Although the vineyards were planted in 1982 the company was only founded in 1999 after Joe sold his previous wine company. The introduction of Michael Fogerty as winemaker should ensure the success of this new venture.

2 Bud Spur   Minuscule amounts of outstanding Pinot Noir

Yaxley Estate   A small business that has its wines contract-made by Andrew Hood. The vines are dry-grown and insecticides are not used. They are close planted and the yield is minuscule, at one tonne per acre.

with Pinot and Chardonnay. Traditional practices are respected here, although in recent times this has given way to a more modern approach, with the purchase of a new air bag press. This small nod to the 20th century is perhaps the only concession that has been made. The must is fermented to dryness in open vats over 7-9 days, and then transferred to French and East European oak barriques for malolactic fermentation and maturation. The wine is then settled off its lees for a month, before being pumped into a tall tank outside, which usually gives a natural cold stabilisation (this ensures that the tartrate compounds are reduced, preventing them from forming harmless but unsightly solids in the bottle). The wine is then bottled unfiltered, to preserve the flavours, and released after a further three months ageing. This attention to detail has ensured that the wine has gained extensive gold medals in shows and been very well received by critics.

Domaine A in Southern Tasmania is just a short drive away from Hobart and was originally established in 1973 by Priscilla and George Park. Initially just over an acre was planted, but this has grown to over 50 today. The Coal River Valley offers a temperate climate to grow grapes, with a maritime weather pattern and low annual rainfall. The growing season is long, dry and mild, which allows the grapes to develop evenly and reach full ripeness at a steady pace. The growth of the foliage is carefully managed to maintain a height of 1.4m, allowing the leaves to take full advantage

of the sunshine. As is consistent with most boutique wineries on the island, all pruning and picking is done by hand - which is both costly and time-consuming but is essential to maintain the quality. The Cabernet Sauvignon is given lavish oak treatment with new French barrels each vintage, whilst the Pinot Noir is placed into two-year-old barrels to maintain its fruit characteristics.

Along with Ten Minutes By Tractor, Elsewhere Vineyard is my favourite name for a wine company in Australia. The name was inspired by a local weather bulletin that informed of snowy weather on the Southern Ranges but reported, "Elsewhere the weather will be fine". This prompted the owner's daughter to comment that she wished she could live elsewhere. The vineyard is located on the Huon River with a magnificent backdrop of the Hartz Mountains. 50% of the vineyard is planted to Pinot Noir (quite a common theme in Tasmania) and the remainder with Chardonnay, Riesling and Gewürztraminer. All the still wines are made by Andrew Hood and the sparkling wines by Stefano Lubiana.

The Meadowbank property was first established in 1850 as a grazing farm on the Derwent River. In 1974, nearly 125 years later, a vineyard was planted on the site for private use but was later expanded into a commercial operation. Another vineyard in Cambridge, with different micro-climates, was added in 1999. The Glenora vineyard has warm days and cool nights but can be prone to frost,

ABOVE: *Cleaning out the seeds and skins from the press, after the racked juice has been removed, ready for the next batch.*

whilst the Cambridge vineyard benefits from the moderating effect of the nearby sea, with milder days and nights. The business also manages vineyards that contract-grow grapes for BRL Hardy, and wines are made in their new on-site winery.

Although BRL Hardy have some of their grapes contract-grown by Meadowbank, they, like the other large companies, do not have a substantial presence here, which has preserved the boutique quality of the state. With the seemingly constant takeovers and mergers of the large global wine companies in the early part of this millennium, it looks set to remain that way. Southcorp, when they merged with Rosemount, went through a period of consolidation and dropped numerous brands from their portfolio to focus on the core names. Not only does this keep shareholders happy, but it is also beneficial to the small-to-medium sized growers in each region equally. It is likely that the wineries producing between 200,000 and 1,000,000 cases per annum will purchase these relatively small offshoots from the major businesses, to avoid being stuck in the mud themselves. This, of course, would allow further economies of scale and expansion and should allow them to cement a sound supply chain, ensuring that their wines reach global markets not only on time, but in a cost efficient manner. At the beginning of 2003, BRL Hardy had just merged with Constellation Brands in the USA to create the largest wine company in the world. Like Southcorp, I am certain that the share holders of this monolithic wine company (although it is still minuscule in comparison to the soft drinks manufactures) will demand that all the under-performing brands are dropped.

This ever-increasing polarisation of the

ABOVE *Before they are crushed and destemmed, the grapes are closely checked for quality. The best quality ingredients will make the best quality wines.*

industry should make additional room for the small producers, allowing them to take full advantage of the niche markets they operate in. It will, of course, also be to the benefit of independent wine merchants. Not only will they be able to look at selling the wines from small volume importers, they will also have a ready market for them since the large retailers tend only to offer the products of just a handful of the bigger Australian companies.

Tasmania, with its multitude of small producers, should take full advantage of the current situation and not see the large corporations as some sort of threat. It, like other small regions, should regard all the takeovers as an opportunity to expand into the market segments that have now been left open for forward-thinking wineries.

ABOVE *General s Tasmania cenic shot*

Queensland is the smallest of all the wine states in Australia - apart from the Northern Territory, which has just one winery (Chateau Hornsby). There are two main viticultural areas here, the Granite Belt and South Burnett. The former is the more important of the two, encompassing an area of 36 miles in length and six miles in width with around 40 wineries.

The Granite Belt's first grapes were planted in 1878, although it was not until the early 1970s that grape-growing really took hold. The region was originally the summer hunting ground of the Kambu Wal Aboriginal tribe, but this was thousands of years prior to its modern-day existence as a tin mining area. The region is based around the town of Stanthorpe, which derives its name from "Stannum" meaning tin and "Thorpe" meaning village. As its name suggests, the soils here are predominantly decomposed granite with large outcrops of solid granite. For a part of Australia that is renowned for its golden beaches and tropical climate, it can get very cold here. In June 2002 the temperature dropped to minus 13ºC - and snow does fall if the conditions are right. Generally the region to the southern side of Stanhope and the western side of the New England Highway tend to have less rain during the growing season, as it mainly comes from the south-east and follows the east ridge of the mountains. It lies at a latitude of 28º 40' and at an altitude of 700-950 metres, giving it a rather mild climate overall. The region itself is on the extremity of the latitude that is generally regarded as ideal for grape-growing, and is regarded as a marginal area. It is not dissimilar to Margaret River, Padthaway and Mt Barker, but cooler than the Barossa.

As well as the obvious grape varieties grown here, there is a strong sense of trying to break away from the norm and make wines from varieties that are not currently in the mainstream within Australia. This is a good move in a crowded market place, but they do need to be careful to ensure the varieties work and are not just planted to offer something different. To this end, two varieties have so far been identified that may well work well here. The first is Gamay, which has been selected to make a light red wine in the Beaujolais style - this is where this grape is most successful as the solids are not so different. The second is an Albarino, due to its resilience to wet weather and Botrytis.

RIGHT & BELOW *The Granite Belt's first grapes were planted as far back as1878, although it was not until the early 1970s that grape-growing really took hold.*

Recommended Producers

Bald Mountain A well-respected winery that has won numerous medals.

Ballandean Estate Angelo Puglisi, the founder of this winery, is a self-proclaimed "Godfather" of the Queensland wine industry. Multi-award wines that deserve the praise that they receive.

Bungawarra Look out for the liqueur Muscat, which is very good. Fine solid reds also.

Golden Grove Estate An ever-popular cellar door, which is testament to the quality of the wines made. Around 16 wines here, including a Muscat using the Solera system.

Heritage Wines of Stanthorpe Originally an apple cold store, which has now been converted into a winery. Most wines are barrel-fermented in new oak casks.

Felsberg Winery Founded in 1983, this winery draws upon its own hand-pruned and picked fruit. Nice wines.

Robinson Family Wines This historic vineyard can trace its roots back to the 1970s when it was founded by John Robinson, who had previously worked in the classic regions of France. In between his time abroad and the formation of the family wine business, he worked alongside the legendary Max Lake at Lake's Folly in the Hunter Valley. It was here in 1974 that he made his first wine. They say that some people are lucky in love and this certainly must have applied to John, as his wife, Heather, comes from a family that had established Saltrams Winery in the Barossa during the 1850s. The vineyards here are situated on a north-east facing slope with infertile granite soils and a portion of heavier clay. The wines produced are very good and compare favourably with those from more well-known regions.

Sirromet Wines A striking winery informs you of the ambitions of this company - to be at the forefront of the wine industry in Queensland. Adam Chapman, formerly of Elderton, Krondorf, and Peter Lehmann have been drafted in as CEO and winemaker. This should ensure the success of this venture.

Stanthorpe Wine Company Located at the northern end of the Granite Belt, wines produced here go under the Summit Estate label. There are 15 acres under vine, with Verdelho, Tempranillo, Shiraz, Merlot, Petit Verdot, Cabernet Sauvignon, Chardonnay, Black Muscat, Pinot Noir and Zinfandel. Quite an eclectic range, considering the region. This diversity has not taken away from quality though, with the Shiraz 2000 winning a Gold Medal at the Australian Small Winemakers show against 83 other Shiraz entries.

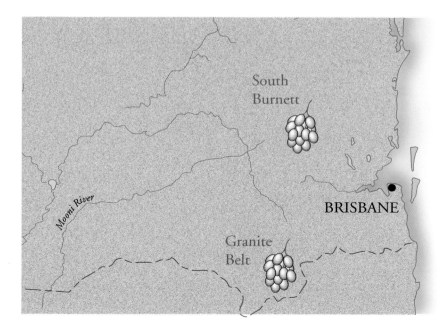

Index

2 Bud Spur 153

A
Abbey Vale 32
Abercorn Estate 144-5
Abercorn Reserve A 145
Adelaide Hills 12, 19, 20, 40, 41, 60, 71, 80-4, 141, 145
Ainsworth Estate 96
    Reserve Shiraz 96
Albarino grape 113, 114, 156
Alcorso, Claudio 153
Aldgate Ridge 83
Alexandra Vineyard 116
Alkoomi 35, 37
    Black Butt 37
    Jarra 37
All Saints Estate 109, 111
Allandale 136
Allanmere 136
    Durham Chardonnay 136
Althaus, Peter 153
Amadio, Caj & Genny 83, 87
Ambler, Ted & Wendy 147
Anakie 118
Anderson, David 102, 103
Anderson, Howard 111
Anderson, James & Diana 145
Anderson, John & Beryl 29
Anderson, John & Margaret 141
Anderson, Stuart 107
Andersons 111
Andrew Harris 145
Andrew Peace Wines 127
Angas family 45, 46
Annie's Lane 63, 64, 70
Annvers Wines 83
AP Birks see Wendouree
Apsley Gorge 153
Aquila Wines 38
Arelewood Estate 32
Arrakoon 60
    Doyen Shiraz 60
    Sellicks Beach 60
Arthurs Creek 96
Ashmead family 50
Ashton Hills 83, 84
Audrey Wilkinson 79
Auldstone 111
Auricht, Christian 52

B
Baily & Baily 18
Bainton Family Wines 138
Baintons Mail 136
Bald Mountain 157
Balgownie Estate 107
    Tignanello 107
    Viognier 107
Ballandean Estate 157
Balnaves 74, 75-6, 79
Balnaves family 75
Bannockburn 119
Banrock Station 19
Barbera 9, 137
Barbera grape 131, 136
Barnadown Run 102
Barnier, John & Elizabeth 126
Barossa Distillery 61
Barossa Valley 11, 12, 13, 18, 19, 20, 27, 32, 39, 40, 41, 42-52, 42, 43, 53, 63, 71, 74, 77, 78, 80, 83, 84, 105, 106, 107, 137, 156, 157
Barossa Valley Estates E&E Black Pepper Shiraz 50
Barratt 83
Barry, Jim 68
Barry, Peter 69
Basedow 32
Bass Phillip 121
Beaumont Estate 136
Beechworth 89, 108, 116-7
Bellarine Peninsular 118
Bendigo 20, 88, 89, 100, 106-7, 126
Beringer Blass 51, 55, 61, 64, 97, 102
Bernkastel 52
Berry, Alexander 147
Berrys Bridge 125
Bertrand, Francois 116
Beson, Daniel 97
Best, Harry 122
Bests 19, 86, 107, 121, 123
Bethany Wines 50, 47
Bialkower, Louis 97
Binder, Rolf 47, 51
Birk, Roly 68
Bissell, Peter 76
Bitter, Chris 52
Black Muscat grape 137
Blackjack Vineyards 107
Blackwood Valley 35
Blanche Barkly Wines 107
Blaxland, John 138
Bleasdale Vineyards 87
    Frank Potts 87
Bloodwood 129, 146
Blue Pyrenees 125
Blue Wren 145
Bobbie Burns Vineyard 109
Botobolar 144, 145
Bowen 74, 79
Bowen, Doug 79
Bradley family 136
Brady, Tony 66-7, 84
Brand, Eric 78

Brands 78, 79
Brangayne 129
Brangayne of Orange 146
Bratasiuk, Roman 58, 60
Breit, Rainer 118
Bremerton 87
    Old Adam 87
Briar Ridge 136
Bridgewater Mill 83
Brindabella Hills 141, 142
BRL Hardy 8, 19, 42, 55, 43, 70, 71, 78, 83, 103, 139-40, 155
Hardys Eileen Hardy 103
Broadbent, Michael 135
Brocksopp, John 30, 31
Broke Estate 136
Brokenwood 97, 120, 133, 136
    The Graveyard Shiraz 136
Brooks, Zar 83-4
Brookwood Estate 32
Broughton, Bartholemew 148
Brown Brothers 117
Bryce family 151
Buller, Reginald 111
Bullers Calliope 111
Bungawarra 157
Burge, Grant 83
Buring, Leo 64
Burnbrae 145
Burton, Murray 37
Busby, James 130
Busby, James 144, 145

C
Cabernet Franc 32, 37, 74, 83, 96, 111, 126, 136, 146
Cabernet Franc grape 12, 24, 29, 36, 61, 79, 101, 141
Cabernet Sauvignon 9, 19, 23, 24, 28, 33, 34, 40, 46, 49, 50, 51, 60, 61, 70, 74, 75, 76, 77, 78, 79, 83, 96, 102, 103, 105, 106, 107, 111, 113, 115, 121, 125, 127, 131, 135, 136, 138, 139, 145, 153, 154
Cabernet Sauvignon grape 11, 11, 12, 27, 27, 29, 30, 35, 44, 45, 54, 57, 64, 67, 73, 74, 77, 78, 79, 85, 85, 87, 88, 91, 94, 95, 96, 114, 120, 121, 125, 127, 140, 141, 146, 148, 153, 157
Cabernet Shiraz 75
Cabernet/Merlot 91
Calais Estate 136
Cameron, Chris 79
Campbell, Allen 109
Campbell, Colin & Malcolm 109-10
Campbell, David 109
Campbell, Isabella 109
Campbell, John 109
Campbells 109-10, 111
    Barkly Duff 111
    Bobbie Burns Shiraz 110, 111
Canberra District 129, 139-43, 147
Cannibal Creek Vineyard 121
Canobolas-Smith 129, 146
Cape d'Estaing 87
Cape Jaffa Wines 86
Cape Mentelle 27, 28, 29, 33, 32, 34
    Ironstone 28
Capel Vale 39
Capriotti, Vin 117
Carmody, Patrick 126, 127
Carosa 39
Carpenter, David & Sue 142-3
Carpenters 142
Carrodus, Dr Bailey 91-2, 97
Cartwright, Bob 30, 31, 31
Casa Freschi 87
Cassegrain 147
Cassegrain, John & Eva 147
Castagna 117
    Genesis 117
Castagna, Julian 117
Castle Rock Estate 37
Catherine Vale 136
    Barbera 136
    Dolcetto 136
Cazzolli family 32
Chain of Ponds 83-4, 87
Chalkers Crossing 147
Chambers Rosewood 109, 110-1
Chambers, Bill & Wendy 110, 11
Chambers, Stephen 110, 111
Chambourcin 19, 147
Chambourcin grape 136, 137
Chapel Hill 60, 62
    The Vicar Shiraz/Cabernet 60
Chapman, Adam 157
Chapoutier, M. 85-6, 101, 137
Chardonnay 39, 49, 60, 61, 70, 78, 82, 83, 84, 87, 88, 89, 91, 94, 96, 97, 99, 102, 105, 111, 115, 117, 118, 119, 129, 132, 133, 134, 136, 137, 138, 142, 146, 147, 148, 150, 152, 153
Chardonnay grape 12, 15, 24, 26, 29, 30, 34, 35, 40, 54, 73, 78, 79, 63, 80, 81, 84, 91, 91, 93, 96, 101, 112, 114, 114, 117, 121, 121, 131, 134, 135, 139, 139, 140, 141, 145, 145, 146, 147, 148, 150, 154, 157
Charles Cimiky 50
Charles Melton 42, 46, 47, 50
    Nine Popes 47, 50

Rose of Virginia 50
Chassala 116
Chateau Dore 107
Chateau Hornsby 156
Chateau Leamon 107
Chatsfield 35-6, 37
Chenin Blanc 111
Chevalier, Louis 116
Cheviot Bridge 127
Chromy, Joe 153
Cinsault 111
Clairault 32
Clare Valley 12, 19, 20, 40, 41, 63-71, 83, 106, 107, 137, 141
Clarendon Hills 58, 60
Claret 116
Claymore Wines 70
Clonakilla Estate 129, 139, 140, 142
clos Clare 64, 70
clos Clare Watervale Riesling 64
Clos du Val 28
Cloudy Bay, 28
Clover Hill Estate 125, 153
Cockfighter's Ghost 136
Cofield 111
Coldstream Hills 94, 96
Collett family 59
Collett, Scott 59
Collings, Ron & Lynne 94, 95
Collis, Marc 118, 119
Concongella Vineyard 122-3
    FHT 122
    Great Western Range 122
    Thompson Family Reserve 122
    Victoria Range 122
Conti, Paul 39
Coolangatta 147
Coombend Estate 153
Coonawarra 17, 19, 20, 27, 40, 41, 64, 68, 71, 72-9, 85, 86, 99, 113, 136, 150
Cootes 83
Coriole 60
    Lloyd Reserve Shiraz 60
    Redstone 60
Cowra 129
Crabtree Watervale 70
Craiglee 126-7
Craigmoor 144
Crappsley, Bill 32
Crittenden, Gary 115
Crosser, Brian 69, 81, 83
Crouchen grape 67
Cullen Wines 27, 28, 28-9, 32, 112
Cullen, Diana 28, 29
Cullen, Dr Kevin 27
Cullen, Vanya 28, 29, 32
Cullity, Tom 27
Curlewis Winery 118, 119
Cutler, Frank 121
Cynge Jones 85
Cyril Henschke Cabernet 43

D
d'Arenberg Wines 32, 48, 56, 56-7, 57, 60, 84
    Broken Fish Plate 57
    Coppermine Road 57
    Dead Arm 57
    Hermit Crab 57
    Ironstone Pressings 57
    Last Ditch 57
Dafarras 105
Dalrymple 152, 153
Dalwhinnie 125
Dalwood 130
David Traeger 105
Davidson, Mark 134
De Bortoli Wines 90, 96
    Botrytis Semillon 129
de Castella, Hubert 91
de Castella, Paul 91
De Iuliis Wines 136
De Iuliis, Joss 136
de Meuron, Adolphe 91
de Pury, Guill 91
Deans, Christa 47, 51
Deep Woods Estate 32
Del Rios Vineyard 119
Delamere Vineyard 153
Dennis 60
Dennis, Peter 60
Derham, Sir Peter & Lady 115
Devil's Lair 32
Dexter, Tod 115
Diamond Valley 94, 96, 98
    Blue Label Pinot Noir 94
    Close Planted Pinot Noir 94
    White Label Pinot Noir 94
Diletti, Nicole 39
Domaine A 153, 154
Domaine Chandon 92, 93-4, 96
Dominique Portet 96
Doole, Norm 60
Doonkuna 140, 142
Dowie Doole 60
Dowie, Drew 60
Doyle, Stephen 146
Drayton, Stephen & Tracey 136
Dredge, Peter 103
Drogemuller, Paul & Kathy 82, 83
Dromana Estate 115
Drummond, Craig & Caroline 37
du Pury family 91
Dubois, Alexander 116
Dunn, Caroline 64

Dunsford, Pam 60, 62
Durham, John 28
Durif grape 114
Dutschke Wines 50
Duval, John 30

E
East Arm Vineyard 153
Eather, Rhys 137
Eckersley, Ken & Juliet 121
Eden Springs 46
Eden Valley 12, 19, 41, 43, 42-52, 78, 80
Edwards & Chaffey 60
Elderton 50, 157
    Command Shiraz 50
Eldridge Estate 115
Elgee Park 115
Ellender Estate 127
Ellender, Graham 127
Elliott Rocke Estate 145
Ellis, John & Ann 101, 102
Elmswood Estate 96
Elsewhere Vineyard 153, 154
Elson, James 39
Erindale Vineyard 100
Esdaile, Nicole 39
Evans & Tate 29, 32, 34
Evans Family Estate 136
Evans, Len 24, 81, 135, 138
Evelyn County Estate 96, 98-9
Excelsior Park 147

F
Fairview 136
Falkenberg, Neville 84
Farmer's Daughter Wines 145
Farnsworth, Keith 125
Farr, Gary 119, 125
Felsberg Winery 157
Fergusson 96
Fergusson, Peter 96
Fermoy Estate 29
Ferngrove 37
Fire Gully 32
Five Oaks 96
Fogarty, Peter 135
Fogerty, Michael 153
Follett, Greg 87
Fosters 55
Fowler, Ralph 86
Fox Creek 60
    Shiraz 59
Francis, Hon James Goodall 126
Frankland Estate 36, 37
    Olmo's Reward 36, 37
Freycinet 153
Frog Rock 145

G
Galafrey 36, 37
    Art Label 36
Galafrey, Ian 36
Galah 83, 84
Gamay 111
Gamay grape 10, 156
Garland, Mike & Judy 37
Garlands 24, 32, 37
Garrett, Andrew 82
Geelong 20, 88, 118-20
Gembrook Hill 96-7
Gemtree 60
    Tally's 60
Geoff Merrill 60
    Reserve 60
Geoff Weaver 83
Geographe 24, 39
George, Spencer 67, 83, 84
Gewürztraminer 23, 68, 106
Gewürztraminer grape 97, 154
Giaconda 33, 33, 117
Gilbert, Joseph 45
Gilbert, Simon 145, 146
Gilberts 37
Gippsland 89, 120-1
Gjergja, Giorgio & Dianne 115
Gladstone, Dr John 24, 26
Glaetzer 50
Glaetzer, Colin 50
Gleeson, Edward 68
Glenara 83
Gnangara Shiraz 32
Goelet, John 124-5
Golden Grove Estate 157
Golders Vineyard 152-4, 153
Goona Warra 126, 126
Gouais 45
Goulburn Valley 18, 88, 100, 104-6, 107, 108
Goundrey Wines 35, 37
Graciano grape 114
Gralyn Estate 32
Gramp, Johann 46
Grampians 20, 88, 89, 121-4
Gramps 19
Grandjoux, Ambrose 116
Granite Belt 20, 156, 156, 157
Grant Burge 46, 50
    Meshach Shiraz 50
Great Southern 20, 24, 35-37
Great Western 39, 74, 122, 123
Green Valley Vineyard 32, 34
Green, Ed & Eleonore 34
Greenock Creek 42, 49, 50
    Cornerstone Grenache 50
    Roennfeldt Road 49, 50
Grenache 51, 58, 59, 60

Grenache grape *12*, 12, 13, 40, 44, 47, 48, 50, 51, 54, 57, 62, 67
Gresswell, Patrick & Christine 37
Grey Sands Vineyard 150-1, 153
Grosset 64-5, 70
  Gaia 66, 70
Grosset, Jeffrey 64-5, *65*, 66, 70, 81, 83
Guestier, Daniel 125
Guigals La Mouline 49
Gurdies Winery 121

H
Haan Wines 50
Hackett, Simon 61
Hallett, Ron 35
Halliday, James 66, 94, 96, 110
Hamburg grape 91
Hamelin Bay 32
Hamilton 86
Hamilton, Hugh 59, 60
Hanging Rock Winery *100*, *101*, 101-2
  Jim Jim 102
  Shiraz *100*
Hanisch, JST 52
Hansen Hilltops 147
Happs 32
Happs, Erl 32
Hardiker family 121
Hardy, Andrew 69
Hardy, Geoff 61
Hardy, Ken 35
Hardy, Thomas 55
Harris, Dr Roger 141, 142
Harrop, Matt 120
Haselgrove 60
Haselgrove, Nick 60
Haselgrove, Ron 60
Hastings River 129, 147
Hawley Vineyard 153
Hazyblur 87
Heathcote 85, 88, 99, 100-3, 106, 107, 120
Heathcote Winery 100, 102
  Mail Coach Shiraz 102
Heemskerk 152
Helm Wines 142, 143
Helm, Ken 143
Helm, Stephanie 143
Henschke 52, 81
  Hill of Grace 43
  Museum Programme 43
Henschke, Cyril 43
Henschke, Johann Christian 43
Henschke, Stephen & Prue 43
Heritage Wines 50
Heritage Wines of Stanhope 157
Hermitage Vineyard 101
Herons Rise 153
High Valley Wines 145
Highbank Wines 78
Highland Heritage 146
  Mt Canobolas 146
Hill Smith family 45-6
Hill Smith, Michael 84
Hillstowe 60, 83
  Buxton 60
Hilltops 129, 136, 147
Hodden, Sue 60, 64, 73-4
Hoddles Creek *91*
Hoffmann Winery 62
Hoffmann, Peter & Anthea 62
Hogg, Don 56
Hohnen, David 28
Hollick Vineyard 78, 79
  Ravensworth Cabernet 79
  Wilgha Shiraz 79
Hollick, Ian 78
Hollick, Peter 113
Holm Oak 153
Holmes, Nick 61
Holt, Jane 125
Hood Wines 150
Hood, Andrew 150, 152, 153, 154
Hooke, Huon 36, 142
Hooper, Derek 86
Hooper, Rod 70
Hope Estate 127, 134, 136
Hope Farm 60, 64
Hope, David 136
Hope, Michael 127, 134
Horgan, Denis 30
Horrocks, John 64
Hoskins, Don & Pamela 146
Houghton Wines 19, 32, 38, *39*
  White Burgundy 38
Howard family 34
Howard Park 32
Howell, Rob 142
Hugh Hamilton 60
Hugo 60
Hugo, John 60
Hungerford Hill 86
Hunter Valley *9*, 12, 19, 20, 28, 32, 35, 50, 61, 79, 81, 90, 97, 120, 127, 128, 129, 130-8, 139, 144, 145, 147, 157
Hunter Valley Elements 136
Huntington Estate 144, 145
Huntleigh Vineyards 102
Hyett, Bruce 120

I
Ibis 146
Ice Wine 99
Indigo Ridge 146
Ingoldby 61
Ireland, Bill 70
Ireland, Scott 119
Irvine Estate 44, 50
  Grand Merlot 44
Irvine, James 50

Ivanhoe 136

J
Jack Mann Cabernet 38
Jackson's Hill 136
Jacobs Creek 8, 19, 42, 46, 51, 52
Jarvis, Darrel 30
Jasper Hill 88, 100-1, 102
  Emily's Paddock Shiraz 101
  Georgia's Paddock Shiraz 101
Jeanneret Wines 70
Jeir Creek 142
Jenke Wines 50
Jenke, Kym 50
Jim Barry Wines 68, 70
  Armagh 68-9, 70
  McRae Wood Shiraz 68, 70
Jindalee Estate 119
Johnson, Hugh 69, 104, 135
Jones, David 125
Jones, Ewan 125
Jones, Phillip 121
Joshua Tree Imports 18
Juniper Estate 33

K
Kangarilla Road 61
Kangaroo Island 40, 86-7
Katnook Estate 73, 74, 75, 79, 99
  Odyssey Cabernet 75, 79
  Prodigy Shiraz 79
  Riddoch 75
Kay Brothers 61
  Block 6 Shiraz 61
Keith Tulloch Wines 137
Kelly, Michael 29
Kelly, Noel 70
Kellybrook 97
Kelly's Creek 153
Kelman, James 130
Kempe, Rodney 135
Keoghan, Wayne & Myriam 83
Kerny, Phil 114
Kevin Sobel Wines 137
Kilikanoon 70
  Oracle Shiraz 70
Killerby 33
King Valley 108, 115
King, James 131
Kinzbrunner, Rick 117
Kirk, Dr John 139
Kirwan's Bridge Wines 105
Kittle, Peter 113
Knapp, Oliver 99
Knappstein Lenswood 83
Knappstein Wines 69, 70, 71, 81
Knappstein, Tim 69
Koppamurra Wines 86
Kozik, Peter 121
Kreglinger 86
Krondorf 157
Kwak, Dr Teunis 95
Kyeema Estate 142
Kyle, Sir Wallace 34

L
Lake Breeze 87
Lake George Winery 142
Lake, Max 35, 135, 157
Lake's Folly 35, 131, 135-8, 157
Lance, Cathy 94
Lance, David 94, 96, 98
Lance, James 94, 98
Langes, Merv 35
Langes, Wayne 35
Langhorne Creek 12, 41, 83, 87
Langmeil Winery 42, 46, 51, 52
  Freedom Shiraz 51 52
Lark Hill 129, 142-3
Laughton, Georgia 101
Laughton, Ron 88, 100, 101
Lawson, Bill & Wendy 136
Lawson's Hill 145
Leamon, Ian 107
Leasingham Wines 70, 71
  Bin 56 70
  Bin 61 70
  Bin 7 Riesling 70
Leask, Ian 61
Leconfield 79, 86
Lehmann, Peter 157
Leland Estate 83
Lenton Brae 33
Leske, Peter 80, *81*, 81-2, 83
Leslie, David and Paula 114
Lethbridge Wines 118-9
Lewis, Don 105, 125
Liebich Wines 46
Liebich, Benno 46
Liebich, Janet 46
Liebig, Baron J von 131
Lillydale Vineyards 97
Lindemans 8, 19, 28, 42, 74, 137
Lindner, Richard & Carl 51, 52
Lockhart, Adrian 136
Logan 146
Logan, Peter 146
Long Gully 97, 99
Longleat Vineyard 105-6
Lovegrove Vineyard 97
Lubiana, Stefano 154
Lynch, Ken 35, 36
Lynn, George 78, 79

M
Macaw Creek Wines 70-1
  Yoolang Shiraz 71

Macedon 104, 106
MacKereth 124
Maclean, Ian & Anne 92, 97
Macquariedale Estate 136, 137, 138
  Four Winds 137, 138
MacRae, Ian 145
Maglieri 61
Main Ridge Estate 114, 115
Majella 74, 78-9
  Malleea 79
Malbec 116
Malbec grape 12, 35, 141, 142
Male, Roger & Robyn 98
Mann, Jack 32
Margan 137
Margan, Andrew 137
Margaret River 12, 19, 20, 23, 24, 26-34, 35, 38, 83, 86, 90, 112, 156
Marion's Vineyard *151*
Marks, Ian & June 96, 97
Marquis, Foxy and Sarah 60
Marsanne 104, 111, 113
Marsanne grape 57, 136
Marsanne/Rousanne 91
Mast, Trevor 122-3, 124
Mataro grape 51
Maximilian's Vineyard 83
Maxwell 61
  Lime Cave Cabernet 61
  Old Vines Semillon 61
  Reserve Shiraz 61
McCall, Lindsay 112, 115
McDonald, Ross 136
McIntyre, Richard 114
McIvor Creek 102
McLaren Vale 12, 13, 19, 20, 32, 40, 41, 48, 53-62, 80, 83, 87, 120, 136, 137
McRae Wood, Duncan 68
McWilliam 79, 97
McWilliams Barwang Vineyard 147
Meadowbank 153, 154-5
Meerea Park 137
Melton, Charles 50
Merlot 39, 50, 78, 83, 84, 94, 105, 111, 121, 150, 151, 153
Merlot grape *11*, 12, 13, 29, 35, 36, 38, 44, 74, 79, 85, 95, 114, 121, 127, 139, 140, 141, 146, 157
Merrebee Estate 37
Metier Wines 97
Miceli 112, 115
Miceli, Anthony 112
Middleton, Dr John 91, 97
Miguet, Jean 151
Mildara 60, 75, 125
Milimani Estate 141, 142
Mills, Andrew 102
Miramar 145
Mitchell Winery 68, 70
Mitchell, Andrew & Jane 68
Mitchell, Sir James 34
Mitchelton Wines 71, 81, *104*, 105, 125
Mondavi, Robert 30
Monichino Wines 105
Montalto Vineyards 115
Moorabool Valley 118
Moorilla 153
Moorooduc Estate 114, 115
Mornington Peninsular 20, 88, 89, 112-5, 118
Morris 109, 111
Moss Brothers 33
Moss Wood 27, 29, 32, 33, 34
Mount Avoca 125
Mount Barker 156
Mount Benson 85
Mount Broke Wines 131, 137, 138
Mount Eyre Vineyard 137
Mount Horrocks 66, 70
  Cordon Cut Riesling 66, 70
Mount Ida 100, 102
Mount Langi Ghiran 23, 121, 123, 124
Mount Lofty Ranges Vineyard 83
Mount Majura Wines 142
Mount Mary 91, 97
  Quintet 97
Mountilford Vineyard 145
Mouvedre grape 12, 47, 48
Mudgee 128, 129, 136, 137, 144-5
Mugford, Keith 32, 34
Muller Thurgau 153
Mulligan family 79
Munari Wines 107
Munari, Adrian & Deborah 107
Murray Darling 128
Muscat 109, 111, 157
Muscat grape 12, 108
Muscatel 116

N
Nadeson, Ray 118, 119
Nagambie Lakes 20
Nairn, Will 39
Napthine, Simon 113
Nebbiolo grape 101, 117
Nelson, David 84
Nepenthe 80, 81-2, 83
New Chum Gully see Ridgeback Wines
Nicholson River 121
Ninth Island 153
No Regrets 153
Noon Wines 59, 61, 62
  Eclipse 61
  Solaire Grenache 61

Noon, David 62
Noon, Drew 59, *59*, 61, 62
Norrie, Dr Philip 137
North Tasmania 20, 148

O
O'Callaghan, Robert 48, 51
O'Leary Walker Wines 71
O'Leary, David 71
O'Regan, Eileen 84
Oakbank 71
Oakridge 97
Oborn, Leon 75
Old Station 70
Olive Farm 38
Oliver, Wendy 118
Orange 20, 128, 129, 146
Orlando 19, 42, 46, 51, 71
Orlando-Wyndhamm 144
Osborn, Chester 56-7, 58, 60
Osborn, d'Arry 56
Osborn, Joseph 56
Oxford Landing 51

P
Padthaway 41, 77, 86, 156
Palandri 29-30
Palandri, Giovanni 29, 30
Palandri, Rob 29, 30
Palmer, Dave & Diane 67-8
Palomino 81
Pankhurst 137
Pannell, Dr Bill 27, 34
Pannell, Sandra 34
Panorama 153
Panton Hills 95, *95*
Paracombe Wines 82-3
Paringa Estate 114, 115
Park, George & Priscilla 154
Parker Estate 74, 77-8, 79
  First Growth 77
Parker, John 78, 79
Parker, Robert 19, 32, 36, 40, 42, 49, 56, 87, 96, 102, 110, 117
Parkinson, Tony & Susie 62
Paul Conti Wines 39
  Mariginiup Shiraz 39
Paul Osicka 102
Paulett 71
Peace, Andrew 127
Peel Estate 39
Peerick 124
Pemberton 24
Pendarves Estate 137
Penfold, Rev John 77
Penfolds 8, 19, 30, 42, 49, 51, 74, 77, 84
  Bin 389 49
  Bin 707 49
  Grange 22, 42, 49, 51, 69, 77, 83, 102
  Padthaway Chardonnay 86
  RWT 49
  Yattarna 31, 49, 84
Penley Estate 77, 79
  Ausvetia Shiraz 79
  Cabernet Reserve 79
  Hyland Shiraz 79
  Phoenix Cabernet 79
  Reserve Cabernet 77
Penmara Wines 137
Penny's Hill 61, 62
  Shiraz 59
Pepper Tree 137
Pepper Tree Wines *16*, 79
Perrini Estate 61
Perriocorta 128
Pertaringa 61
Perth Hills 24, 38
Petaluma 30, 69, 71, 74, 83
  Petaluma Tiers 31
Peter Lehmann *18*, 46-7, 51
  Stonewall Shiraz 47, 51
Peterkin, Michael 32
Petit Verdot 9, 136, 147
Petit Verdot grape 35, 60, 61, 157
Petrus 44, 50
Pfeiffer 111
Phillips, Eric & Jette 153
Piccadilly Shiraz *39*
Piccadilly Valley 83
Pierro 29, 31, 32, 33
Pinot Blanc grape 97
Pinot Grigio 113, 134
Pinot Grigio grape 112
Pinot Gris 19, 23, 115, 150, 151, 153
Pinot Gris grape 113, 145
Pinot Meunier 86, 122
Pinot Meunier grape 97
Pinot Noir 23, 28, 37, 74, 81, 82, 83, 84, 88, 89, 91, 93, 94, 95, 96, 97, 106, 111, 113, 115, 118, 119, 120, 121, 126, 127, 142, 143, 146, 148, 150, 152, 153, 154
Pinot Noir grape 12, 30, 34, 40, 80, 81, 91, 93, 94, 95, 101, 112, 114, 117, 119, 120, 121, 139, 140, 141, 142, 146, 147, 152, 154, 157
Pipers Brook 86, 150, 153
Pirie, David 150
Pirie, Dr Andrew 150, 153
Pirramimma 61
Plantagenet 37
Poets Corner 144, 145
Pooles Rock Wines 136
Port Phillip Estate 115
Portet Brothers 28
Portet, Dominique 99, 125, 152
Portet, André 99
Potts, Michael 87
Powell, Dave 49-50, 51, 70, 83

Pratten, Dr Peter 39
Preece, Colin 105
Preston, Dr Peter & Rosemary 141
Prince Albert Vineyard 119-20, 121, *120*
Provenance Wines 119
Providence Vineyard 151-2, 153
Puglisi, Angelo 157
Purbrick, Alister 104, 105, 106
Purbrick, James Escott 104
Pyrenees 88, 99, 124-5

Q
Quelltaler see Annies Lane

R
Ralph Fowler Wines 86
Rathbone, Darren 93
Ravenswood Lane 83
Razina Park 137
Red Edge 100, 102, 103
Red Frotignac 45
Red Hill see Red Edge
Red Hill Estate 115
Redgate 33
Redmans 32
Reid, Michael 111
Reynell, John 54-5, 57
Reynolds Winery 128, 146
    Little Boomey 129, *146*, 146
    Yarraman 129
Reynolds, John 146
Rhone 105
Richman, James 64
Richmond Grove 51
Richter, Robert 157
Riddoch, John 73, 75
Ridgeback Wine 94, 97
Riek, Dr Edgar 157
Riesling 16, 19, 23, 36, 43, 46, 50, 63, 64, 65, 67, 68, 69, 70, 71, 78, 79, 81, 83, 84, 96, 97, 99, 105, 106, 116, 122, 145, 153
Riesling grape 12, 15, 30, 35, 40, 44, 45, 64, *64*, 65, 67, 73, 97, 139, 140, 146, 148, 153, 154
Riggs, Ben 61, 62
Riggs, Ian 133, 136
Ringland, Chris 51
Riverina 128, 129
Riverland 41, 48, 50, 77, 86
Robinson Family Wines 157
Robinson, Jancis 36, 117, 143
Robinson, John & Heather 157
Rochlitz, Mr 116
Rockford Winery 46, 48, 51
Roe, John Septimus 38
Rosemount 8, 19, 42, 107, 128, 144, 145, 155
    Mountain Blue Shiraz Cabernet 145
    Roxburgh 133
Rothbury Estate 81
Rouge Homme Estate 74
Rousanne grape 57
Rousseau, Celine 147
Ruche, Anthony 110
Rutherglen 12, 19, 39, 48, 88, 89, 107, 108-11, 117, 128
Ryan family 136
Ryecroft 32
Rymill Wines *74*, *76*, 79
    MC2 74, 79
Ryrie, Donald & James 90, 93
Ryrie, William 90, 91, 93

S
S Kidman 79
Salter, William 73, 75
Saltrams Winery 46, 61, 157
Sandalford Wines *27*, 29, 32, 33, 38
Sangiovese 23, 60, 113
Sangiovese grape 11, 35, 59, 117
Saperavi grape 59, 60
Saracen Estate 32, 33, 34
Saraceni family 32
Sauvignon Blanc 16, 19, 22, 23, 28, 37, 50, 81, 82, 83, 84, 85, 96, 97, 102, 113, 121, 145, 146, 152
Sauvignon Blanc grape *9*, 12, 24, 28, 29, 30, 35, 40, 80, 81, 120, 141, 153
Sauvignon/Semillon 32, 33, 92, 137
Scarborough 137
Scarpantoni 61
Scarpantoni brothers 83
Scarpantoni, Domenico 61
Schrapel, Geoff and Rob 50
Schubert, Max 49, 77
Schultz, Peter 105
Scotchmans Hill 118, *118*, 119
Seaview 153
Seldom Seen Vineyards 145
Semillon 19, 23, 60, 61, 70, 113, 132, 133, 134, 135, 136, 137, 138
Semillon grape 12, 24, 28, 29, 34, 35, 38, 40, 44, 131, *131*, 134, 138
Seppelt 48, 74, 86
    Great Western 123-4
Seven Mile Vineyard 147
Sevenhill Cellars 64, 71
Seville Estate 97
Shadowfax 119, 120
Sharmans 153
Shaw & Smith 83, 84
    M3 83, 84
Shelmerdine, Ross 105
Sher, Jeff 115
Shiraz 9, 19, 23, 32, 33, 37, 39, 40, 44, 48, 49, 50, 51, 53, 58, 60, 61, 62, 63, 67, 68, 70, 71, 75, 76, 78, 79, 83, 86, 87, 88, 89, 91, 93, 96, 99, 100, 101, 102, 103, 105, 106, 107, 111, 114, 117, 118, 119, 122, 124, 125, 126, 127, 128, 136, 137, 140, 145, 157
Shiraz grape 11, 12, 24, 26, 35, 38, 40, 44, *44*, *45*, 45, 47, 48, 50, 51, 52, 54, 57, 59, 64, 67, 68, 71, 73, 78, 83, 85, 92, 93, 104, *107*, 116, 117, 120, 123, 125, 127, 131, 139, 134, 140, 141, 142, 144, 146, 157
Shiraz/Cabernet 79
Shiraz/Viognier 142
Shoalhaven 147
Shottesbrooke 61
Silk Hill 153
Simon Gilbert Wines 145
Simon Hackett Wines 61
Sirromet Wines 157
Skillogalee Wines 67-8, 71
Smith, Brenden 37
Sneddon, Bill 136
Sobels Wines 64
Sobels, Carl 64
Sobels, Kevin 64, 137
South Burnett 156, 157
South Tasmania 20, 148
Southcorp 19, 32, 42, 49, 55, 71, 74, 94, 96, 155
Spray Farm *119*
Sprigg, John & Katie 36
Squance, Kevin & Marian 33
St Andrews Vineyard 122
St Hallett 51
    Old Block Shiraz 51
St Henri 83
St Huberts 91, 97
St Leonards 111
St Marys 79
Staniford, Michael 35
Stanthorpe Wine Company 157
Stanton & Killeen 111
Stefano Lubiana 153
Stehbens, Wayne 75
Stevens, Neil 133
Stevens, Tim & Connie 144-5
Stevenson, Phil 146
Stonier Wines 71, 113, 114-5
    Reserve 115
Stonier, Brian & Noel 114
Strathewen Hills 96, 97
    Tribal Elder 96
Straws Lane 106
Stump Hill 56
Stumpy Gully Vineyard 112-3, 115, *113*

Suckfizzle 33
    Stella Bella 33
Sumerfield 125
Summit Estate 157
Sunbury 88, 126-7
Sundstrup, Dr Bertel & Anne 152
Swan District 12, 24, *38*, *39*, 38, 86, 88, 127, 128
Swarbrick, Eric & Joan 147
Sweetwater grape 81
Sylvaner grape 145

T
T'Gallant 115
Tahbilk *18*, 19, *103*, 104, 105, 105, 106, *106*, 117
    1860 Vines Shiraz 104
Tallarook 120
Taltarni Vineyards 28, 99, *124*, 124-5, 152
Tamar Ridge 153
Tamburlaine Vineyard 134, 137
Tarrawarra Estate 97
Tatachilla Vineyard 55, 61
    The Foundation Shiraz 61
Tate, John 32
Temple Bruer 87
Tempranillo 82, 98
Tempranillo grape 59, 60, 114, 157
Ten Minutes by Tractor 115, 154
Thomas Hardy & Son 56, 61
Thomas, Adrian 118
Thompson family 122
Thompson, Frederick 122
Thompson, Viv 122
Three Rivers 42, 51
Tim Adams 71
Tim Gramp 71
Tokay 45, 110, 111, 116, 117
Tokay grape 108
Tolley, Kym 77
Toole, Stephanie 66
Torbreck 42, 49, 51, 66, 70, 83
    Factor 47
    Juveniles 51
    Run Rig 49, 50, 51
    The Descendent 51
    The Steading 51
Townsend, Arthur 58, 59, 61
Traeger, David 105
Traminer 23, 71
Traminer grape 67, 141, 142
Trebbiano 110
Treloar, Francis 64
Trestrail, John 67
Trevelen Farm 36-7
Trevor Jones 51
    Wild Witch Shiraz 51
Trotanoy 50
Trott, Greg & Roger 61
Tuck's Ridge 113, 115
Tulloch family 138
Tulloch, Keith 137
Tullochs 32
Tumbarumba 129, 147
Turkey Flat 51
Turramurra Estate *112*, 114, 115
Tweddell family 81
Tyrrells 61, 86, 101, *130*, 132-3, 137, 147
    HVD 133
    Lost Block 133
    Old Winery Semillon 133
    Rufus Stone Shiraz 61
    Stevens Reserve 133
    Vat 1 Semillon 133
    Vat 47 133

U
Ullinger, Bill 33

V
Vale Vineyard 114
Vale, John 114
Vasse 26, 30
Vasse Felix 27, 29, *30*, 32, 33
    Heytesbury 33
Verdelho 19, 45, 117, 134, 137, 147
Verdelho grape 12, 33, 60, 121, 131, 133, 134, 157

Veritas 42, 46, 47-8, 51, 52
    Hanische 51
    Heysen 47-8, 51
Vertumnus 28
Vice, Dennis & Bonnie 78
Viognier 85, 86, 93, 102, 124, 137, 140
Viognier grape 12, 35, 50, 51, 54, 57, 59, 60, *73*, 117, 117, 120
Virgin Hills 127, 136
Voyager Estate 32

W
Walker, Nick 71
Warrabilla 111
    Durif 111
Water Wheel 107
Watervale 71
Watsons Creek 96
Wattlebrook Vineyard 137
Waugh, Michael & Annabelle 49, 50
Waurn Ponds 118
Weaver 81
Wendouree 63, 64, 66-7, 68, 71, 84
West Cape Howe Wines 37
White, Nat 114
Wiencke, Richard 46
Wigley, Robert Strangeways 61
Wild Duck Creek 102-3
    Duck Muck 102, 103
    Springflat Shiraz 103
Willespie 33
Willow Creek 114
Wilson, Craig & Mignonne 87
Wilson, Lucy 87
Wilson, Rebecca 87
Wimbaliri Estate 140-1, 142
Winborne, Mike 136
Wine Vault 19
Wirra Wirra 61
    Church Block 61
Wolf Blass 51
Woodstock Winery *57*, *58*, 59, 61
    The Stocks 59, 61
Wrattonbully 41, 78, 86
Wyndham, George 130
Wyndhams 19, 133, 146
Wynn, David 46, 73
Wynn, Samuel 73
Wynns 19, 73-4, 79
    Black Label Cabernet 74, 79
    John Riddoch Cabernet
    Sauvignon 74, 79
    Michael Shiraz 74, 79

X
Xanadu 33

Y
Yaldara 51
Yalumba Wines 44, 45, 46, 51
    Virgilius Viognier 51
Yarra Ridge 97
Yarra Valley 10, 12, 19, 20, 23, 28, 38, 88, 89, 90-9, 92-3, 97, 104, 107, 126, 127, 152
Yarra Yering 90, 91-2, 97
    Dry Red No 1 92
    Dry Red No 2 92
Yaxley Estate 153
Yellowglen Winery 125
Yering Station 91, 93, 93, 96, 97, 99
    Baraks Bridge 93
    Reserve 93
    Reserve Bottling 97
Yeringberg 90, 91, 97
Yunghams family 75

Z
Zantvoort, Frank & Michael 112-3
Zarephath Wines 37
Zema Estate 64, 74, 76-7, 79
    Cluny 79
Zimmerman, John August 116
Zinfandel 28, 32, 82, 83
Zinfandel grape 136, 145, 157

Acknowledgements

I would like to thank the following people for their support in helping me to write this book.

My wife Sarah and my son James, who did not complain when I told them that I would be going to Australia for five weeks on a research trip. Also to Sarah for proof reading the entire text and correcting all my grammatical errors.

To my mother for putting up with my idiosyncratic mannerisms and uninformative nature – thank you.

To Mark Sargeant for allowing me to be his personal taxi service whilst at college together, and for the endless discussions about food and wine - three Michelin stars surely beckon...

To David Avery for realising that cooking was not my strong point and allowing me to focus on wine.

To Ruan Courtney who chauffeured me around countless vineyards throughout Australia in the 1990s.

To Graeme Kelly for his persistent encouragement for me to complete this book.

To Chrysalis for having faith in me, and especially Marie Clayton for all her hard work.

To Qantas for their kind co-operation and excellent service.

To Hazel Murphy from the Australian Wine Bureau in London, for her support in organising travel arrangements and making appointments at wineries, which proved invaluable.

To Rona and David Pitchford at Reads Restaurant for putting up with a wine anorak for eight years.

And finally to all the winemakers in Australia for their generosity and time.